BALE

THE BIOGRAPHY OF THE
100-MILLION MAN

FRANK WORRALL

Design by www.envydesign.co.uk

Printed in Great Britain by CPI Group (UK) Ltd

1 3 5 7 9 10 8 6 4 2

© Text copyright Frank Worrall 2013

Cover image © Rex

Gareth Bale and Real Madrid president Florentino Perez © Rex

Gareth Bale salutes to Real Madrid fans © Rex

All other images © Action Images

JB

JOHN BLAKE

Published by John Blake Publishing Ltd,
3 Bramber Court, 2 Bramber Road,
London W14 9PB, England

www.johnblakepublishing.co.uk

www.facebook.com/Johnblakepub facebook
twitter.com/johnblakepub twitter

First published in hardback in 2011
This updated edition published in 2013

ISBN: 978-185782-679-1

Papers used by John Blake Publishing are natural, recyclable products made
from wood grown in sustainable forests. The manufacturing processes
conform to the environmental regulations of the country of origin.

Every attempt has been made to contact the relevant copyright-holders, but some
were unobtainable. We would be grateful if the appropriate people could contact us.

This book is dedicated to
Steven Gordon, a true Tottenham fan –
and a true friend

CONTENTS

'Bale's got everything. He's incredible…I would go so far as to say that Gareth is the best player to come out of Wales since Ryan Giggs. As an Englishman, I am highly disappointed he is Welsh.'

Harry Redknapp, Tottenham manager

'Tottenham have a cyclone on the left wing whose name is Gareth Bale. He combines the height and build of an 800m runner like Steve Ovett with the acceleration and directness of a rugby winger like Bryan Habana. And when he gets to the byline he delivers curling crosses like a Brazilian. He left Maicon for dead and then a wily old fox like Lucio was left in his wake like someone trying to follow the vapour trail of an aeroplane.'

Spanish newspaper *El Mundo*

'Gareth Bale is today the No. 1 player in the world.'

Fabio Capello, England manager

ACKNOWLEDGEMENTS

SPECIAL THANKS: John Blake, Allie Collins and all at John Blake Publishing. Andy Bucklow, the *Mail on Sunday*. Alan Feltham, the *Sun*. Alex Butler, the *Sunday Times*. Bruce Waddell, the *Daily Record*. Dominic Turnbull, the *Mail on Sunday*. Zoe King, literary agent extraordinaire.

THANKS: Gary Edwards, Kevin Nicholls, Danny Bottono, Ben Felsenburg, Carole Theobald, Colin Forshaw, Ian Rondeau, Russell Forgham, Roy Stone, Tom Henderson Smith, Dave Morgan, David and Nicki Burgess, Denise Hannay, Pravina Patel, Meg Graham, Martin Creasy, Celee and Desmond Campbell, Angela, Frankie, Jude, Natalie, Barbara and Frank, Bob and Stephen, Gill, Lucy, Alex, Suzanne, Michael and William.

Chapter 1

MY LEFT FOOT

He didn't sulk one little bit when the PE teacher informed him of his decision. Instead, the 13-year-old boy simply trotted away up the football pitch and determined that he would still be the best…at school today and, if his dream went to plan, in the professional game one special day in the not too distant future. Minutes later Gareth Bale went some way to proving that dream could become a reality as he was mobbed by his young team-mates after scoring with his right foot. Then, when he trooped off at the end of the match, he shook hands with the PE teacher who had banned him from using his left foot in that secondary school games lesson because 'that foot was so accomplished it was unfair'.

After all, the way Gareth saw it the ban had brought an indirect bonus: it had paved the way for him to develop his weaker right foot. He would now make it his aim to strengthen it and become a complete all-rounder…that was the inspirational nature of the Welsh boy wonder from even such an early age.

'We had to make up special rules for him,' Gwyn Morris, the head of PE at Cardiff's Whitchurch High School and the man responsible for the ban, would say years later by way of explanation. 'In a normal game we had to limit him to playing one touch and he was never allowed to use his left foot. If we didn't make those rules he would have run through everyone, so it was the only way we could have an even game when he was involved.'

Gareth Frank Bale was born on July 16, 1989, in Cardiff. His father, Frank, was a school caretaker (now retired) while mum Debbie was an operations manager with a law firm (a job she still holds to this day). His sister Vicky, who is three years older and now a primary school teacher in Wales, was also always a big supporter of him and his budding football career – regularly travelling with Gareth and their parents from Cardiff to Southampton and back for training sessions from when he was 14.

Gareth attended Eglwys Newydd Primary School in Whitchurch and then moved up to the High School in the same essentially middle-class suburb, three miles north of Cardiff city centre. It was at Eglwys Newydd that, at the tender age of eight, his talent on the football pitch was first noted by those in the professional game.

Rod Ruddick, who helped run Southampton FC's satellite academy in Bath, spotted Gareth playing for a youth team called Cardiff Civil Service in a six-a-side tournament in Newport. Ruddick would later recall, 'Even then, at that age and despite his small size, I could tell Gareth was something special. It was small-sided mini football, six-a-side, but Gareth was head and shoulders above anyone else at the tournament.

I used to attend various competitions in south Wales looking for talent, but never have I come across anyone quite like him.

'Even back in those days, he would race past players down the left wing and score goals.'

Ruddick's belief that Gareth would always have the pace to see off defenders was confirmed when he subsequently witnessed him finishing second in the Welsh national schools Under-11s 50m sprint.

Gareth was brought up in a family crazy about sport. He would say, 'My dad was always into sport and my mum was when she was younger, as was my sister. I kind of followed in the family footsteps. My dad played either rugby or football.' His father also loved golf and his uncle Chris Pike showed Gareth the way forward towards his dreams by making a name for himself as a pro footballer with Cardiff City. At the age of three, Gareth would go to Ninian Park with dad Frank to see Chris play – and Pike proved a fine role model, ending up Cardiff's top scorer in 1992, the season Gareth joined Frank on the terraces.

Gareth had a steady, stable upbringing in a solid family setting. He was a happy boy who spent most of his time kicking a ball about outside the family's modest three-bedroom terraced home.

'Everything was very local in terms of friends and people we knew – my best friend Ellis lived across the back from me. I remember my childhood spending time in the back garden or down at the park with my friends, playing football, messing around – doing what all kids do,' he would say.

He was interested in many sports – he was also good at rugby, hockey and distance running – but football was always his No. 1 priority. Gareth admitted, 'From literally the age of three, I just liked football. I always used to ask my dad to take me over to the park to practice – it was always football for me and I was left-footed from the start I think.'

'He wasn't the best at the traditional school subjects but he was absolutely outstanding at football, easily the best in the school and the best I've ever seen close up,' said Carl Morgan, a fellow pupil. 'He was lucky in that he had such a supportive family; his dad was always at the side of the pitch urging him on and taking him here and there for matches. They were a very close family and anything Gareth needed he got, even though they weren't well off.'

By the age of 14 Gareth was also making trips to the Southampton academy itself, as well as their satellite centre in Bath. Dad Frank would accompany him around the country and Gareth would later admit the debt he owed to him, saying, 'My dad's the one who's always been there; he's my hero, you could say. Even when he was working, he'd do anything for me. He's been the biggest influence in my life.'

Even at such a tender age the search for perfection was apparent as Gareth spent hours alone working on his skills and technique on the training pitch – long after the other boys had showered and left.

It was a trait that had been foreign to British footballers until six years earlier when Eric Cantona had arrived at Manchester United. Until 1996, the Brit pack would do their training and then head straight off home. But something stirred at Old Trafford when young men like Ryan Giggs and David Beckham saw the Frenchman Cantona still working alone as they jumped into their cars.

Beckham would later admit that it 'opened my eyes' and he also began to delay his exit from training, working with and learning from the French master. Cantona would help David with his technique and encourage him to perfect his free kicks – to great effect, as it would turn out.

So when Gareth worked on his skills as the new boy at Southampton's academy in 2002, it was nothing new. But it was still not the norm – he usually ended up training alone after the other trainees had left. 'The first time I saw Gareth play was when he was 13. He was playing as a left-winger then and had such a lovely left foot. Repetition is the best way to improve – the more repetition you have the better, and I often saw Gareth taking free-kick after free-kick in his own time,' Frenchman Georges Prost, the former technical director of Southampton's academy, would later confirm. 'All that practice gave him accuracy and made him believe, and now he takes them with so much confidence. He hits them with pace and a lovely technique.'

When Gareth stayed in Southampton to learn at the club's academy he roomed with another youngster who would go on to make a big name for himself – Theo Walcott. The two had planned to buy a flat together until Walcott left the club for Arsenal in January 2006. Gareth's mum Debbie told the *Sun*: 'They were planning to buy a TV and get a flat together until Theo moved to Arsenal. Theo used to pinch Gareth's aftershave before he met his girlfriend, Mel Slade.'

It was Walcott whom many of the staff initially believed would be the bigger star of the two. He also had great pace, control and technique – and he seemed to be the fitter of the two. Even as a youngster Gareth was bedevilled by injury and fitness problems – and the Saints academy staff also worried about his height. 'He was a lot smaller back then,' recalled one source close to the club. 'And he seemed surprisingly shy. The staff had their work cut out bringing him out of his shell and beefing him up. But it worked out eventually – he became bigger and taller – and it became clear that he had everything needed to become a big star.'

But the doubts had been very real. Indeed, it later emerged that Southampton were so unsure whether Gareth would make the grade as a professional footballer that they even contemplated releasing him at the age of 15. 'Between the ages of 14 and 16 he had growth spurts which affected his mobility and strength,' Ron Ruddick would add. 'He had a horrendous three years because he had a couple of injuries as well. But because of his character he kept going. There was some doubt whether he would get a scholarship but I never had any doubts about him. You could see from an early age he had something special.'

Gareth himself accepted he had a problem, admitting, 'At 14 growing pains almost forced me out of the game. I was quite small then shot up. My back was out of alignment. I couldn't run properly.'

Gareth left Whitchurch High school in the summer of 2005 with a Grade A in PE among his GCSE results. In his final year at school, he was awarded the PE department's prize for services to sport. In the presentation, PE teacher Gwyn Morris said, 'Gareth has a fierce determination to succeed and has the character and qualities to achieve his personal goals. He is one of the most unselfish individuals that I have had the pleasure to help educate.' It was a wonderful tribute from an early mentor to the boy who, although not the brightest academic star in the school, had certainly helped put Whitchurch High on the map in the world of professional sport. Gareth was the jewel in Whitchurch's crown; its greatest ever pupil in terms of sporting achievement and certainly its most famous ever. Before leaving, Gareth even helped Whitchurch win a trophy that earned them major bragging rights in Cardiff – the Cardiff and Vale Senior Cup.

His perseverance and dogged determination to make the grade at Southampton FC would also soon pay dividends. Within his close circles, it is often contended that the key match in his life was not the one that propelled him on to the world stage against Inter Milan in 2010, but one back in January 2005 – when he starred for Southampton Under-18s against Norwich Under-18s. After a series of injury setbacks it was made clear to him and his family that he now had to deliver the goods – or suffer the consequences. Which, in stark terms, would have meant he would not have been offered an academy scholarship with the Saints – and could have ended up on the footballing scrapheap.

Given his fame and acclaim now, it is almost unbelievable that he flew so close to disaster; that his career could have ended before it started. Luckily, he had a brilliant match, flying down the left flank and destroying poor Norwich with the help of his mate Walcott, who grabbed a first half hat-trick in the 5-1 romp.

Gareth, then 15, was now on his way and it was no surprise when 15 months later – on April 17, 2006 – he became the second youngest player at 16 years and 275 days ever to play for Southampton (the youngest being Walcott) when he made his debut and played the whole match as Saints beat Millwall 2-0.

Gareth made a confident debut in a match that then boss George Burley had earmarked as a good opportunity to blood some of his youngsters as the game meant little to Saints. It was no easy run-out for Gareth, though – Millwall were fighting a desperate battle against relegation but goals from Kenwyne Jones and Ricardo Fuller helped send them down from the Championship to League One.

Afterwards Burley would throw an arm around Gareth and tell him he had done well on his debut. Burley said, 'We have played with quality in the last few games and this was an opportunity to blood young players.'

He later added: 'I was particularly pleased with young Gareth on his debut; he was solid and composed. He has a big future in football, no doubt at all about that.'

The 2005/06 season was almost over but Gareth managed to make one more appearance before the curtain fell – a fortnight later in the home win over Leicester, by the same 2-0 scoreline.

The next season – 2006/07 – would see him much more involved in the thick of the action as he made 43 appearances and scored five goals for Saints. His impact was immediate as he netted in the opening match of the campaign, the 2-2 draw at Derby.

It arrived just after the hour mark from what would eventually become known in the trade as 'one of Bale's trademark free kicks', bringing Saints back into the match after they had trailed to a first-half goal from Seth Johnson.

Southampton's official website, www.saintsfc.co.uk, certainly sat up and took notice of the goal. It had already commended Gareth's efforts early on in the match for 'pushing on powerfully down the left' and now rhapsodised about his first professional goal in this way, 'Saints deservedly levelled with a first league goal for Gareth Bale, just three weeks after his 17th birthday. And what a peach it was! In only his third league start he had the self confidence and stature to demand the free kick when it was awarded 25 yards out. Being in the inside right channel it suited a left-footer but he pushed himself to the fore in front of dead ball specialist Skacel and curled a superb shot into the top right corner. It fired Saints forward...'

As if that in itself were not a story worthy of Roy of the Rovers, Gareth then trumped it by scoring in his next match as well, opening the scoring in the 2-0 home win over Coventry City on 61 minutes, just a minute earlier than the goal he had scored at Derby.

He then had to wait until November for his next goal, in the 1-1 draw at Sunderland. But it was a vital strike, coming in the last minute and saving Saints from defeat. The BBC summed it up in this way, 'Bale drove in a powerful shot from the edge of the area which appeared to take a deflection off Steve Caldwell on its way past Darren Ward. Southampton controlled the majority of the game but until Bale's goal had been defied by Ward, who produced a string of saves to frustrate the visitors.'

Saints boss Burley did not single Gareth out in his post match analysis. But a sure sign of the impact the Welsh wonder boy was starting to have came from the post- match comments of Burley's Sunderland counterpart, the enigmatic but legendary former Manchester United captain Roy Keane. Keano said, 'I'm disappointed we conceded a goal so late in the game, but we played a lot better at Norwich last week and lost, so that's football. The only way I thought they would find a way past Darren Ward was like that. The last player you want the ball to fall to is Gareth Bale. He's an exceptional player.'

It was a telling tribute from a man who, as a player, had won every honour going in the domestic and international club game: if anyone knew what a star of the future looked like, it would surely be Roy Keane.

Gareth also netted in the 4-2 triumph at Hull City and the 2-1 win over Norwich as Christmas 2006 loomed. The goal at Hull typified why Gareth was becoming renowned, and feared, in equal measure. Yes, it was another of his 25-yard thunderbolts that gave the keeper no chance. The win would also be the final nail in the coffin of under-pressure Hull boss Phil Parkinson – he would be forced out the following week.

Gareth also notched a similarly outstanding goal against Norwich – this time from 30 yards out. Again, his talent was applauded by the opposition. The official Norwich website, www.canaries.co.uk purred, 'Promising teenager Gareth Bale levelled before the break with a sensational 30-yard free-kick...a brilliant curling effort into the top corner which gave Gallacher no chance...'

Two days before Christmas Gareth chalked up another first – but this time it was an unwanted gift, his first yellow card, for unsporting behaviour, in the 3-3 draw at Sheffield Wednesday. It would be the first of four yellow cards in his debut full season.

The dawn of 2007 saw Gareth maintain his place in the Southampton first team as he continued to deliver the goods, defending and raiding down that left flank. Just as his efforts were being applauded by his rivals, so they were not going unnoticed by the media either. The papers were full of praise for him and even BBC *Match of the Day* commentator John Motson allowed himself to get carried away by the euphoria – publicly linking him with a move to Manchester United.

And it wasn't as if his talent was unnoticed within his own club. 'Gareth has come on in the last few months and filled out a bit,' then Saints captain Claus Lundekvam said. 'He is just going to get better and better. He is playing like someone who has been around for a long time. He can be as good as he wants to be.'

That was evident in April 2007 when he was honoured at the Football League awards ceremony in London – taking the Young Player of the Year prize.

But with such talent came, much to the anguish of all Saints fans, the inevitable Premier League predators. Ferguson and United were certainly keen, but did not back up their interest with hard cash – much, it would emerge a few years later, to Sir Alex's eternal regret.

No, it would be Tottenham Hotspur and then boss Martin Jol who would firm up their interest with enough money to twist Southampton's arm in May 2007. In total, Gareth made 45 appearances for Southampton, scoring five goals, before moving to Spurs for an initial fee of £5 million.

His last match for the Saints was the 2-1 home defeat by Derby; ironically the team against whom ten months earlier Gareth had grabbed his first goal as a professional player. It was a match that could have led Saints towards the Premier League – the first leg of their Championship playoff semi-final. But two goals from Steven Howard sent Saints into despair and their anguish was compounded when Gareth was substituted on 56 minutes after picking up an injury. He was later seen leaving St Mary's on crutches and would miss the second leg at Pride Park, which finished with Derby marching into the playoff final courtesy of a 4-3 penalty triumph after brave Saints had won 3-2 on the day, leaving the aggregate scores level at 4-4.

It was a terribly sad way for Gareth to end his Saints career. But in ten short months he had transformed from a 17-year-old with glittering potential to a 17-year-old who was set for the Premier League – albeit at a different football club than Southampton.

It had certainly been a roller-coaster journey for the boy who had almost been released by Saints two years earlier – and the twists and turns would continue to come fast and furious as he now headed for his new home at White Hart Lane, in North London.

Chapter 2

SPUR OF THE MOMENT

With Manchester United in the frame, Tottenham knew they had to act decisively and fast if they were to secure the services of Gareth Bale. So Spurs manager Martin Jol and the club's sporting director Damien Comolli quickly put together a £10 million package to signal to Saints – and Gareth – that they meant business.

While United dithered, Spurs roared in and won the day. Gareth put pen to paper on a four-year deal on May 25, 2007, just days after the rush for his signature began in earnest. 'It's true that Gareth was impressed by Spurs – and how much they clearly wanted him,' says a White Hart Lane source. 'They didn't mess about and he appreciated that. He liked the club and what they had to offer.'

It was a blow for Fergie and United and a coup for Tottenham. They had signed the biggest prospect in British football, and on their terms. Spurs agreed to make the immediate payment of £5 million they had promised earlier, with further additional payments that could see the transfer fee rise to £10 million.

It was a snip for what they were getting; a no-brainer. Saints could probably have got more up front if they had pushed harder, but they were aware that Gareth only had one year left on his contract and that he wanted to join Spurs. After the deal went through, he said, 'I'm just excited to be coming to a massive club like Spurs. It's pushing forward and I want to be part of its future.'

Martin Jol had hoped to secure Bale's signature the previous January but had been sent packing. Gareth had made it clear then that he had hopes of making the Premier League with Saints, who were in the running to make the play-offs. But when that dream died with the defeat to Derby in the play-off semis, Gareth decided to make the switch.

He said, 'I really want to play in the Premiership. That's very important to me and this is a fantastic opportunity. I've thought long and hard about it and feel the time is right to move on. I could have gone in January but I wanted to try and help Saints win promotion. I felt I owed them that and I didn't want to move mid-season.

'I wanted to keep my focus on learning and developing my game at a critical stage of the campaign.'

Tottenham were also delighted, of course, having seen off the competition of United and, it would later emerge, bitter local rivals Arsenal. Spurs sporting director Damien Comolli said, 'We have been following Gareth for a long time now and have been very tenacious, so we are absolutely delighted to get him here.

'He's a player of great quality and, as we always say, our

aim in each window is to improve the quality of the squad. He has the ideal combination to become a top, top player.'

And even United veteran Ryan Giggs paid tribute to Gareth – hiding his own disappointment that Bale had not joined United – and predicting he would be a major success in the Premier League. Giggsy said of his fellow Welshman, 'He has talent, temperament and should not have any problems. My advice for Gareth is to just carry on with what he is doing, that is why clubs have been interested in him.

'It has been totally his own decision where he goes, he has plenty of advice I am sure. But a talent like that deserves to be in the Premiership...he has all the attributes to be a top player. He has a good attitude, good behaviour and the way he conducts himself suggests he is also mature.'

Giggsy, a Welsh national team-mate of Gareth, was also convinced he would be a success in the Premier League. He said, 'Gareth's a great talent. When he first came into the Welsh squad he took to it like a duck to water and just watching him in training and his previous games for us you can tell he is a fantastic player.

'It's a tough jump from the Championship to the Premiership but I'm sure he will relish it because he's just world class and he would have the best stage in the world to show off his talents.'

Gareth was given the No. 37 shirt on his arrival at White Hart Lane and settled in quickly, making his debut in the pre-season friendly against Irish side St Patrick's. There was a certain amount of panic on the Spurs bench when he limped off towards the end of a 1-0 win with what was initially diagnosed as a thigh problem, but later appeared to have been simply a dead leg.

He was certainly fit and raring to go for his competitive first start – and it didn't come much bigger than Manchester United away in the opening match of the new 2007/08 Premier League season. Gareth's mum and dad Frank and Debbie sat proudly in the Old Trafford stands as their son finally began his career in the big-time.

But their pride and Gareth's own joy would be tinged not only by the 1-0 defeat but also, as time went by, the unpalatable fact that it was the first game in what would become known as 'the Bale jinx'. It was the beginning of the longest run of games by any Premier League player without being on the winning side – 24 appearances, over more than two seasons – and would even lead to United boss Alex Ferguson jokily suggesting to his eventual Spurs counterpart Harry Redknapp that he should flog Gareth if he planned on winning many games! Tottenham had not beaten United in 18 years prior to that opening match of the season in 2007, so it was no real shock that Gareth's competitive debut should end in defeat (courtesy of a goal from Luis Nani). But he did enough on the left flank – setting up Ricardo Rocha for a free header from one of his free kicks – to suggest that here was a young man on the brink of something wonderful. Gareth told friends it had been a 'great experience' and that he had enjoyed himself, apart from the result of course.

It was what he had always dreamed of and aimed towards from those days with his local youth team and on through the academy ranks at Saints. All the hard work and sacrifice had been worthwhile: Gareth Bale was now heading only one way. To the very top.

But there would still be agonising twists and turns on the journey – in particular the injuries that would bedevil his progress and the instability at Tottenham that saw Martin Jol and his successor Juande Ramos hit the rocks before the era of Redknapp finally dawned in October 2008.

After his side's defeat at United 14 months earlier, on August 26 2007, Jol claimed he was not under pressure and applauded Gareth and his team-mates' efforts. Jol said, 'I am bitterly disappointed because we absolutely deserved something from this game - maybe even the win. We just needed a bit of luck or a decision to go our way. I'm not under pressure. The chairman's backing me and you can see today how the players are desperate to play for this team so there is no problem.'

But there was a problem as his team struggled for results. They were away again in their next Premier League clash, exiting Craven Cottage with a 3-3 draw against Fulham – a match many pundits expected them to win. For Gareth, there was consolation as he grabbed his first goal for the club, taking a pass from Robbie Keane and leaving the Cottagers' backline for dead as he crashed the ball home on the hour. He would later tell friends it was one of the best moments of his life – but, being the perfectionist he is, was also just as disappointed they allowed the hosts to sneak a point through a last-minute equaliser by Diomansy Kamara.

Gareth was on the scoresheet again in the next Premier League encounter – but again it ended in agony. This time the grief was much worse and the pressure on Jol much greater as Spurs lost 3-1 at home to local rivals Arsenal in the middle of September 2007.

Gareth had put Spurs ahead with a fine free kick after 15 minutes but a brace from Emmanuel Adebayor and another from Cesc Fabregas condemned the Welsh wonder boy, his team-mates and the fans to a miserable weekend. It couldn't have been worse? It was – the win also lifted the Gunners to the top of the league. The visiting Arsenal fans rubbed salt in the wounds by taunting under-pressure Jol with chants of 'You're getting sacked in the morning'.

He wouldn't – but the end was not that far off. The Spurs boss conceded he was 'very pleased' with Gareth's cool-headed goal, but added that he was disappointed that his men had not been able to convert other chances. Gareth himself was 'as sick as anyone' that Arsenal had once again secured local bragging rights.

There would be temporary relief with the 6-1 thrashing of Cypriot minnows Anorthosis Famugusta in the first round of the UEFA Cup five days later and the 2-0 dispatching of Middlesbrough in the third round of the League Cup six days after that. Gareth celebrated his third goal for the club in the win over Boro, grabbing the opener with much confidence. He was released on goal by Robbie Keane, beat one defender and then ran the ball into the net past hapless keeper Brad Jones. Tom Huddlestone wrapped up the win with a headed goal three minutes later.

Afterwards Jol tried to relieve the growing pressure on himself by pointing out that he had achieved fifth-placed finishes in his first full Premier League seasons – and claiming he could win silverware in a competition like the League Cup. He said: 'I am in a very good position here, and that is what I deserve; I gave them a bit of success over the last couple of years – no-one could have done better.'

They were defiant words but the instability continued for the Dutchman, Gareth and the other Spurs staff as it emerged club officials had flown to Spain to sound out Seville manager

Ramos about taking over. The uncertainty appeared to be taking its toll in the league campaign as Tottenham now drew 4-4 at home with Aston Villa, 2-2 at Liverpool and then crashed 3-1 at Newcastle. Gareth was injured in the clash at St James's Park and would be sidelined for a month. It had been feared he had broken a bone in his foot after a rash challenge by Newcastle's Geremi – but a relieved Jol said after the match, 'We've scanned the injury several times and nothing is broken. There is significant bruising, it is still painful and we'll know more once the bruising has gone down. I feel he will be fine though and will only be out for a week to 10 days.'

The Dutchman was wrong on that score...Gareth would need a month to recover, but at least it wasn't another long-term injury. The first match he missed turned out to be Jol's farewell after a three-year stint as boss as Spurs lost 2-1 at home to Getafe in the opening match of the UEFA Cup group stage. It was a low moment at the Lane; many fans were disturbed by the way the club had dismissed a man who was a favourite on the terraces. I am told Gareth himself was 'saddened' that the man who had brought him to the club was now gone.

'I shall never forget the Spurs fans,' Jol said as he packed his bags. Well, they would never forget him and the new man had a hard act to follow. He would have to prove himself – and quickly. Ramos was certainly not slow to move into the job...the day after Jol was sacked he resigned as coach of Seville and 24 hours later became Tottenham Hotspur manager on a four-year deal, worth £5 million a year, making him one of the top paid managers in the Premier League.

Gareth Bale would play just three games for the Spaniard in

what was both men's debut campaign at the Lane and in the Premier League. He started at left-back in the 1-1 draw at West Ham in the league on November 25, 2007, and the 3-2 win over Danish outfit Aalborg in the UEFA Cup group clash four days later. But calamity struck and despair followed hot on its heels on December 2 as Gareth was injured in the 3-2 home defeat by Birmingham in the league.

He was subbed on 75 minutes after a challenge from Fabrice Muamba left him with a foot injury. A scan showed that Gareth had suffered ligament damage to his right ankle, and the really bad news was that it would mean he would be out for at least three months. It was a devastating blow just as Gareth had cemented his place at left-back in the first team, having made 12 appearances and scored three goals.

Spurs' sporting director Damien Comolli confirmed the situation in a statement on the club's website a week after Gareth suffered the injury. Comolli said,

'Gareth will now undergo an examination under anaesthesia to determine the damage sustained to the foot. The decision has been taken to bring him back slowly. Gareth is obviously disappointed to be sidelined for this length of time but he is still young and we have to do what is best for him in the long run.'

The Bale injury jinx had struck again – and it would not be the end of the matter. Worse news was to follow. In February 2008, Comolli stuck his head above the parapet once again, this time to rule Gareth out for the rest of the season. Comolli said, 'Although the surgeon was happy with the results of the X-rays he does not anticipate Gareth playing any further part this season. We are all disappointed, but his long-term fitness is our priority.'

Gareth was also disappointed. He would miss out on a season that saw Ramos set down a marker by guiding Tottenham to Premier League safety and also taking them to their first silverware for nine years.

Of course, Gareth was delighted for his team-mates as they beat Chelsea 2-1 to lift the League Cup at the new Wembley stadium in March 2008 (they had also won the same competition by beating Leicester 1-0 back in 1999) – but it was hard not being a part of the glory day at the end of February 2008.

Still, he was an optimist and was working hard on his rehabilitation. Yes, he was determined that he would also be part of a Wembley final for his new club when he got back to full fitness – and that it wouldn't take years to get there. He wouldn't have to wait long for that dream to come true – just 12 months, in fact.

And there was one unexpected high note as the season drew to its close – Gareth won praise from the man who was continuing to prove himself as a managerial genius, if also a hate figure of many Tottenham fans. Yes, even though his first Premiership season had been wrecked by that foot injury, Gareth was acclaimed by former Chelsea boss Jose Mourinho, who included him in his Fantasy Football XI.

Mourinho, by now in charge of Serie A side Inter Milan, said he believed Bale was destined to reach the very top of world football when he recovered from his enforced lay-off. Praise indeed from the man who would the following season win the Champions League with Inter – his second success in the competition after landing it with Porto in 2005. Even in a season that had been disrupted by injury, Gareth had clearly been making waves – and special ones at that.

Chapter 3

THE WING COMMANDER

It had been a long, lonely, arduous road back to fitness for Gareth during the first seven months of 2008. He would spend hour after hour with physios and rehab experts in the gym and on the training field as he slowly but surely pounded the road to recovery. Many footballers I have spoken to over the years have told me how frustrating and testing those long hours can be – and how they can take you to the limit mentally and emotionally, as well as physically.

Roy Keane, for example, would admit that he was 'terrible company to be around' when he was out injured. The Irishman is one of the strongest, most determined people you would ever meet in terms of mental durability. But even he would concede that doubts crept in about whether he would ever play again as he was forced to spend almost a whole season on the sidelines after suffering cruciate ligament injury in the 1997/98 campaign.

Keane said his long-term recovery programme pushed him to the limit emotionally and mentally and that he had many low periods as he struggled to regain his fitness. But, of course, he did return and eventually to the level of aggression and talent for which he had already become famed.

Gareth would face a similar mountain to climb in those challenging eight months on the sidelines. But he is more of a measured, balanced individual than Keano – less susceptible to bouts of the black dog and with a more positive outlook. Of course, as we have mentioned already, he was gutted not to be playing every week and particularly to have missed out on the League Cup final win over Chelsea.

But he kept his spirits up and was fully supported by his family and friends. He had also experienced the physical battle before – he was no stranger to injury and physical demands on his body. After all, it had been a tough ride during his early and mid teens when growth spurts put pressure on his back. Yes, pain was no stranger.

Certainly Ramos, Comolli and the backroom staff at the Lane were impressed by his resilience and optimistic attitude. 'He's a fighter and a winner,' the Spaniard would say in his broken English. 'He will be back – and better than before.'

That probably explains why in August 2008 Ramos put him straight back into the first team for the start of the new 2008/09 season and also boosted his spirits even more by awarding him the No. 3 shirt for the campaign – even though Lee Young-Pyo was still at the club – and a new contract, even though he had only put pen to paper to a four year deal 14 months earlier.

Gareth happily signed the new four-and-a-half year deal offered to him by the club. It gave him improved terms on the deal signed in May 2007 – I am told his salary increased from £15,000 a week to £25,000 – and provided both sides with security until at least 2012. Spurs hoped that by that time their wonder boy would appreciate how much he was wanted and loved by the club, and would stay well beyond. It was a piece of shrewd management and shrewd business sense by Tottenham. It showed Gareth that they believed he had a big future at the Lane – and that they were also convinced he would not only recover from his injury but come back stronger than ever.

By acting early, I am told Spurs hoped they had taken the important first steps in tying up a superb young talent for what they hoped would be his whole footballing career.

But his season would once again be disrupted by injury and instability behind the scenes.

Gareth's first competitive appearance since the foot injury was in the 2-0 loss at Middlesbrough on Saturday August 16, 2008, when he came on as a 65th-minute sub for Aaron Lennon. He started the next match on the left of a five-man midfield and ended up getting booked as Spurs crashed 2-1 to Sunderland in their first Premier League match of the new campaign at the Lane.

The joy and glory of winning the League Cup almost six months earlier was beginning to evaporate for Tottenham fans – as was goodwill towards boss Ramos. A sign of the crevice between supporters and manager was their restlessness not only at the poor results but also that he had not ingratiated himself more within the club and their affections. It was a fact that he still could not communicate in English – and there were growing suggestions that the team were suffering as a consequence.

Once again it was left to Ramos's trusty assistant, the likeable Gus Poyet to face the media after the latest defeat. He said of the loss to the Mackems, 'Defeat is difficult to take because we really tried very hard to go and create chances, and we had a few, to change the result. They did their job – Sunderland really worked very hard.'

By deduction, Spurs had not done their job nor worked very hard. Ramos was on the rack and it got worse – the Spaniard would lead the club to their worst ever start to a league campaign, with the team rock bottom of the table with just two points from their opening eight matches. Clearly it couldn't continue and the board put him (but mostly the fans, seeing as he would pocket a fat compensation fee) out of their misery on October 25, 2008.

Gareth had played in 11 matches under Ramos that season. The disastrous run of results had also seen Gareth sent off for the first time in his career, as they lost 2-1 at Stoke, a week before the Spanish manager's demise. Bale saw red on 17 minutes for a tackle on Tom Soares which gave City their first spot-kick. Danny Higginbotham made no mistake from the spot, opening the scoring for the Potters.

It was more a clumsy blunder than a deliberately bad tackle on Soares and Gareth could count himself unlucky that he was forced to take that early bath. But he would say later that he was still disappointed with himself at conceding the penalty and that he had certainly had better days at the office.

He was sad to see Ramos go and, along with him, Comolli, who had been so instrumental in bringing him to the Lane in the first place. There was a sense of despair and anxiety around the club but it would not take long to lift – just 24 hours, in fact.

Luckily, the board had the good sense to line up as the dour, uncommunicative Spaniard's replacement a man who was the exact opposite: the bright, talkative Harry Redknapp, who was never without an opinion or a quip. He was also the right man for the job: talented, experienced in the whims and ways of the English player and the Premier League and a true breath of fresh air after the claustrophobic despair of the Ramos regime.

Just 12 hours into his new job, Harry led Spurs to their first win of the season – a 2-0 home triumph over Bolton. Gareth missed the victory; he was serving his suspension after being dismissed at Stoke. But he was also caught up in the feelgood factor as the Redknapp era began in earnest. The good times were about to roll and Harry, whose services had cost £5 million to secure from Portsmouth, was determined they would come sooner rather than later.

Redknapp, who the previous season had led Pompey to the FA Cup, told Sky Sports: 'It's a great opportunity for me. It's a big club, Tottenham. They have a decent squad on paper, although it's not a well-balanced squad, it's a squad with good ability, very skilful players – but maybe a bit of a soft centre.

'We need a little bit more strength and aggression about the team if we're going to survive. You don't pick up two points (so far this season) if you're that good. They've been on a horrendous run of games and we've got to get cracking and turn it around as quick as we can.'

Gareth's first start under Redknapp came the following week – and it couldn't have been much bigger or important, in London terms – against Arsenal at the Emirates. The match ended in a thrilling 4-4 draw, with Gareth speeding down the left midfield flank, with Benoit Assou-Ekotto in the left-back slot.

The *Sun*'s Mark Irwin best summed up the new spirit of optimism at Tottenham when he wrote, 'Arsène Wenger has already seen off eight Tottenham managers during his 12 years at Arsenal. Harry Redknapp could prove a bit more difficult to shift. His team might still be stuck at the foot of the Premier League and chucking goals away like there is no tomorrow.

'But in the space of just four days Redknapp has already restored the pride and fighting spirit to a team which had become a laughing stock under Juande Ramos. Aaron Lennon's 93rd-minute equaliser provided an unforgettable ending to a night of heart-stopping drama in North London. Lennon was the first to react when Luka Modric's desperate, last-gasp effort came back off a post and set up scenes of utter jubilation among the Spurs fans.'

Utter jubilation...who would have guessed it a week earlier when gloom and doom was the order of the day in the dying embers of the Ramos era.

Harry now led Spurs clear of the drop zone in his first two weeks in charge, winning ten out of the twelve points available – although Gareth would be in and out of his team. He brought back Jermain Defoe from his old club Portsmouth for £15.75 million, Robbie Keane for £12 million from Liverpool and signed Honduran midfielder Wilson Palacios from Wigan for £12 million.

But still Gareth could not end his jinx of not being on the winning side when the boss selected him in Premier League matches.

Still, Bale did make an impression as Spurs marched to Wembley for the League Cup final against Manchester United on Sunday March 1, 2009. The match held a double significance. Firstly, it gave Gareth a chance to make up for missing out on the previous season's final which Tottenham had won. And secondly, it was an opportunity to get revenge on United after they had ended Gareth's dream of getting to the FA Cup final by beating them 2-1 at Old Trafford just five weeks earlier.

Yet it wasn't to be. Gareth didn't even start the match; Harry preferring to go with Assou-Ekotto at left-back and Jermaine Jenas in midfield. He eventually arrived on the scene on 98 minutes, replacing the aforementioned Jenas. That gave him just 22 minutes to change the outcome at Wembley; it was asking too much. He didn't even get to take a penalty in the shootout after the game ended goalless after extra time. Jamie O'Hara and David Bentley missed from the spot, with only Vedran Corluka saving face as United won 4-1 on penalties.

It was a disappointing end to a disappointing day – certainly not the glory-laced occasion Gareth had dreamt of. Indeed, from dreams of glory, Gareth and his team-mates now had to confront the very real possibility that they might get drawn into an unexpected relegation scrap. 'Yes, Gareth was down and deflated after the final,' a Spurs source said. 'He had built up his hopes after missing out the season before – he really wanted to win some silverware with the club. There was not much party spirit at the post-match bash – they were all just glad when it was all over and they could get home.'

Boss Redknapp was also downhearted and confirmed that he feared getting sucked into the relegation battle. He said, 'There's injuries, there's fatigue – we've spent all our resources. But I thought we were super. It was a great performance and it came down to a lottery in the end. They couldn't beat us in 90 minutes plus extra time, we didn't deserve to lose and I thought we were fantastic.'

His team were two points above the relegation zone and set for a match at Middlesbrough, who were also fighting to beat the drop, three days later. 'We have to make sure we are focused for that match and get something from it,' Harry added.

Tottenham's form would pick up and they would eventually finish in eighth position in the league table, missing out on a Europa League spot by just one place to fellow Londoners Fulham. Gareth would still be in and out of the team in the home straight and when he did play, they still did not win. After the League Cup final, some pundits and fans even suggested he should be sold off.

He played just three league games that season after that League Cup final setback – the first one being, ironically, as a late sub at Old Trafford as United rubbed salt in the wound by winning 5-2 on April 25, then starting in the 0-0 draw at Everton on 9 May and the 3-1 defeat at Liverpool on May 26.

In his second season at Tottenham, Gareth had made 30 appearances, scored no goals and been sent off once. It had clearly not gone as planned after that promising opening when he was told he was going to get a pay rise and a new deal.

There would be another setback a month after the season ended when it emerged he would need surgery on his knee. A scan confirmed he had a medial meniscal tear and a Tottenham spokesman relayed the bad news that he would now be out for possibly two months. It would mean he'd miss the club's pre-season and training.

It couldn't really get much worse could it? He was injured again and hadn't yet been on the winning side when he had turned out for Spurs in the Premier League. But this was the end of the beginning for Bale at Tottenham: he would now fly on an extraordinary upward trajectory in tandem with new mentor Redknapp.

The 2009/10 campaign – Redknapp's first full season with the club and Gareth's second – would see them work together to bring Tottenham their most successful Premier League season ever. At the end of it they would be dreaming of the Champions League after finishing fourth, Redknapp would be named Barclays Manager of the Year and Gareth would be on the brink of world stardom.

The campaign began with four straight wins but it was not until September that Gareth got involved in the action after recovering from his latest injury. He missed seven games in total – six in the league and the 5-1 romp over Doncaster in the League Cup – before returning to action on 23 September, 2009. It was a happy comeback as he helped Tottenham to another 5-1 League Cup win, this time at Preston in the third round.

Three days later, as if to confirm his dark days were now over, he finally finished on the winning side in a league match with Tottenham. It was September 26, and four minutes from the end of the match against Burnley at the Lane, with Spurs 4-0 up. Spurs scored again and Gareth was simply delighted to have taken part in a winning Premier League game for the first time in 25 appearances. 'It was a real weight off his back,' a club source revealed. 'The more games that went by, the harder it seemed to be to beat the jinx. He was cock-a-hoop when the final whistle went. It was also a fine piece of man-management by Harry [Redknapp]. To bring him on when there was no chance of the team drawing or losing. Mind you, if they'd lost after being 4-0 up, both Gareth and Harry would have been pulling their hair out!'

Gareth would later tell the *Daily Telegraph*, 'It was just one of those freak things; we had a bit of banter about it in the changing-room but it never really affected me as a person.'

He may have finally beaten the jinx, but now Gareth faced another problem – the fine form of Benoit Assou-Ekotto. At this time, Redknapp appeared to view Bale purely as a left-back, and that meant he could not get into the team – he simply could not dislodge the Cameroon international. To be fair to the boss, it would have been cruel to have axed Assou-Ekotto. The solution was already staring Redknapp in the face, but he seemed unwilling to apply it, although, of course, within a couple of months, he would see sense and have Gareth playing in front of Benoit in left midfield.

It all meant Gareth would not be on the winning side as a starter in the Premier League for Spurs until the end of January in 2010...another four months after tasting victory in the league as a sub against Burnley! In those four months, he did start in the Carling Cup and the FA Cup and taste success – as they beat Everton at the end of October in the former and Peterborough in the latter in January.

One man's misfortune became another's good fortune. Assou-Ekotto suffered an injury, allowing Gareth in via the back door for the 4-0 thrashing of Posh in the FA Cup, with the young Welshman putting in a fine performance. So, finally, on Tuesday January 26, 2010, Gareth finally put to bed that long sequence of games without a win as a starter in the team as goals from Peter Crouch and David Bentley put Fulham in their place with a 2-0 triumph at the Lane.

The BBC's Sam Lyon summed Gareth's relief up in this way, '...And that was pretty much that as far as the competitive edge in the match was concerned, with Tottenham happy to move the ball around comfortably and injury-ravaged Fulham apparently just happy to keep the score down. It will do nothing to take away from what was a red-letter day for Gareth Bale, though, who – at the 23rd time of asking – secured his first ever victory as a Premier League starter.' 'Yep, Gareth was relieved,' says a Spurs source. 'But he had also been just as concerned about playing well. The aim was to get in the first team – and stay there.'

And he did just that. From that day onwards, Gareth Bale was a guaranteed starter for Tottenham, one, if not the, first names on the team sheet. Benoit Assou-Ekotto would also be one of the select band who could count on being picked in the first eleven when he finally returned to action on February 24, 2010, in the 4-0 drubbing of Bolton in the FA Cup fifth round. How? Simple. As we have already said, the answer to the dilemma of how to fit two such talented left-sided players into the same team was to play the Cameroon international at left-back – and push Gareth forward, where he could attack and destroy teams, rather than simply having to destroy them.

It was a role he would quickly grow accustomed to and grow to love – while world-class defenders such as Maicon would rue the day Redknapp had taken the logical step to set Gareth free.

Remarkably, Redknapp said recently that he still considered Gareth would be better as a defender than a left-midfielder/winger. I am convinced that old Harry is wrong on that one. Certainly I know for sure that Gareth loved the freer role – and he even admitted as much, although being careful not to antagonise the boss, when he was asked what he thought of Harry's assessment. Gareth said: 'I think the best part of my game, whether I'm playing left-back or left mid, is going forward. But it's up to the manager where he sees my future and where he wants to play me.'

Gareth's rich vein of form was officially acknowledged on March 1, 2010, when he was named EON Player of the Round by the FA for his brilliance in the two FA Cup fifth round encounters with Bolton. He had set up Defoe for the equaliser in the original 1-1 draw at the Reebok on February 14 and then made the third goal in the 4-0 slaughter of Wanderers in the replay at the Lane 10 days later. Gareth zoomed down the left and crossed a dangerous ball that the hapless Andy O'Brien could only deflect past his own keeper Jussi Jaaskelainen. Gareth amassed a resounding 61 per cent of the votes for the award with Crystal Palace's Darren Ambrose in second place – and the still shell-shocked Jaaskelainen was also on the shortlist!

April started badly but got much better for the wonder boy. On the 11th of the month he suffered more heartache in the latter stages of the cup competitions. Last year it had been in the final against Manchester United, now it was agony in the semi of the FA Cup as he and his team-mates surprisingly slumped to a 2-0 loss against Portsmouth at Wembley.

It was a shock of a scoreline against a team that had already been relegated from the Premier League. Gareth was downhearted – he had believed he had set up an equaliser for Crouch but ref Alan Wiley disallowed it for a foul by Nico Kranjcar on David James. TV replays would show that Wiley had got it badly wrong and that only added to the sense of injustice felt afterwards in the dressing room. 'Of course Gareth was low afterwards,' says a Spurs source. 'They all were. No one had believed that Pompey would have won, it was an absolute shocker. The only saving grace was that they still had a carrot to play for – if they finished fourth in the league, they would make the qualifiers for the Champions League. And everyone knew that was a much bigger prize than the FA Cup winners could hope for [a place in the Europa League].'

Gareth led the way in two crunch home games after the loss to Pompey – against Arsenal and Chelsea.

Youngster Danny Rose put Spurs ahead at the Lane against the Gunners and Gareth side-footed the ball home to make it 2-0 just after the interval. Nicklas Bendtner pulled one back, but it was too little, too late. Tottenham were now fifth, one place and one point behind Man City who were still clutching on to that all-important fourth place.

Afterwards Redknapp praised Gareth and Rose for their goals and added, 'It was a great win because we came here on the back of a disappointing day on Sunday. To lift ourselves after that and turn in a performance like that said so much for the players, especially when we were so patched up. All round it was a great night for us, everybody worked hard and did a great job.'

They did indeed. And they would do the same great job three days later, this time beating Chelsea by the same score. Defoe put Spurs ahead from the penalty spot on 15 minutes after Terry handled in the box and Gareth made it 2-0 just before the interval, leaving Paulo Ferreira for dead and hammering the ball home...with his right foot!

Lampard pulled one back for the Blues on the stroke of full-time, but it was Spurs who took the three points. Spurs fan Alan Fisher summed up Gareth's showing when asked his views by the *Guardian*. He said, 'Bale was outstanding, the physicality and shrewdness of his game; he is a world-class prospect.' He named Gareth as his star man – awarding him 10 out of 10. 'Gareth was well chuffed with the win – and to have scored with his right foot!' a Spurs source confirmed. 'Everyone knows he is a genius with his left foot – well, his right ain't that bad either, you know!'

There was more good news. Manchester City had lost 1-0 at home to Manchester United and Tottenham were now in those oh-so-important Champions League places – replacing City in fourth place. The stage was now set for a four-game shootout that would decide if Spurs or City grabbed the big prize.

After the jubilation of the wins over their London rivals, Spurs suffered a big setback in the first of those four matches, losing 3-1 at Old Trafford to Manchester United. Two penalties from Ryan Giggs and a goal from Nani brought about Gareth and Co's downfall, with only a Ledley King headed goal to ease the pain of the defeat as the lads travelled back to London. Gareth at least had earned the kudos of having set up Ledley for the goal with a pinpoint corner as he eased into his seat on the coach for the three-hour journey. And the day after he would learn he had been named Barclays Player of the Month for April – the first time he had won the coveted award, and the first time a Welshman had won it since, ironically, Giggs in February 2007.

There was one other consolation after the defeat at Old Trafford – and it was a big one. Man City had only managed a 0-0 draw at Arsenal, so Spurs stayed in fourth place, still a point clear of their rivals.

One game down, three to go for Gareth and Co.

They would win two and lose one – but it was enough

because one of those victories was against...Man City, away. On May 1, Tottenham beat Bolton 1-0 at the Lane and four days later headed back up north for the big date with City at the City of Manchester Stadium. A late goal from Crouch sealed the points for Tottenham as they scampered away from Manchester with a 1-0 win – and a potential £30 million windfall as they had now secured that vital fourth place finish in the Premier League, and with it a Champions League qualifying spot.

Tottenham now had 70 points to City's 66, which meant the last match of the season away at Burnley was largely irrelevant. Gareth and the boys had done it...and in some style, too. He hailed the achievement as 'fantastic' and said he couldn't wait to play in the Champions League. He also made it clear he loved it at White Hart Lane – and had never felt the need of going to another club to fulfil his ambitions. 'He felt at home,' says a Spurs source. 'You could see that from the Tottenham dressing room at City afterwards as the team celebrated with each other – they were all friends as well as team-mates, and Gareth was a very popular lad indeed.'

The season couldn't have ended better for Spurs, Gareth or the fans.

Well, maybe they could have won at Burnley...

But no one at the club was too anguished when they crashed 4-2 at Turf Moor in the final game of the season. And at least Gareth grabbed another goal – his third of the season for the club, all of which had come in the last six matches. Gareth opened the scoring with a fine drive on three minutes but tiredness inevitably affected the boys after that season-defining win at City just four days earlier. Redknapp admitted as much after the game, saying, 'Perhaps I should have rested a few, but I wanted to give them the chance to finish the season off.'

To be fair, even if they had won at Turf Moor, they still would not have finished third in the table as, at the same time, Arsenal were thrashing Fulham 4-0 at the Emirates.

So the Gunners finished the campaign on 75 points, five ahead of Tottenham.

Gareth had certainly come on a bunch during the season and inevitably, as it concluded, there was talk that he might be a transfer target for other clubs. But, as we have already pointed out, he had already made it quite clear that he was happy at the Lane – and Redknapp certainly had no doubt he would stay at the club, saying he was 'the future of this football club'.

Harry added, 'We're looking to build a team here. We wouldn't be looking to sell players like him. His game has gone up so many levels this season. He's got stronger, he's a fantastic athlete, great ability. He can do everything. He's got the ability to run all day. He's grown up. He's still only a boy, but physically he has got stronger this last year and he's looking as good as any left-sided player in the country.

'The ability to run like he does is amazing. He runs 60 yards, recovers, runs 60 yards again, recovers, runs 60 yards, he just doesn't stop. When you are playing against him it must be very difficult because he just keeps going at you and going at you. Eventually, unless you are very fit, you are not going to run with him for 90 minutes.'

There was one final act in the drama. As if to prove that he backed his manager, club chairman Daniel Levy called Gareth to his office and presented him with a new contract as a reward for his brilliant development from January 2010 to the end of the season in May. Gareth had no hesitation in putting pen to paper on the four-year deal which would tie him to the club until 2014.

He was still only 20 and had played 70 times for Tottenham. After an unsteady start to his career at the Lane, Gareth Bale had settled and become a major player. But it was only the beginning of a remarkable surge to the top: yes, the next season would rocket him into a completely new universe of acclaim...and stardom.

Chapter 4

A SPECIAL ONE

As the 2010/2011 season dawned, Gareth Bale must have felt the usual nervous excitement. He had enjoyed a good summer break, relaxing and unwinding after the last busy season. But this pre-season also felt different than previous ones – and it seems Gareth felt differently about it, and the prospects it held. It was as if he knew that it would be his defining season: the one that would make him a recognised name in world football, not just at Spurs and in Wales.

Perhaps that explained his even more vigorous approach to pre-season training and an even more determined attitude as he launched into the pre-season friendlies. Yes, it was as if his moment had now come on the world footballing stage – and he would do everything in his power to ensure he didn't fluff his lines.

A Spurs source said: 'You could see it in his eyes and in his demeanour when we got down to pre-season work. It was almost as if he were possessed. He was like a demon in training and it was quickly apparent that his game had gone up to an altogether different level. Almost overnight, he had become a superstar.'

That theme was picked up by lifelong fan Stevie Turner. He told me: 'Yes, he seemed to have got bigger and better. He reminded me of Cristiano Ronaldo – he had that big, tall frame and yet could dance around the opposition as if he were small like Aaron Lennon. And he must have been working on his conditioning – he certainly seemed much faster when he got the ball. He had become a phenomenon – he was like a tornado running down that wing. Even before he really came to prominence against Inter Milan, we had been seeing all the signs of his remarkable development.'

There were suggestions that the change had also been brought on by a sudden elevation of confidence – and that this in turn had been brought on by an attempt by one of the world's biggest clubs to buy him in that summer. The Spurs source added: 'Gareth had been watching a lot of the World Cup and that whetted his appetite for the new season. It made him think that he wanted to be part of games like that but, of course, the problem is that Wales rarely qualify. I got the impression that he decided that summer that he therefore needed to play in the biggest games at club level – which meant the Champions League.

'There was a strong rumour that Real Madrid put in a bid for him during the summer, but it was rejected out of hand. Of course, any footballer worth their salt would have been interested if Real came in for them, but I was told that Gareth was happy enough staying at Spurs – as they would be in the

Champions League, anyway, and he loves the club, the manager and especially the fans, who have always been on his side.'

Credence to the claim that Bale had been targeted by Real Madrid in the summer of 2010 came a couple of months later from then Wales national team boss John Toshack. He said: 'It was a big-money bid – it's big money to me anyway. You'll have to ask Tottenham, they know about it. Gareth is aware people are looking at him and people are interested.'

When asked which club it was, Toshack would only say: 'I wouldn't do that out of confidence for the people who have informed me.'

But given that the former Liverpool frontman had managed at the Bernabeu during two spells in the late Eighties and early Nineties, and still had good contacts there, it was widely assumed he was talking about Real Madrid.

Pre-season went well. Gareth had not let his fitness drop that much during the weeks away from the Lane. He was not that kind of footballer. Being abstinent from booze and not indulging in food binges made it easy for him. It was Gareth who scored the only goal in the final pre-season friendly: the 1-0 win in Lisbon over Benfica.

The win was another big confidence booster. While Spurs would have to qualify for the Champions League proper via a play-off, Benfica were already through.

So, what was there to worry about? If they could beat one of the teams who had already qualified in their own backyard, surely they could see off the challenge of a fellow qualifying hopeful in the play-offs?

Plus Benfica had beaten Aston Villa 4-1 the previous Saturday, so they were certainly no mugs.

Gareth was 'very pleased' with his performance and that the

club had won the Eusébio Cup – named after the club's most famous player ever, the brilliant Eusébio da Silva Ferreira – by beating the Portuguese giants.

Boss Redknapp had not been as pleased that his team were facing their sixth pre-season match. He called the fixtures pile-up 'crazy' and had pointed to 'pre-season fatigue' as being one of the reasons Spurs had crashed 4-1 at home to Villarreal in the previous friendly, just five days before the match in Lisbon.

But at least he was smiling after lifting the Eusébio Cup. Redknapp said: 'It was a good performance, Bale and Luka Modric were excellent down the left in the first half and Jermaine Jenas passed the ball well. It's now a case of trying to get everyone fit and strengthen the squad if I can.'

Gareth had made two key contributions before his goal. In the first minute he sent Giovani Dos Santos away down the left flank, but the Mexican blew the opportunity. Then Gareth set up Peter Crouch with a fine cross – only for the big hitman's goal to be controversially disallowed for offside.

Dos Santos later made amends for his earlier howler by setting Gareth up for the winning goal on the hour. His cute back-heel giving Bale an easy chance to score from just 10 yards out.

There were now 11 days to go before the start of the season – and the big Premier League kick-off. Redknapp, his assistant manager Kevin Bond and first team coach Joe Jordan now stepped up the ante in training. Each day would be harder and more stamina-building as the three men pushed the players to maximum fitness and tried to build up their stamina. The intensity left several of the players gasping for breath, but Gareth Bale was not one of them.

A naturally fit, lean and energetic young man, he roared through the sessions and was one of the few who stayed out on the pitch for more work-outs and practice after the management team called time at the club's training ground in Chigwell, Essex.

By Saturday August 14, Gareth was like a prize fighter who had been locked away training in the mountains for weeks – and who could not wait to get in the ring to work off the pent-up energy. He was truly ready to go to work and the fixture list computer had certainly thrown up a tantalising opener.

Spurs would begin their campaign against the team that had become their biggest rival for that fourth Champions League spot...yes, the club bankrolled by the Arab sheiks' oil money, Manchester City.

The clubs had met just three months earlier in the vital Premier League clash at Eastlands that would decide which of them headed into the Champions League. Spurs had kept their nerve and outplayed the City millionaires, winning 1-0 to secure the Champions League spot that could bring a potential £40 million jackpot. Peter Crouch had headed home the late winner.

City's directors had applauded politely at the final whistle but disappointment and anger lay behind their rigid grins. City boss Roberto Mancini had been brought in specifically to ensure the Sky Blues made it into the Champions League, and his failure led to many pundits doubting whether he would survive the summer. He was given a reprieve – but on the strict understanding that any subsequently similar failure would lead to his dismissal.

So there was much resting on that first fixture of the new season. Mancini knew he could not afford to lose – there would be no gradual easing into the new campaign for him and his under-pressure team. And Harry Redknapp and Bale and the boys wanted a good result to put down a marker for the season.

Given the heightened stress and pressure, it was hardly a

surprise that the match should fizzle out to a 0-0 draw. But Italian Mancini certainly owed a debt to his goalkeeper Joe Hart. The newly-installed England No. 1 (after the World Cup debacle that had seen England crash 4-1 to Germany in the last 16) made a string of top-notch saves in the White Hart Lane sunshine.

The big stopper denied Jermain Defoe, Tom Huddlestone, Benoit Assou-Ekotto and Roman Pavlyuchenko. Inevitably perhaps, the only man who had the beating of him on the day was Bale, but the Welshman's left foot shot rebounded agonisingly off the post to safety.

Gareth gave City's Micah Richards the runaround throughout the 90 minutes, and could have had a penalty at one stage when the big right-back floored him in the box. Gareth was also the villain of the day when he fluffed an easy chance when one on one with Hart a few minutes before the final whistle. But, a Spurs dressing room source told me: 'No one made a big deal of it afterwards. OK, it would have won us the three points but the way Hart was thwarting us we never looked like breaking through – and don't forget that the chance fell on Gareth's right foot. If it had been his left, the boss would have been moaning like mad!'

Gareth was disappointed afterwards – he felt Spurs should have got off to a winning start – and the dressing room was a rather muted, frustrating place. Boss Redknapp was also convinced it was two points lost although he had the grace to congratulate Hart on his heroics: 'Sometimes you can play that well and still not get a result. We did everything that we'd worked on. We moved the ball about with great style and you can't ask for more than that. We couldn't get the breakthrough but their keeper had a fantastic game, which was good for the England manager and good for England.'

But bad for Tottenham, as they aimed to show from the start of the campaign that their fourth place finish the previous season had been no fluke. They were handed a swift opportunity to show what they were made of three days later, when they travelled to Switzerland for another key match, the first leg of their Champions League qualifier – against Young Boys on their controversial Astroturf pitch.

Once again, the result was not the signal of intent Redknapp had demanded, his side going down 3-2 on the night. But it could have been a lot worse as Gareth and co were trailing 3-0 after half an hour in Bern – and Redknapp was pleased at least by the fighting qualities of his team.

The Spurs Odyssey fans' website summed up the night brilliantly, saying: 'The travelling army of Spurs fans thought they were in Bern to witness a historic Spurs debut in the Champions League, but after half an hour must have thought they had taken a wrong turning to Disneyland. By that time Spurs were three down to a rampaging Young Boys team, who looked like scoring a hatful more goals against a defence that looked like Bambi on Ice, never mind the Astroturf.'

Spurs were run ragged on the hosts' plastic pitch but the two goals they scored – courtesy of Bassong and Pavyluchenko – meant they were still very much in the tie and that their dream of making the Champions League proper was still very much alive.

Gareth's corner set up Bassong for Spurs' first goal, three minutes before the break, and Pavyluchenko grabbed the vital second seven minutes from time.

Gareth was a relieved man in the dressing room after the match. He knew Spurs had got away with it; that they were somehow still in with a chance of realising their Champions

League dream despite struggling with the icy conditions and the Astroturf.

Redknapp summed up his feelings when he said: 'That was a great defeat if there is such a thing. At 3-0 we were staring down the barrel. We were in desperate trouble. We didn't look happy on the surface, we were not confident in our play. It was a great goal from Pavlyuchenko to put us back in the tie, though otherwise he had a very quiet night. He can do that.

'I had a nasty feeling about the game. I watched the players train on the pitch and watched them feel not happy about this and that. It's not an excuse but I played on Astroturf myself and hated every minute of it. I don't agree with Astroturf and I don't think Astroturf should be used in a competition like this. Jermain Defoe and Luka Modric have both picked up strains and are doubtful for the weekend. Young Boys started the game excellently. They pressed us. We couldn't get to grips with holding the ball. We didn't look sure of ourselves and suddenly we were almost out of the tie.

'It took some character to come back. At half-time, I said, "Come on, we've got a lifeline and we've got to go and get another goal". Luckily enough we managed to do so.'

They had lost but had battled back – a theme that would become something of a constant as the season progressed. Spurs could certainly score goals, but they were guilty also of conceding too many of them, a failing that Gareth knew could well cost them dearly if they ever came up against opposition such as Barcelona.

But for now, even though they had lost the first leg, there was hope and belief that they would see the job through as they relaxed on the plane journey back to London.

Even Young Boys suspected they may have had their chance

– and blown it by not making Spurs pay more on their Astroturf. Young Boys' Enfield-born right-back Scott Sutter – a Spurs fan – summed up the feeling of anxiety in their dressing room: 'It was a dream for me to play against Tottenham. As a player it doesn't get better than this, walking out in front of a full house to play Tottenham – I could never have imagined it like this.

'We tried to look for the fourth goal and we had a couple of very good chances to extend our lead. I just hope we can keep as concentrated.'

Gareth and the boys definitely had to keep their concentration levels high – no sooner had they arrived home than they were back training at Chigwell in preparation for another crunch game, the Premier League clash away at traditionally hard-to-beat, dogs-of-war battlers, Stoke City.

This would be the match in which Gareth Bale's season truly came alive: the match in which he would be the two-goal hero after the damp squibs of the Man City and Young Boys outings. It would also be a turning point for the boy – the first time he had scored two goals in his professional career and the moment he truly announced himself as a potentially major star in the domestic game at least. Plus Gareth finally put to bed the embarrassment of being red-carded at the Britannia Stadium in the reverse match back in October 2008. Then, Spurs were at the wrong end of a 2-1 scoreline, with Gareth being dismissed after just 17 minutes for bundling over Tom Soares in the box – a foul that led to Danny Higginbotham scoring for Stoke. The defeat was probably the lowest point of the Juande Ramos reign: after the match Tottenham were four points adrift at the bottom of the Premier League table and had already lost six league games.

Fast forward two years and Spurs were now rocking and

rolling under Redknapp and Gareth's first goal in the win over Stoke arrived on 19 minutes when Aaron Lennon set him with a defence-splitting ball. Gareth's first shot was blocked by keeper Thomas Sorensen but the Welshman bundled home the rebound. If the first goal had a touch of luck, the second was an absolute belter as Bale fired home on the volley with his left foot.

In between, Ricardo Fuller scored for the Potters, and they were then denied what appeared a legitimate equaliser when Jon Walters's late header appeared to cross the line, but no goal was given.

Gareth was beaming afterwards, saying his two-goal salvo had iced the cake on 'one of the best days of my life'. Gareth said of his volley: 'I don't think I've ever caught a shot as sweetly as that, It's a great feeling when you hit one like that. The first one went in off my nose, but they all count and now I feel I am repaying the manager for giving me a regular run in the team.

'I still don't know if my role is left-back or left midfield but I always knew my confidence would increase with more games.'

Boss Redknapp was full of praise for him, explaining that this sort of show had been what he had expected Gareth to finally deliver after many previous days of disappointment – days when he had been forced to deliver 'tough love' to the Welsh wonderboy.

Redknapp said: 'When I first came to the club he was still a baby. Every time he got touched he'd limp off the training ground and then be all right again in five minutes. I made him realise he had to be mentally tougher if he was going to make it in the Premier League. And to be fair to the lad, that's what he's done. He's come on leaps and bounds and his confidence is sky high.

'I just said to him, "C'mon Gareth, stop f*****g about with your barnet and toughen up". Real good tactical stuff – but it worked.'

Harry admitted that he had worried about the boy in that demoralising period during which the team never won a league game when Gareth was in the starting line-up. He said: 'That record was a burden for him – and a burden for me. Even Alex Ferguson asked me, "how can you pick him?" and I couldn't. I'm a superstitious person and it was difficult to keep putting him in my team. But at the same time I always knew there was a player in there and there was no way I was going to sell him. On top of that he's also a smashing lad. You couldn't meet a nicer kid.'

But despite Gareth's two goals, Harry surprised the press corps listening to his every word when he said he believed the boy would eventually return to left-back; that he thought he was more suited to that than the left wing. Redknapp said: 'I think Gareth will be as good as Ashley Cole, the best left-back anywhere. Cole started out as a winger at Arsenal and ended up as a full-back and this kid will be the same. He played at left-back against Benfica the other week and I've not seen a performance like it. He kept running from deep, crossing balls from their by-line and then getting back. I can't think of a better British left-sided player.

'That left foot of his is amazing, he can run all day, he's 6ft 2in and can head it and his technique is unbelievable. He's got everything and I couldn't even begin to put a value on him.'

Gareth had been voted Man of the Match against Stoke, with even Potteries boss Tony Pulis being heard to comment that 'the boy's a phenomenon; he could be world-class'. He temporarily basked in the glory of his performance and the adulation but, true to form, was hardly carried away by it all. Just as he had been forced to knuckle down and keep up his spirits and self-belief during his rough spell, so he would now wave away the plaudits.

Gareth Bale wanted to be a world-class footballer but he knew that it wouldn't just happen by luck; he was a grounded lad who was always willing to dig deep and work hard for his success. And, anyway, neither Harry nor his team-mates would tolerate anyone within the squad getting carried away if they were singled out for praise. The Spurs lads quickly took the mickey out of anyone who started to act the 'big I am'; bringing them down to earth with a bang...or by playing practical jokes on them.

But Gareth soon had another chance to show how he was developing into a class act, with the return leg at White Hart Lane of the Champions League qualifier against Young Boys. Their two-goal comeback had given them hope (and what could turn out to be key away goals) in the 3-2 loss a week earlier, but now they had to do the business in front of their own fans...or face an ignominious, early exit from the competition and the end of their dreams of playing in the world's premier club competition (for another year at least).

Redknapp issued a rallying call before kick off, urging his men to smash the Swiss with an avalanche of goals. He said: 'We've got to swarm all over them from the start. Our pride is at stake and we want to get into the Champions League proper. The place will be jumping and that will be a big thing in our favour. I wouldn't say we are favourites. But the bottom line is if we can't win, we don't deserve to be in the competition. We have got to win – draw and we are out.'

This time his boys would make no mistakes, thrashing the

Swiss 4-0 at the Lane and setting up a party atmosphere as they finally made the Champions League proper. A Peter Crouch hat-trick helped them on the way, with Jermain Defoe adding to the rout that saw Spurs advance 6-3 on aggregate.

Crouch may have scored the hat-trick, but it was Bale who, for the second time in less than a week, left the critics purring with delight. The *Guardian*'s Kevin McCarra summed it all up when he wrote: 'Tottenham Hotspur ambled into the Champions League proper and looked as if they belong among the type of clubs who consider this tournament their natural habitat. Young Boys, by contrast, were entirely ill at ease, and had Senad Lulic sent off after he brought down Gareth Bale to concede the penalty from which Peter Crouch notched his side's fourth...

'The striker, all the same, was overshadowed. Bale contributed to each of the goals and, at 21, personifies a side that appears to have come of age. By now his left-footed deliveries are in the thoughts of all rivals, but no amount of planning nullifies the threat entirely.'

Gareth set up Crouch for the opener within the first five minutes with a fine cross to the far post and provided another for Defoe to make it 2-0 just after the half hour mark. Just after the hour Crouch headed home the third from a Bale corner, and in the 77th-minute the Welshman was brought down in the box by Lulic.

Crouch gratefully stepped up to claim his hat-trick and Tottenham's fourth on the night. Afterwards the big man paid tribute to Gareth. Crouch had been voted Man of the Match for his hat-trick, but said: 'It should have gone to Baley really, shouldn't it? He set up all the goals and was our star performer. I'm always delighted when I see him out on that left wing…I know it means there's a chance I'll score, because of the quality of his crosses!'

Redknapp had now taken the club from the bottom of the league to the Champions League in 20 months – but he was determined they would not call success simply qualifying for the group stages. No, he wanted to get out of the group and into the knockout stages.

He said: 'We'll take on anybody now. We're in the group stage and we'll give anyone a good game here. We are a good side with good players and it will be a great experience for us. It's fantastic. When I came here the dream was to get into the group stage and we've achieved that, so that is something to look forward to.'

Gareth and his team-mates were nervous but excited when the draw was made for the group stages, but were happy to draw holders Inter Milan as one of the three teams they would face (along with FC Twente and Werder Bremen). 'It'll be brilliant to get Inter down here at the Lane,' Gareth said. 'And to play against them in Milan is also something I'm really looking forward to. I have always wanted to play in games like this – now I am actually going to get the chance. I can't wait.'

But there was much to think about before they played Inter. Like the Premier League clash with Wigan just three days after Gareth and the boys had seen off the Young Boys of Bern.

Inevitable really that it would be anti-climatic. After the highs of reaching the Champions League group stages, Spurs now struggled against a team they would normally expect to beat – and comfortably – at the Lane. But it was not to be…in a dismal, embarrassing showing, Spurs lost 1-0 to the Latics, their European hangover plain for all to see. The *Sun*'s Pat Sheehan summed up the worries that now faced Tottenham, writing: 'Forget about Jekyll and Hyde. This season for Tottenham will be more like Jekyll and no place to hide. Brilliant when booking their Champions League place on Wednesday, distinctly average as they were beaten by the team who were bottom of the Premier League.

'It was the best (or maybe worst) example of a wannabe top performer's split personality. Competing with the best one minute, getting turned over in the worst possible way the next.'

Too true, and it was all the more unacceptable given that just under 12 months previously, Redknapp's boys had crushed Wigan 9-1. Jermain Defoe's five goals had eased Spurs on to their highest top-flight win – a win that was achieved without the injured Bale.

Hugo Rodallega's winner at the Lane came after 80 minutes when stand-in keeper Carlo Cudicini failed to block his shot.

The defeat left Redknapp worried and he spoke unusually pessimistically after the match, saying: 'We lack that bit of guile. I have felt it all along with us. We've got no real dribblers if Modric doesn't play. Chelsea, Man United and Arsenal are stronger than us – that's why they finish where they do every year. I came to the ground thinking it would be a difficult day.

'But it's easy after a good result to think you should rotate or you should do this. If you change the team today and go and get beat, and you leave Crouch out everyone goes "What did we change the team for?"

'It's no hardship to play a couple of games in a week, is it? It shouldn't be a real problem for them. People turn up and they expect you to win, don't they? We all expected to win today, but we knew it wouldn't be that easy because they are going to come here and close you down.

'Wigan gave us a warning when they missed two great

chances and then we should have gone, "Okay, lads, make sure we don't get done here". But we were still open as a barn door, wanting to run forward and score, and we got done. The preparation was right, we'd heeded the advice about winning Premier League games after playing in the Champions League.

'Today we just lacked ideas and the longer it goes it becomes harder and harder.' I felt at the time he was a bit harsh – especially the bit about having no real dribblers if Modric was out. Bale would certainly go on to prove that assessment wrong as the season progressed.

A week later and Gareth was on the road to the Midlands in another match you might have expected Spurs to win. West Brom away, at the Hawthorns. But again, they would be thwarted, taking the lead through Modric on 27 minutes but ending up with just a point after Chris Brunt headed them level just before the interval.

'Gareth and all the lads were quiet and looked lost in thought after the match,' says a Spurs source 'It was a muted, downbeat return to London. Two bad results in a week – just one point from a possible six and all of a sudden people are writing them off as no-hopers. But there was a feeling that maybe the point at West Brom wasn't *that* bad.

'Remember, they had suffered a Champions League hangover after seeing off Young Boys in the qualifier – now maybe they were suffering from pre-Champions League anxiety as they were off to Germany on the Monday after West Brom for the first group match against Werder Bremen.'

Spurs went with a 4-5-1 formation against Bremen, with Harry keen to pack the midfield once again. He knew that a defeat in their first group game was to be avoided at all costs:

it could damage the team psychologically and could make qualification seem an uphill struggle.

Luka Modric didn't make it after limping off at The Hawthorns with a leg injury but Harry still started with a powerful-looking five across the middle – Lennon, Huddlestone, Jenas, Van der Vaart and Bale.

Gareth was the man who answered Harry's clarion call for his troops to step up to the plate as the big European adventure finally began. The Welshman is used to his team-mates converting his fine crosses, and was just as delighted when the hapless Petri Pasanen turned the ball into his own net from one of those crosses, on 13 minutes.

Five minutes later Peter Crouch made it 2-0 with an accurate header.

Everything seemed to be going Tottenham's way: this Champions League looked a lark rather than a tough test. Then Bremen pulled a goal back minutes before the interval as Hugo Almeida headed home and a goal from Marko Marin a couple of minutes after half-time wrecked Gareth's big night.

From a position of strength, Spurs had thrown away what could turn out to be two vital points when the group came to be decided in December. Gareth had given Clemens Fritz a torrid time down that left wing, but now returned home feeling a little disappointed. 'We were brilliant in the first-half but let it slip and that is so frustrating,' he confided to a friend on the plane home. 'We need to be more clinical in finishing teams off.'

His boss was much of the same mind.

Redknapp said: 'Yes, I'm frustrated, but I can't be angry. That first half was as good as you could wish to see. Barcelona might be better but that was as good as Tottenham can do.

'That first 42 minutes or so was the best you could ever see us play. We passed the ball and opened them up time and time again. But then we conceded a bad goal which suddenly brought them back into the game.

'At 2-1 it gave them a massive lift and they got the early goal in the second half. But we had our chances with Gareth and Peter [Crouch] at the end but overall it was an excellent performance. We came here for an away game in a very difficult place to come and play.

'They're a good side, they had a few missing but we had four very important players missing.'

Both Gareth and Harry would need to overcome their frustrations – and quickly. Big Mick McCarthy and his Wolverhampton Wanderers were due in town four days after the trip to Bremen and they would be sure to pose a tough physical examination. Already they seemed set for a battle against relegation, so Harry Redknapp knew what his team would be in for – it was hardly the best of rewards after their strenuous Champions League efforts over in Germany. And a few days beyond that they would face another tough test...against arch rivals Arsenal in the Carling Cup. The games continued to come thick and fast...but that didn't worry Gareth Bale one bit. On the contrary, he loved the challenge...the way he saw it was the more games, the more successful he and Spurs must have become. They were the thoughts and instincts of a natural born winner.

Chapter 5

THE TOTTENHAM TORNADO

'Look, it's all very well drawing in Bremen in the Champions League, but now you've got to show you can do it against the teams who are struggling in the Premier League. The likes of Man United and Chelsea do it in Europe – and then come home and also do the business in the league. That's how we've got to be – that's our aim.'

Gareth and the Spurs players all nodded in agreement as Harry Redknapp outlined his philosophy for success on the training ground at Chigwell a couple of days after their Champions League group stage induction in Germany. He was right; there was no argument, they all knew that.

Gareth had spent the best part of two years looking for more consistency in his own game at White Hart Lane. Now he was almost there; he felt it, that feeling that he could achieve something big, that he was on the brink of becoming a world-class footballer. But he couldn't do it alone: as a team Tottenham now needed to dig in and grind out results against lesser teams if they were to emulate the likes of Chelsea and United.

Being show ponies that performed well against some of the giants but self-destructed against teams they should easily beat needed to be a thing of the past. Harry was determined that they would become consistent performers – and that they would battle for the points if necessary.

Starting with Wolves at the Lane. Which meant it was important the team did not enter that match blurred by thoughts of the mouth-watering clash with Arsenal the following Tuesday. 'Harry made it clear that many of the team who played against Wolves wouldn't even be in the squad against Arsenal, anyway,' says my dressing room source. 'So they might as well give their all against Wolves – because it would be another week before they played again. It was a clever move because it killed off any hint of complacency.'

Ledley King was also on message after Harry's pep talk. The defender said: 'No disrespect to Wolves, but these are the games we need to win to build on last season. We are a good side at home – we try to win every home game. The way we started against Wigan was not good enough and we were sloppy.

'We will have to start a lot better against Wolves and try to get an early goal to get them to change their tactics.'

The pep talks and pledges of determination worked well as Spurs avoided another European hangover, winning 3-1, when they had previously lost 1-0 at home to Wigan after thrashing Young Boys in that Champions League qualifier.

Not that Gareth could ever be accused of complacency. No, once again, in this, his season of destiny, he was the best player in a Tottenham shirt as he delivered some great crosses and left Wolves full-back Richard Stearman dizzy.

Yet it was Wolves who had taken the lead – raising fears that Tottenham *were* suffering another hangover – when Stephen Fletcher put them ahead on the stroke of half-time. Spurs drew level on 77 minutes after Stephen Ward had tripped Alan Hutton in the box. Rafael Van der Vaart took the spot kick sending Marcus Hahnemann the wrong way. Late goals from Hutton and Pavyluchenko secured the three points and left Bale a very relieved man. 'He and the other players had been afraid they would get a right bollocking if they let it slip,' says a Spurs source. 'They didn't want it to be another Wigan – they knew they had to deliver or face the wrath of Harry!'

A smiling Redknapp admitted he was a relieved man after the victory. He told the *Guardian*: 'I wasn't disappointed with the way we were playing because we were trying to do the right things but I'd be a liar if I said I wasn't sitting there thinking we might not get back into this game.'

Next up was a match no Spurs player would need any motivation for – Arsenal at home. But Gareth would miss out on the Carling Cup encounter. Initially he was disappointed – this was, after all a lad who, similar to Manchester United's Wayne Rooney, wanted to play in every match – but when the boss explained his reasoning, he accepted his night off. Later Harry would also spell out exactly why he had taken the decision to the press, saying he felt Gareth was simply worn out. He told the *North Wales Daily Post*: 'I can't destroy Gareth Bale. He played for his country, then ran a million miles in Germany against Werder Bremen down that left flank. He's still a youngster. He's running on empty. I've got to protect him a bit.'

It was one of those matches where players' reputations are enhanced by *not* being picked. Spurs crashed 4-1 after 120 minutes as Arsenal chalked up their biggest win at the Lane in 32 years and gained revenge for their 5-1 hammering in the same competition two years ago. 'Gareth was still as sick as the rest of the lads about the result,' says my Spurs source. 'OK, he wasn't playing but it was still hard to digest. None of them like losing to Arsenal, whatever the competition.'

Gareth was back for the trip to north London rivals West Ham four days later – but again the result was a miserable one as Tottenham lost 1-0 to the relegation candidates. The win temporarily took the Hammers off the bottom and was their first against Spurs for over four years. It was also a particularly miserable defeat for the boss – Redknapp had not lost to West Ham since he left the club in 2001. Harry said afterwards: 'They started strong and their front two were a real handful. They worked their socks off. It was a great team effort from West Ham and it could have gone either way. It was an exciting game, end to end stuff.

'It was more of a basketball match. They attacked, we attacked. If Tom Huddlestone had scored when he was clean through in the second half it would have been different. They would have been on the floor and we would have been in the ascendancy.'

Harry may have sounded fairly upbeat, but he was far from it, as was Gareth. Neither man liked the fact that they had lost two games on the trot, and both knew that they had to get back on track soon, or the season would be over before Christmas as far as the Champions League or that vital top four Premier League finish was concerned. The following Wednesday they were at home to Dutch outfit FC Twente, their second match in the group stages. Defeat or a draw could prove disastrous after they failed to win in Germany in the first group match. 'We don't want to be playing catch-up,' Gareth confided. 'We need to get a result against Twente. We don't want to make it difficult for ourselves.'

Well, they did – but they still came through smiling. Rafael van der Vaart got himself sent off (for two yellow cards), but also scored (and missed a penalty) as Spurs came home by four goals to one on another incredible night of European football involving the North London entertainers.

The *Telegraph*'s Henry Winter succinctly summed up the efforts of Bale and Co. He wrote: 'Now that's entertainment. Now that's a rebuke to those who decry the Champions League group stage as boring. Even with 10 men, even with Twente far from makeweights in a thrilling Group A tie, Tottenham showed what this club and Harry Redknapp are all about: attacking football...

'"Champions League – we're having a laugh," chorused the delighted Spurs faithful, singing in the rain, even ending an epic second half with chants of "olé" as Gareth Bale and company continued to flood upfield. UEFA should thank Redknapp and Tottenham for reminding everyone that it's about the goals, about the glory.'

Roman Pavlyuchenko also scored from the spot twice and Bale – who else? – iced the cake with a fine late fourth goal. Gareth arrived in the box at speed and lashed the ball past hapless Bulgarian keeper Nikolay Mihailov in the Twente goal.

Gareth was buzzing after his late goal and delighted with the result. 'He and the lads were on a real high in the dressing room,' I am told. 'They were all messing about and having a laugh. It was a great night.'

The boss was also pleased that his team had notched up their first Champions League win – and in such style. His gamble of going for the jugular, with Modric also told to 'get in there and destroy 'em' had certainly paid dividends. And Harry made a point of singling Gareth out for praise for destroying fullback Nicky Kuiper and for the way he took his goal. Redknapp said: 'It was exciting stuff. The first two penalties were blatant. 'Crouch was pulled down, wrestled to the floor. For the second one Bale beat the fellow like he did all night and was pulled down. It was a blatant penalty. On the third, the ball travelled a long way and it was a soft penalty but you see them given.

'There was nothing wrong with Van der Vaart's goal and it was a fantastic finish from Bale at the end.

'We picked an open team who went for it. We could have played with one up with Van der Vaart behind, but went for it and got four goals. It was a fantastic result. We won 4-1 so I picked the right team. It's not a problem. You pick different teams for different games. I felt we'd take a chance but there are certain games where you wouldn't do that.'

Gareth now had just three days before the next match. He trained well at Chigwell and rested well at night. He knew it was vital to live the right way if he was to achieve that aim of becoming a world-class star. There were no booze binges or wild late nights on the cards for this man. He was a model footballer; always had been. He was not interested in living it up, he preferred a quiet night in and to let his feet, rather than his mouth, do the talking.

He wasn't one for nightclubs or bars. He had a steady girlfriend, his childhood sweetheart Emma Rhys-Jones, who was the same age. They preferred nights in with a takeaway and a DVD. Emma had told how they had initially been long-distance lovers, travelling down the M4 between Cardiff and his flat in Essex. She even suggested it had been like the long-distance England/Wales romance in the BBC sitcom, *Gavin and Stacey*. Emma told friends: 'We made it work like Gavin and Stacey did. We always joke with each other and I even call Gareth Gav in a soppy accent.' They now live together in Gareth's Essex home.

By the time of the FC Twente match, most of his displays for Spurs were now consistently excellent and he wanted to maintain that level, both in domestic and European encounters. Sure, he knew that the big European matches would make the biggest headlines – and propel him to world stardom if he delivered the goods as he knew he could. But his mindset was like boss Harry's; both wanted to do equally as well in the Premier League. It was, after all, their bread and butter; what paid the bills.

Aston Villa followed FC Twente to the Lane on the Saturday. It saw the return of Gerard Houllier to London; the former Liverpool boss was now in charge at Villa Park and was looking for a big result. Houllier would be out of luck. Despite going ahead through a 16th-minute goal from Marc Albrighton, Villa ended up losing 2-1. Rafael van der Vaart grabbed a brace and even outshone Bale, who picked up his first booking of the season in injury-time.

Van der Vaart had played in the hole just behind Crouch to score his third and fourth goals in three games, giving Redknapp a potential headache when Defoe returned from injury. The boss explained: 'If you play two up front with Rafa in behind, what do you do with Gareth Bale? You could play a diamond in midfield, but that would be asking Bale to play somewhere he doesn't play.

'It makes balancing the team difficult. Villa played with one striker up and Ashley Young behind, in the hole, and we went that way after the break. I put Rafa in behind Crouchy, with Aaron Lennon on the right, the balance looked better.

'He likes that position. He is never going to stay wide. If you start him on the right, he is going to come inside because he always wants to be involved.'

There would now be a two-week break in which the players would go off to represent their various countries in Euro 2012 qualifiers. Gareth scored for Wales in Switzerland, but a 4-1 defeat would spell the end of their hopes, and of Brian Flynn's time in charge. More of all that in a later chapter on Bale's international career.

Gareth was glad to be back among his Spurs team-mates the following week, and was anticipating with relish their Premier League trip to West London rivals Fulham on Saturday October 16. It would provide him and his team-mates with an opportunity to make amends to their fans after their last two meetings with fellow London clubs – West Ham and Arsenal – had ended in such depressing defeats.

Plus there was the small matter of setting up a confidence booster to take with them when they flew out the following Tuesday for Wednesday's Champions League group stage clash with Inter Milan. It would almost certainly be the toughest match of the group and they would need all the confidence, luck and help they could muster against the reigning champions.

So it was just the tonic required as Gareth and the boys came away from Craven Cottage with a 2-1 win under their belts. Typically, given the fightback nature of Tottenham's season thus far, it was a triumph carved out of adversity. Yes, they had to come from behind (yet again) to secure the points.

It was also a match swathed in controversy; one that left home manager Mark Hughes bemoaning his team's luck and verbally lashing referee Mike Dean. The ref had initially ruled out Spurs' second goal, from a low drive by Tom Huddlestone, for offside.

But after Huddlestone complained and a consultation with ref's assistant Martin Yerby, Dean allowed it to stand. Hughes moaned, 'We feel the goal should have been wiped out because William Gallas was offside as the ball was struck. Huddlestone was first in Mr Dean's face and obviously made a compelling argument for him to talk to his assistant.

'But Gallas was in Mark Schwarzer's vision and it affected his timing in diving for the ball. It is unusual for a referee to overrule a linesman. Perhaps he lost trust in him, but I think he should have backed him.'

Also typically in this exciting season for Spurs and their fans, it was Gareth Bale (yet again) who set Huddlestone up for the goal, swinging over a cross that the midfielder lashed home from just outside the penalty area.

Diomansy Kamara had put Fulham ahead only for Pavlyuchenko to equalise. The win also ended Fulham's unbeaten start in the Premier League.

Afterwards Gareth was jubilant in the dressing room. 'He was just glad to end what had become a bit of a jinx against fellow London teams – and to set down a marker for the big match against Inter the following Wednesday,' said a Spurs source. 'He and the boys all knew they had to put in a shift to prepare physically and mentally for the Milan match. Gareth said he was planning a nice relaxing day on the Sunday – one were he would just put his feet up, and go out for a nice meal with his girlfriend and unwind. It is his simple way of dealing with the pressure when it gets heavy, as would be the case with the match in Milan.

'As Gareth said, games don't come much bigger than playing the European champions in their own back yard.'

Boss Redknapp was also looking forward to the trip to Italy with a certain relish. He said that, like Gareth, he planned to relax the following day and then the hard work would begin again on the Monday: 'What a day [Sunday] it will be! My missus Sandra has bought me some kippers so I'll have them with a bit of toast and nice mug of tea.

'I was going to go and see Milan play, but they're on TV. So is Liverpool at Everton, then Blackpool playing Man City... Sandra has to go upstairs and watch the portable. I hardly watch telly. I never sit down to watch a film. The last film I really saw was Dr Zhivago. The only other time was when we got invited to a premiere in Southampton. It was a Bond film. I fell asleep after five minutes, had a kip for two hours. It was lovely.'

Gareth and Harry both did enjoy their days off that Sunday, but come Monday morning both were raring to go. They knew the time for talk was over; now it was time to walk the walk. For Tottenham's biggest game since their league and European glory days of the early Sixties. They were on their way to Milan for a date with destiny: and both they and their loyal fans hoped they would not be humiliated. That they would instead come home covered in glory. For Gareth Bale, the match would also be easily the most important of his relatively short career...for it was the match that propelled him to world stardom.

Chapter 6

THE GIGGS TIME

Inter Milan away on Wednesday October 20, 2010, would be the making of Gareth Bale. But before we chart his remarkable ascent that balmy autumn day in the fashion capital of Europe, let's now look at how his meteoric rise mirrored similar steps to stardom for a fellow Welshman: the great Ryan Giggs.

The comparisons between the two are relevant. Both were born in Cardiff, both ply their trade down that left wing and both are similar in style and outlook; honest, down-to-earth guys who put their football as their No. 1 priority after family. Both willingly made sacrifices to reach the top.

Is Gareth the new Ryan Giggs? In those characteristics of style, professionalism and sheer generosity of spirit, certainly. But in terms of their style on the pitch, there are a couple of differences to mingle in with the obvious similarities. Both maraud and terrorise down that left wing but Gareth reminds me more of Cristiano Ronaldo at times. That is partly down to his size, he is 6ft 1ins and weights just over 13st, like the Real Madrid man, and he has incredible speed...again like Ronaldo.

Giggsy is smaller and was always more of a dribbler than Gareth. He was also never as fast. Yet the beauty of both men was that they managed to get their crosses and shots in. They are both a nightmare for full-backs.

Of course, Gareth has a long way to go if he is ever to match Ryan's long list of honours. Giggs is the most decorated player ever in the English game – after winning 11 Premier League titles, four FA Cups, three League Cups and two Champions League winners' medals in 19 Premier League seasons.

He has also won the PFA Player of the Year and BBC Sports Personality of the Year in 2009.

Right now, Gareth's biggest domestic honour is a Carling Cup runners-up medal, which he picked up while facing Giggsy in the 2009 final, and having played in a Championship play-off semi-final for Southampton in 2007.

But time is on his side while Giggsy's days at the top are now numbered.

There was one huge difference in their family backgrounds. Giggs grew up against the backdrop of a troubled relationship while Gareth has known only warmth, happiness and stability in the home.

Giggs was born Ryan Joseph Wilson in Cardiff on 29 November 1973, to labourer and rugby-playing father, Danny Wilson, and children's nurse and cook mother, Lynne Ceri Giggs. The couple met when they were still at school and by the time Ryan arrived on the scene, they were both still only seventeen.

Lynne was Welsh and hailed from the more tranquil Pentrebane in west Cardiff; Danny was born to a Welsh mother and a father from Sierra Leone, and would become a promising halfback with Cardiff Rugby Union Club. His mother Winnie – a hospital cleaner – and Danny senior – a merchant seaman – hailed from the then rough dockland area known as Tiger Bay.

Ryan's first home would be with his mum and his dad on the Ely council estate. The surname on his birth certificate was registered as Giggs, and his mother gave her parents' address in Pentrebane. The space where his father's name should have been entered was left blank.

The relationship between Lynne and Danny hardly augured well from the start. Life was tough: at times, Lynne worked two jobs, and had to rely on her parents to look after Ryan. That was the one solid base the youngster had throughout his life – the love, care and reliability of his maternal grandparents, Dennis and Margaret. He would alternate his time as he grew up between staying with his parents in Cardiff and with Dennis and Margaret in Pentrebane. He would become a regular sight in the district as he played with a football and a rugby ball for hours on end outside his grandparents' home.

Staying with them provided him with the stability he needed. The rows between Danny and Lynne would worsen as the years rolled by and their relationship was in no way cemented when another son, Rhodri, was born three years after Ryan. Indeed, Ryan has admitted that the arguments took on a more unpleasant aspect – not just shouting and crying, but 'physical'.

Ryan has said that as he grew up and came to realise the

way his father treated his mother, he found he liked him less and less, He was a self-confessed 'mummy's boy' and drifted apart from Danny, rarely talking to him as he grew from boy to man.

The growing rift would lead to Ryan eventually changing his name from Wilson to Giggs when he was sixteen. He would take the decision then, two years after his parents' separation, so 'the world would know he was his mother's son'. The rift would also, inevitably maybe, lead to him becoming a more inward-looking, insular boy.

Gareth was a much different commodity. He benefited from a settled upbringing with dad Frank and mum Debbie. It helped him become a much more naturally sociable, easy going lad than Ryan in his formative years – although Ryan would come out of his shell as his football started to do the talking and his dad left home.

And while Ryan's father was often not around, Gareth's dad was always there, supporting and encouraging his boy. Gareth said Frank would always have time to play football with him in the local park, even when he was exhausted after a hard day at work. Gareth told the *Independent* in 2008: 'He liked playing football, was a parks player but maybe could have gone further himself. Unfortunately his family didn't have the money and so on to help him with transport. But he's always been there for me. He's put in a lot of hard work, giving up his weekends and supported me.'

It helped too that he came from a more salubrious area than Giggsy's. Gareth was brought up in Whitchurch in north Cardiff, a leafy area that was a village back in the 19th century but has since become a natural extension of the city. Locals say it is certainly a notch or two up from the more troubled housing estates where Ryan was brought up. It has its own golf club and is home to the Presbyterian Church of Wales and the Conservative Party in Wales.

Both Gareth and Ryan excelled at football at school-boy level, and again Gareth would benefit from the support of his parents.

With his troubled early background, it was little wonder Ryan Giggs would suffer something of an identity crisis and strive to find himself in later years. Manchester United and Sir Alex Ferguson would play a vital role in helping him come to terms with his life and himself. Like a surrogate father and family, Sir Alex and the cosseted world of United provided him with the background he had in some ways been denied as a boy.

Fergie would protect him from the outside world and virtually wrap him in cotton wool – Gareth had no such immunity from fame, and no figurehead to put him in bubble wrap until he met Harry Redknapp. He was more able to look after himself, he was more confident and he was growing up among similar top talents to himself, such as Theo Walcott.

Ryan was at the time a one-off genius – the likes of Beckham, Scholes and the Nevilles would come through a few years later. Fergie knew he had a special talent on his hands with Giggs, but resisted the heavy temptation to throw the wonder boy into the first team at once. He decided on a softly-softly approach with the lad who would become a United legend – and in doing so, formulated a programme of development that he would similarly employ with the other young stars during the next 20 years of his reign.

He used Ryan sparingly, keeping him well away from the wolves of the media, whom he did not trust back then (and largely still does not now). Ferguson would tell the pack to back off; that no, the boy was not available for a chat after a particularly inspiring showing, and no, he was not going to be doing columns, adverts or promotions until he, the manager, decided the time was right to do so. Fourteen years later Ferguson would sum up his methodology for treating Ryan and his so-called 'fledglings' over the years when he spoke about how new boy Wayne Rooney would be handled. He said, 'We won't ask the lad to climb a mountain tomorrow. The important thing is that he is a major player in five years' time. We have a job to do to make sure he fulfils his potential. We have a reputation for looking after young players here. He will get the same protection the others have had.'

Of course, United were more wary than other clubs may have been with Giggs – little wonder given that they'd had the original whiz kid in George Best under their wings. Two decades on, United as a club still felt some guilt over Best – that they had not done enough to help him, and to get help for him. It hadn't been the done thing in the Busby era; you didn't talk through problems, you just fronted it out. Busby was hardly a therapist or a psychologist, and he never wanted to be.

Ferguson was from the same sort of upbringing – the idea that 'we're all big boys who don't cry' – but, to his credit, he matured and moved on as the years rolled by. He knew that Ryan Giggs would need his attention – and his protection. He knew there would be comparisons with Best and that some pundits would sniff out Ryan's background – that he was from a broken home – and suggest he could easily go the way of the late, great Georgie Boy.

So he determined, from day one, that it would not happen:

that Ryan would not be George Best Mark 2, he would be Ryan Giggs Mark 1.

Paul Parker, the former United fullback who played in the United team of Ryan's early career, summed up Ferguson's influence in this way: 'The boss brought Ryan through from a troubled childhood and always saw him as one of his own. Ryan [also] got very close to Paul Ince, and Incey took him under his wing. Ryan would also socialise quite a lot with Lee Sharpe. But he was always his own man and made his own decisions.

'He didn't go out looking for publicity. Apart from doing a few promotional things for his boot company, he was content to be known as Giggs the footballer.'

Fergie's protectiveness helps explain why it was only in August 1993 – three years after he joined United and a good two after his debut – that he was allowed to have an agent to find him marketing deals. The lure of the boy was apparent when the agent quickly tucked up a £500,000 deal for Ryan with a boot manufacturer. Then, the press got their bite of the cherry, as he did his first major interview in the men's magazine, FHM.

Gareth had no such father figure within the game early on. A Spurs source said: 'It was only when Redknapp became Spurs boss in 2008 that he was given some sound guidelines and advice. Juande Ramos, understandably, had enough on his plate learning to speak English – and trying to keep his job! He was never going to have the time to mentor young lads like Gareth. Harry was what Gareth needed. He spent time with him, told him he needed to raise his game and how to do it and encouraged him to reach for the sky. He always knew Gareth was good enough to become world-class, he was willing to wait and be patient – people claim he wanted to sell Gareth in 2009, did he hell! Why would he sell a player he knew had the pace, skill, talent and potential to be another Giggs or Ronaldo? He nurtured him like Ferguson nurtured Giggs in that sense, yes.'

Bale and Giggs also had very different journeys from Wales to England. At 16 Bale trained at Southampton's satellite academy in Bath, but returned home to his parents before finally moving to England when he signed for Saints. It was all gradual and softly-softly, slowly-slowly.

Ryan's move to England was much more abrupt and traumatic. The United winger attended Hwyel Dda infant school in Ely but surprisingly remembers his time there not for playing football – he never played for the school team – but for learning the Welsh national anthem 'Mae Hen Wlad Fy Nhadau' ('Land Of My Fathers').

One day in 1979 six-year-old Ryan came home from school and found his mother and father deep in conversation. Danny had been offered the chance to switch rugby codes – to swap from union to league – by Swinton, a team in Salford, a few miles north of Manchester. It would be the turning point of his life, a move for the better, although both Ryan and his mother Lynne were against it at the time. It would mean moving away from her mother and father, Ryan's beloved grandparents.

Danny insisted they had to go. He talked of it being a new start for them all; the money was good and he could make it in the big time. The family moved into a house owned by the club and Danny was welcomed as a conquering hero.

But the move meant more adapting for young Ryan. Growing up in multiracial Cardiff, they had never thought about the colour of their skin. In north Manchester, they had to learn how to cope with racist taunts and being laughed at and abused. Ryan would later admit it was a shock to hear the abuse when he attended Grosvenor Road School in Swinton, but that he dealt with it by dismissing it with contempt.

Gareth, of course, had no such problems and, when he did encounter difficulties at school or youth football, his dad Frank was right behind him.

Ryan found another way of deflecting the abuse and getting his schoolmates to see him in a different light – through his sporting prowess. He excelled at rugby and football. His progress in rugby surprised everyone – apart from his father – as he was such a sprightly, wiry figure. Yet he stuck with the game all the way through comprehensive school from the age of ten to fourteen, and turned out for local side Langworthy and Salford Boys. He did well at stand-off and out on the wing – and was also good enough to represent Lancashire, playing one game for the county.

It was a busy time, but somehow he had enough energy in his tank to keep his hand in at football, playing up front for Sunday League outfit Deans FC and representing Salford Boys at football as well as rugby.

It was at Deans that he would make an impact – even though his first game for them ended in a crushing 9-0 loss – and at Deans that he would meet the man who would put him on the first rung of the professional ladder. The team was coached by milkman Dennis Schofield, who set him up for a trial with Manchester City.

Only problem was Ryan was a staunch United fan and hardly endeared himself to the City youth team bosses by wearing a red United top for training! His dream of playing for the Red Devils became reality, thanks to another man who had his interests at heart – a newsagent by the name of Harry Wood.

Wood was a steward at Old Trafford and he persuaded Alex Ferguson to take a look at the boy. Ryan headed to Old Trafford for a week-long trial and the rest is history. Returning home from school on his 14th birthday, Ryan saw a gold Mercedes parked outside the house. He hurried anxiously inside and saw Sir Alex Ferguson sitting in an armchair, sipping a cup of tea out of some of the best china Lynne could find. Ferguson didn't beat about the bush, quickly offering his protégé a two-year deal as an associate schoolboy with Manchester United.

Ryan was fourteen, captain of England Schoolboys, and he had signed for Manchester United. The world was now at his feet…literally.

Gareth also played rugby at Whitchurch High, but was never at the level of Ryan. However, as we also noted in Chapter One, he certainly excelled at a similarly early age at football – when he was told not to use his left foot! – and also had a panache for hockey and, hardly surprisingly given his incredible pace nowadays, distance running.

And just as Ryan became at 17 one of the youngest lads to play for United back in March 1991, so Gareth became the second youngest to pull on a Southampton shirt in April 2006, at the age of 16 years and 275 days.

In May 2006 Gareth notched up another record – this time for his country as he became Wales' youngest international at 16 in his debut against Trinidad & Tobago. Ryan had not been that much older (17) when he played his first game for the national team, against the Germans, in 1991.

Dean Saunders, manager of Wrexham and assistant to

John Toshack as Wales boss for three years, certainly believes there are similarities between Ryan and Gareth that cannot be ignored.

And he knows what he is talking about when it comes to top Welsh forwards – he is still fourth on Wales' all-time scorers' list with 22 goals from 75 internationals. He also confirmed the view that Gareth is a really nice guy and a great pro.

In November 2010, Saunders said: 'I could see what is happening to Gareth now two years back. He's always been a pleasure to work with and it's been obvious for some time that he has a terrific talent.

'His tremendous ability to do things with the ball in full flight reminds me of Ryan Giggs and I can't pay him a higher compliment than that.

'He's a totally down-to-earth lad who keeps his feet on the ground. He just loves the game and I can't see any of the adulation affecting him. I can see him staying loyal to Spurs and Wales is very fortunate to have him.'

Inevitably, given the natural link between the two players, there were suggestions that Bale might be a ready-made replacement at Manchester United when the ageing Giggs finally decided to hang up his boots. Also, as inevitably, those suggestions were in the main from Manchester United fans. Back at the Lane, the Tottenham supporters could only shake their heads at the perceived arrogance of their Old Trafford counterparts...as if Spurs weren't a big enough club to provide a proper platform to achieve Gareth's ambitions.

One United website, manutdonly.com, put the argument for Baley to replace Giggsy at Old Trafford this way: 'Going through the names [of players they would like to see join

United] there is just the one that stands out and that is the Tottenham wing-back Gareth Bale. He has been immense this season and has really begun to shine on the European stage. The unfortunate issue for Manchester United is that Ryan Giggs is getting older, if age was not a factor then the Welsh wizard would simply be playing into his fifties, he is that good.

'Sadly that will not be the case and trying to find a long term replacement for such a gifted player can surely go one way, and that's in the direction of North London to Tottenham Hotspur's Gareth Bale. He certainly has the promise to be as good as Ryan Giggs over a period of ten to fifteen years but at the end of the day only Bale himself will be able to make that decision.'

For another view on the Bale/Giggs debate, I asked a footballing expert for his analysis. Andy Bucklow has worked for the *Mail* for many years and is widely respected for his views on the beautiful game. Bucklow had this to say: 'Ryan Giggs and Gareth Bale comparison websites were springing up from the minute Bale hit his spectacular second-half hat-trick against Inter in the San Siro...and hardly died down after Bale's even more effective performance in a winning cause in the return at White Hart Lane.

'Indeed, the feeling of out with the old, and in with the new was reinforced when Giggs made his 600th Premier League appearance against a side with Bale in the opposition in January 2011, in a tightly fought game in which neither the Old Maestro or the Young Pretender were anywhere near their best.

'But direct comparisons between the two are erroneous, if not quite in the "Is Bale now better than Ronaldo?" category which did the rounds after Gareth had spent 90 minutes destroying the reputation of Macion, the best right back in the world, no less, according to FIFA.

'Bale and Giggs are Welsh, and, yes, both are highly skilled natural left-sided players who can (and still can in Giggsy's case) demolish any defence on their day. But if the end product is the same, the mechanics are more than subtly different. And it will be at least another five years before we can even begin to compare properly the effectiveness of the pair. Both sprang to prominence as 17-year-olds, and the talent in each was obvious. But whereas Giggs was eased into the team to play an almost instant part at the start of Manchester United's 20-year glory period, Bale's evolution into the player all major European clubs now covet and fear in equal measure has been rather fractured.

'Barely a year earlier, it seemed Bale's early promise at Southampton, and irregular progress through the ranks at Tottenham, had hit the buffers. There was talk of a loan deal to Championship also-rans Nottingham Forest, and the statistic that it took Spurs two dozen games and three managers to win a Premier League game with Bale in the starting eleven was still fresh in the memory. This was never a problem that the young Giggs had to encounter.

'But, putting their differences in playing style to one side for a moment, I believe the one obvious thing that links both players, more than so than the ability which helped divert Bale from a road to nowhere on to the road to world-class stardom, is temperament. Giggs has always been blessed with a calm, level-headed persona which neglected to embrace more senior colleagues at the time (most notably Keane and Cantona). The odd polite query of a dodgy ref after a Paul Scholes mistimed tackle aside, Giggs has carried this demeanour throughout his career and into his last years as a pro.

'Bale is blessed with the same gift, and there's no doubt that his own level-headed mindset helped him through the mini crises in his early years at White Hart Lane to allow his burgeoning ability to burst into bloom in what seemed like overnight. The game is littered with histories of young starlets, who failed to deliver on early promise, either because they couldn't handle the pressure, or didn't have the mental strength to clear the inevitable hurdles placed in the path of every career.

'Bale has indicated, so far, that he will not be one of these. His stable family background obviously helps, and this was something not enjoyed by Giggs, but it also takes something from within oneself. And the relative successes Bale has enjoyed in the past season are the fruits of this. Like Giggs, he comes across in interviews as the sort of sensible lad any father would want their daughter to marry. Compare this to the behaviour of other would-be superstars, most notably Balotelli at Manchester City.

'Where Giggs was the luckier of the two at the start of a stellar career was that at the beginning of the 1990s, he was assimilated into a team of hardened, yet hungry pros – Bruce, Schmeichel, Hughes, Robson, later to be joined be Cantona and Keane – at a time when the smell of impending and overdue success was becoming intoxicating. Yet, as a 17-year-old he was still encouraged to go out and play his natural game without fear – "like a piece of silver foil flitting about in the wind", according to Ferguson.

'Bale didn't have it quite so easy, trying to make an impact in his first couple of seasons at a struggling Tottenham, who were facing the unthinkable prospect of relegation under Juande Ramos before Redknapp transformed the club from laughing stock to members of the Big Four. Even then though, Bale was still more of a slow-burner than Giggs had been, and despite flashes of brilliance, and no one doubted the boy's potential, it was only into his third season in 2010/11 at the Lane that all the pieces started falling into place.

'Without ever having Giggsy's dribbling ability, Bale, with pace to burn, is more direct, and his shooting ability more powerful and accurate, than the early Giggs. Bale is obviously also more versatile at this stage of his career, as he can already play full-back, wing-back and out and out winger, whereas I can't recall Fergie ever considering giving Giggs a stint in the back four. Ryan's crossing was also occasionally more wayward as a youngster than Bale's.

'Having said all that, while Bale still has the whole of what could be a stellar career ahead of him, he'll do well to come even close to Giggs's personal trophy haul, or matching the United star's longevity. Hard as it is to imagine now, at some point in his late 20s or early 30s, one of Bale's biggest assets – his pace – will gradually drop off and he will have to adapt his game. That adaptation might even have to come even sooner if teams decide the best way to negate his effectiveness is to double up on him.

'Then there is the challenge of consistency. No one expects him to put in the performances, such as those which so shook up Benitez and Inter, every week, but now Bale must show that even if he doesn't always get star man in the ratings, he's capable of putting together regular eights out of ten. The odd blip aside, Giggs has done this for 20 years.

'Giggs also had to reinvent himself, replacing quickness of foot with quickness of thought. He possessed an intelligence to draw on all his experience to play in a deeper, more considered midfield role is a template for Bale later in his career, as is Giggs's ability to prolong his time at the top level by looking after his body, yoga and all.

'Whether Bale's career is still flourishing at Tottenham in two, three, five, or even ten years' time is questionable. Giggs's record-breaking appearances for one club is also something that is unlikely to be surpassed in the brave new world of £200,000-a-week pay packets, but even he once seemed destined to leave Old Trafford for Italy during a rocky period in 2002/03. I think at some time soon, you'll see Bale terrorising defences in the Nou Camp or the Bernabeu if he's chasing medals, rather than the piles of lucre in the vaults within the City of Manchester Stadium.

'One place where he could have already picked up a gong or two to start off his collection, of course, would have been Old Trafford, but, in contrast to Sir Alex Ferguson's successful purloining of Giggs from Manchester City's youth academy two decades earlier, Bale is likely to join the likes of Paul Gascoigne and John Barnes on Fergie's list of those who got away. Just as Gazza opted to join Spurs, and Terry Venables, when Fergie thought he had a deal all sewn up, so Bale did likewise with Martin Jol, when Fergie refused to match Tottenham's bid of £5 million, rising to £10 million. There's not much Fergie has had cause to regret during his unsurpassed tenure at Old Trafford, but there's little doubt that's one he'd like to have back. He had already shown his willingness to invest heavily in youth four years earlier with a £12 million plunge for a little-known winger called Cristiano

Ronaldo. Not to mention the £7.4 million the maestro paid out in 2010 for the even lesser-known Bebe.

'Fergie originally saw Bale as a promising left-back, but now must wonder if he has lost out on Giggsy's long-term replacement. If he were to buy him now, it would cost him ten times as much as the original £5 million quoted years ago.

'The one area where Bale can eclipse Giggs, of course, is on the international stage, by inspiring Wales to the final stages of either the World Cup or European Championship. Bale leading out Wales as captain in Brazil in 2014 or Russia 2018...with Giggs as manager? Now there's a thought.'

There was one other area in which the two men similarly excelled – scoring goals that established them as world-class talents against Italian teams. In the 1997/98 season Ryan scored a cracker against Juventus in the Champions League, flying past two challenges before finishing perfectly in the bottom left hand corner. And, as our next chapter illustrates, Gareth was quite capable of matching that landmark – as Inter Milan found to their cost in the San Siro in October 2010...

Chapter 7

INTER THE BIG TIME

It was a night when at various stages Gareth Bale would go from being a potentially good player to a potentially great player to a potential legend to a legend full stop. Yes, the night when the boy from Wales announced himself on the European and world stage with an unforgettable show in the San Siro in Milan, crowning a wonder display with a hat-trick.

This was also the night when Spurs finally made it back in the real big-time – OK, they had already played two games in their Champions League group and one qualifier to get there, but taking on the might of Inter Milan was a sign they really were back with the big boys after that painful hiatus from European football's top club tournament spanning back to 1962.

No disrespect to FC Twente, Werder Bremen and Young Boys, but they were hardly names to set the old pulse racing. Internazionale of Italy certainly were. European Champions

League opposition didn't come much bigger – or better – than the reigning champions. Of course, the Italian outfit's Svengali was long gone: Jose Mourinho had packed his baggage and headed off into the Madrid sunset the previous summer, making way for the former Liverpool boss Rafa Benitez.

That in itself gave Bale and Spurs hope that they could not only cope, but surprise Inter. Benitez, with his psychological problems and lacking the sheer brilliance and motivational skills of Mourinho, was never expected to take the Milan giants to any new level. OK, Benitez had won the Champions League in his six years at Liverpool but he was certainly somewhat lucky to have got the nod for the Inter job. In his last season at Anfield, Liverpool exited the Champions League early on and did not make the top four of the Premier League – ironically losing out to Spurs. If Benitez could maintain Inter's status quo – and that was hardly an easy task given they were also Italian as well as European champions – that would be heralded a major success. And it was hardly as if he would need major surgery on the team and squad bequeathed to him by Mourinho. No, the Portuguese had kept to his word and not snaffled any of Inter's big stars.

They were all still there – and lying in wait for Gareth and his team-mates as they headed to Italy for the crunch encounter on Wednesday October 20, 2010. Maicon, Javier Zanetti, Samuel Eto'o and the brilliant midfield schemer, Wesley Sneijder.

Officially, there were 5,000 Spurs fan in Milan for the match – but unofficially there were probably a couple of thousand more than that. The boys from the Lane bought tickets in the Milan sections and had an away day they will long remember.

Earlier Inter had said that the 5,000 tickets they would send to White Hart Lane for the away supporters would cost £48 apiece. But Spurs learned that the Inter fans would be attending the match for just £18. The Italians had unwittingly broken UEFA rules that say visiting supporters should pay the same as home fans. Inter were forced to lower their prices – and Spurs fans were rightly celebrating having to pay just a third of the original price. It was a small victory given that many fans ended up spending more than a grand on the trip – but a principled victory nonetheless.

Masses of supporters from London gathered at Milan's Duomo Square behind the world famous cathedral during the Tuesday and Wednesday, all in good spirits and good voice. Lifelong Spurs fan Kev Simpson said: 'Milan is renowned as the fashion capital of Europe but it was us Tottenham fans who were all the rage as the locals looked on a bit amused from the cafes and bars as we chanted, sang and enjoyed a glass or two. It was a great couple of days away, no real trouble and lots of good experiences. We travelled independently to the match, getting the tram from the city centre. They gave us the worst seats in the ground – right at the very top of one end, but that didn't bother us. Apart from being out of breath having to climb what seems miles, that is!

'We were told later by the local police that Spurs fans had been on the whole well behaved and good ambassadors for the club.'

But Kev hadn't expected Gareth Bale to be the hero of the night? 'No, not really, sure we knew he was getting better and better but I wouldn't have picked him out as a potential match-winner – or match saver – before kick off.

'With Defoe being out injured you'd look to Crouchy, Lennon or Modric. But after the Inter Milan, Baley definitely became the man who could work miracles!'

The match in the San Siro gave Harry Redknapp an idea of just how far Bale and his Spurs team had come – and how far they still had to go if they were to compete regularly with the cream of European football. With his side gelling together well as the season started to bed in, Redknapp went into the game with much optimism – although that optimism was tempered by the loss of new signing Van der Vaart. The Dutch midfielder had settled in seamlessly to the team's tempo and rhythm and it would be a major loss that he would not play in Milan due to the one-match ban incurred following his sending-off in Spurs' last Group A outing against FC Twente.

Redknapp would be hoping to put yet another one over on Benitez after Spurs nicked Liverpool's Champions League spot before the Spaniard left for Milan – but admitted he would be happy to come home with a point. Harry said: 'I couldn't say we're going to go out and be wide open. You've got to go there and play sensibly against the better teams. You've got to be difficult to beat, first and foremost as we're away from home.

'I wouldn't sit here and kid ourselves, if we came away with a point we'd be delighted. You go out there, you want to win, obviously, but you've got to hit them on the break. You're not just suddenly going to go out and swarm all over them, they are a top team. So you've got to be aware of that and they've got real dangers. Eto'o is playing fantastic at the moment for them.

'So, it will be difficult, but it'll be a great game for the players to go and play there and show what they can do.

We've always got attacking players, whoever we pick, we'll have more than our share of players who want to go forward and want to create and score and make goals, that's how we play.

'We've got it all on now, we've got Milan home and away. We need some points out of those games, otherwise, the other two teams in the group will catch us up. It can all turn. These two games against Inter are vital – otherwise suddenly we will find ourselves in a worse position.'

Benitez and his veteran skipper Zanetti were worried by Spurs as an attacking threat as the build-up to the match continued. Benitez wanted to make clear that he felt Tottenham had become even better than during his final season at Anfield – and that he was fully aware of the threat of players like Bale and Modric. He said: 'I believe that Tottenham have improved quite a lot. They invested a lot of money and now they have a lot of quality players in the squad. So I believe that tomorrow we have to be very attentive – especially to players like Modric and Bale who can catch you out with their speed and skill.'

And he admitted it had not been easy taking over from Mourinho: 'It's true that always it's difficult when you have won a lot of trophies to change things,' he said. 'But I felt the players were quite happy to change something and try to keep the same mentality, the same idea, when they were playing counter-attack, and try to improve a little bit in possession. It was easy for me because, talking with them, they were saying, "OK, we like to do this and we will try to do it".'

Zanetti was also wary of the Tottenham's flair players. He said: 'I believe Tottenham are a very good team and, above all, they are dangerous on the counter. They have very, very speedy players in players like Lennon and Bale. We need to pay particular attention, too, to the set-pieces because they are very dangerous.'

No one had really highlighted the potentially crushing damage that Gareth could individually inflict on the Milanese – simply because he had not, until the match itself, yet risen to the highest level. The Press Association probably came closest with this assessment of the potential clash between Gareth and the Brazilian wonder full-back Maicon: 'Maicon has developed into arguably the best attacking full-back in the world and was unsurprisingly named UEFA's club defender of the year last season. Bale, meanwhile, has been one of the stars of the current campaign both at home and abroad and the prospect of seeing him go toe to toe with the Brazil star is arguably the most mouthwatering of all the head-to-head clashes at the San Siro.'

As kick off approached Baley was coolness personified – he is not one for nerves as we have already noted. 'I'm really looking forward to the game,' he said. 'This is what it's all about, playing against the best teams in the world. It's what I got into the game for in the first place.'

And boss Redknapp couldn't resist one more rallying call to Gareth and the troops as kick off loomed ever closer. He told his team they could join the pantheon of Spurs greats if they produced at the San Siro and told the press they were already a great team – and could only get better and could even win the English league one day soon.

Harry said: 'Tottenham may be one or two signings away from being a team that could win the championship. One or two players in the right positions – and I am talking about top, top players in the right positions. If we could do that,

Tottenham could win the championship in a couple of years. The squad is just so full of talent anyway, who have made their mark.

'And Daniel Levy has done a great job in backing my judgement and improving the squad and the club.'

Harry then gave Baley a namecheck as he outlined the talent already at his disposal. He said: 'The players are playing with confidence, they've improved. Gareth Bale has come on a bundle, the goalkeeper [Gomes], who obviously has talent, is showing what he can do.

'The players we brought in – Crouchy and Defoe – have given us something. Even Robbie Keane and I genuinely feel bad for him that he is not in the team. A night like this is the ideal stage for them, that's why I am looking forward to it.

'It is great to be playing the holders in the San Siro. If you looked at this a couple of years ago when I first arrived at the club, you wouldn't have believed it.'

Eventually all the talking was over and it was time for action – and the match that would propel Gareth Bale into world stardom. The teams lined up like this:

INTER MILAN: 1 César, 13 Maicon, 6 Ferreira da Silva, 25 Samuel, 26 Chivu, 5 Stankovic, 4 Zanetti, 29 Coutinho, 10 Sneijder, 9 Eto'o, 88 Biabiany. Substitutes: 11 Muntari, 23 Materazzi, 19 Cambiasso, 2 Cordoba, 39 Santon, 12 Castellazzi, 27 Pandev.
TOTTENHAM: 1 Gomes, 3 Bale, 19 Bassong, 13 Gallas, 32 Assou-Ekotto, 2 Hutton, 6 Huddlestone, 8 Jenas, 7 Lennon, 14 Modric, 15 Crouch. Substitutes: 9 Pavlyuchenko, 23 Cudicini, 12 Palacios, 5 Bentley, 4 Kaboul, 21 Kranjcar, 10 Keane.

Of course, it did not go exactly to plan. Spurs' big European night was ruined as early as the second minute when Zanetti scored the opener, becoming at 37 the oldest scorer in Champions League history. The goal was set up by the evergreen Eto'o, and Spurs were on the back foot.

Things went from bad to worse seven minutes later when keeper Gomes was sent off after he brought down Jonathan Biabiny in the penalty area. Slovenian referee Damir Skomina pointed straight to the penalty spot.

He also showed a red card to Assou-Ekotto, only realising Gomes was the guilty man after consultation with the fifth official.

Eto'o, inevitably and coolly and calmly, stepped up to make it 2-0 from the resultant spot kick – although stand-in keeper Carlo Cudicini did get a hand to the powerful strike.

Going two-down was bad enough, but it wasn't the only consequence of the Brazilian keeper's act of foolishness. Redknapp now had to sew the team back together in an emergency operation – he had taken off Luka Modric so that Cudicini could go between the sticks. That was all well and good but, of course, it meant Spurs' creativity was now racked down a notch.

The English visitors appeared to be falling to pieces in front of our eyes as three minutes later – and with just 14 minutes gone – they fell 3-0 behind as Dejan Stankovic slammed the ball home. The goal highlighted all too well the defensive nightmare that Spurs appeared unable to wake up from on their Champions League travels – they allowed Inter to make over 20 passes before Maicon found Stankovic, who then worked the ball home after a fine piece of passing with Eto'o.

It looked all over bar the shouting when a shot from Eto'o made it 4-0 just 10 minutes before the break.

In comparison to the excellence of Inter, the visitors' best chance of the first half was wasted by Crouch. It fell to him on 26 minutes after a fine solo run by Aaron Lennon and an equally excellent cross. Crouch met the cross, but headed it over the bar when he only had Julio Cesar to beat.

As the Tottenham players trooped off dejectedly at the interval, it was an equally heartbreaking scene for the thousands who had followed the team from London, spending hundreds of pounds in the process – and it would surely take a miracle to even return home with pride salvaged.

Well, cometh the hour, cometh the power – Gareth Bale stepped forward to the plate to transform the fortunes of his struggling team. Losing 4-0 at the interval with 10 men already tired and asking a team to revive was asking a hell of a lot. Even Redknapp's half-time team talk couldn't have inspired the amazing comeback that followed. Harry had told his men to keep it tight, to try not to concede another goal and to maybe nick a consolation. Never did the naturally optimistic boss anticipate they might come close to nicking the match, let alone just a goal.

Indeed, he later admitted: 'We just started the game sloppy. In the first minute, we find ourselves 1-0 down, suddenly we're down to 10 men with the goalie sent off. We were bang in trouble, and at 4-0 down any kind of score could've come. You could be sitting on the end of a seven, eight, nine goal defeat playing with 10 men against Inter.

'But in the second half we got at them at every opportunity, and found that if you attack Inter you can score against them.'

The boss's words were spot on – but it was all down to

Baley, whose initiative and talent nearly pulled off the greatest of escapes for his team. At the very least, his superstar show meant Tottenham returned home with their pride salvaged.

His one-man superman show began on 52 minutes when he hit the ball home into the bottom right hand corner from the edge of the box. Those are the bare facts of the goal: they do not elucidate upon the wonder of it. Gareth embarked on a solo run from his own half, beat a couple of players and still had a lot of work to do as he scored with a sensational finish.

It appeared that Redknapp's request for a mere consolation goal had been answered.

But that wasn't the end of it. Oh no. In the last minute of normal time, Baley sent another shot powering home into that same bottom right hand corner to make it 4-2.

And two minutes later he collected the hat-trick with a further strike into that favoured spot.

Pandemonium ensued in the stadium. The Inter players and their supporters could not believe what was happening in front of their very eyes. Indeed, how could it be happening? After all, they were the European champions and had been cruising to a 4-0 win at half time. Internazionale just didn't do drama: under Mourinho they had been the kings of tight defence and miserly possession.

Now, here they were – being played off the park by a lad of 21 who many of them had never heard of (they would never forget his name after this traumatic turn) and letting slip a mighty comfortable advantage. 'In the end, it was Inter who were lucky,' crowed Spurs fan Kev Simpson. 'They were holding on – if we had got another 10 minutes to go, Baley could have scored another couple and won it for us!'

He was only joking, but there was an hard edge to the jest.

For as the final whistle blew Gareth Bale and Spurs knew they could now see off this team off European winners. The tide had turned – and irrevocably. Baley's second-half super show had given them the confidence to think, 'Wait till we get them back to the Lane – then we'll find out who's really the best when it's 11 against 11.'

Gareth was mobbed by his team-mates and his mum, who had burst into tears as he completed his hat-trick, was one of the first to congratulate him on a brilliant performance. All the years of effort, dedication and sacrifice by her son had now been worthwhile in her eyes. He had earned this moment; she knew he had worked so bloody damned hard to achieve it. No wonder she had cried those tears of joy.

All of a sudden, the sense of balance had tipped Tottenham's way as they contemplated the return fixture with the European champions in London.

Yes, the natural inbuilt confidence and swagger of Eto'o, Schneider and Co had suffered a severe dent. The supermen had been shown to be only mortal – they would not be anticipating the trip to London with such an easy relish now. They feared what Baley might do to them again given the chance.

As the Tottenham fans were held back for an hour after the game, high up in the stands, their chants were full of hope. The depression of the 4-0 half-time lashing was but a memory: they also knew that the Welsh wonder boy could destroy Inter in the return at the Lane, and they made their journeys back to the city by coach and tram and then the flight home to London savouring the super show they had witness – and relishing how Baley might once again destroy Maicon in the return.

The winger had humbled the Brazilian with his speed and work at the San Siro. This was the man who was supposedly the best defender in Europe yet Baley brought him down to earth with an almighty thud.

After the game Maicon had tried to recover some of his credibility by claiming he had been suffering from a bug. Well, yes, Douglas...a bug by the name of Gareth Bale!

At least Maicon had the good grace to shake hands with his tormentor and congratulate him on his performance. Gareth would later say that Maicon was a 'nice man' who 'kept apologising to me'.

No wonder he was so sorry – the only way he could stop the boy wonder that night was to bring him down.

The *Sun*'s Pat Sheehan summed up the effect Bale had had on European football in the San Siro when he wrote: 'Gareth Bale stuck another £10 million or so on his price tag with a stunning hat-trick here at the San Siro. The Wales star made a mockery of Tottenham's shambolic first-half display and underlined just why he is one of the most wanted men in European football.

'Tottenham have already fended off enquiries for Bale and their resolve will now be tested to the full as he showed he is worth £30 million of anyone's money.'

And even Inter Milan president Massimo Moratti paid tribute to Bale. He admitted he was 'very keen' on signing the Welshman and bringing him to the San Siro, but that he worried the price might now even be beyond his club's reaches. He said: 'He had a great game and we were right to track him during the summer. You can see he's an excellent player. Now? After that hat-trick he'll cost a lot more...'

Bale's disgraced team-mate Gomes also pitched in with his

backing, saying Gareth was good enough to play for Brazil. Gomes said: 'He is a great player and he showed it again. The team as a whole showed lots of character to come back from four-nil but Gareth scored three unbelievable goals.

'When you watch him playing like that on the ball, he looks like he is Brazilian. And playing like that he would get in the Brazil team, I'm sure.

Defender Alan Hutton was another Spurs player keen to add his praise. He said: 'Gareth's finishing is deadly. You might expect it from natural goal scorers like Jermain Defoe but Gareth has that in his locker.

'He has that magic touch for goals and he proved that again. The sky is the limit for him. To get three goals anywhere is good for your pride but to get three goals against the champions, in their own back yard, is special.'

Hutton said Bale's display was particularly impressive when seen against the fact that he was up against the man supposedly the best defender in the world. Hutton added: 'Maicon is supposed to be one of the best full backs in the world but Gareth caused him all sorts of problems. I'm sure he can do that anywhere in the world but we're desperate to hold on to him. He's a great talent on the big stage.'

Two more of Gareth's team-mates were queuing up to back his credentials as a world-class star after the hat-trick in Milan. Benoit Assou-Ekotto explained how he loved playing at left-back behind Gareth – and how he had noticed the vast advancement in his star potential over the previous year.

Assou-Ekotto told the *Sun*: 'At the moment he is the best left midfielder in Europe. He has been that way for the last few weeks. He is young, he likes to hit and he defends to help me. I take pleasure in playing behind him.'

And Younes Kaboul said he had always suspected that Gareth would become 'the best player in Europe in his position'. Kaboul, who joined Spurs in July 2007, two months after Bale's arrival, said: 'Gareth is absolutely amazing. You know, when I played with him three years ago – when they signed him – I knew straight away that he was a big player with a big future. For me, he's the best player in Europe in his position.

'In the past he had a lot of injuries and that stopped him – his condition. But now he's strong, he's not getting injured any more and he's just the best. It's not a surprise because he's powerful, he's got everything and for any right-back it's very difficult. I'm glad he's on my side. You can't forget that he's only 21. Can you believe that? So he's still got another 15 years or so in front of him – that's unbelievable. At a professional level, I've never seen anyone better, no one.'

Meanwhile, Italian national Cudicini, who came on for Gomes when the keeper was red carded in Milan, was questioned by the Italian media after the game about how good he thought Gareth could become. He explained that Gareth had not yet, in his opinion, reached anywhere near his peak!

Cudicini was forthright in his opinions: 'Bale?' he roared. 'He's a player who will improve even more with experience, I'm sure of that. You saw what he did tonight, but he's far from the finished article.'

Gareth, typically given his naturally modest nature, wanted to focus on the team's showing rather than his own wonder display. He said: 'We started off sloppily and we paid the price in the first half. With 10 men we showed what a good team we are, and if we'd had 11 on the field it would've been a different game.

'I'm not too sure what went wrong. It just wasn't a lively start from us and we paid for it. The next time we will learn from those mistakes and go into the game differently.

'I got the ball and put it in the back of the net. I wasn't thinking about me, just about getting back into the game. It's just that time ran out on us, and back at White Hart Lane we can do a better job and get the victory.'

Asked about whether he would honour the four-year deal he had signed with the club the previous May, he added: 'Yeah, I want to keep playing at Tottenham and enjoying my football. I enjoy playing at Tottenham, I'm happy here and I want to keep progressing as a player. I don't take too much notice of the speculation about me - I think we can achieve what we want at Tottenham.'

Redknapp was naturally unwilling to countenance any prospect of Gareth leaving the club – even if Spurs were offered £30 million. The boss said: "You couldn't buy him for £25 million or £30 million. If he had a value, if we wanted to sell him, it would be way in excess of that. He is an amazing young player. We wouldn't entertain a bid. The chairman said he is not for sale and that's good enough. Tottenham is a club who are looking to progress, not to sell their best players. If Tottenham sell Gareth Bale now, it would send out the wrong signals.

'He's a player we hope to build a team around. He signed a new contract and, hopefully, he'll be here for a good few years to come. He gave Maicon a torrid time and he's one of the best right backs in the world. Every time we got the ball to Gareth, he gave them problems.'

Tottenham – from boss Redknapp to the players – were realistic enough to know that Baley's hat-trick could not cover up the underlying defensive problems Spurs were facing on their travels in Europe, where they were continuing to leak goals. Peter Crouch admitted as much, saying: 'It was a ridiculous start, we had a mountain to climb and we can't do that against top teams. We can't give them goals, that's what we did but credit to us, we came back at them in the second half. 'We've got to cut that out but if we do cut that out we've got enough about us, we've got some top quality players, I think we kept the ball well in the second half. If we cut out the silly goals we'd have had a chance but we got punished for the start we had. It was very difficult having 10 men but we showed good character.'

But Crouchy was another one full of praise for Gareth, saying: 'He's been magnificent for two years, obviously at the top level here at the San Siro to score a hat-trick for him is magnificent.'

The glitter and triumph was all Bale's – but it was reassuring for Spurs fans that the players and management were not being allowed to camouflage the fact that their team had now lost its first game in the competition this season. That meant the pressure could be on in Group A to qualify for the next stages if Bremen or FC Twente went on a good run – it meant that Spurs now needed a good result against Inter at the Lane. The pressure was on.

Redknapp himself also conceded the defensive showing in Milan was not acceptable, saying: 'At half-time we'd have all gone home at 4-0. You could see more damage coming. We started sloppily and everything that could go wrong did. All we had to play for was pride. We had to make sure we were not embarrassed by a crazy score. I thought we were quite bold in the second half. We tried to have a go and got some rewards – not in terms of points, but reward in terms of a bit of pride.'

He predicted Tottenham would be a different entity in the return at the Lane, saying he could see a different result: 'At White Hart Lane we're a good team and it will be a great atmosphere. In the end the result in the other game in the group [a draw] was a good one for us. The Inter game at home is something to look forward to. Our defeat didn't do too much damage.'

But would Harry be right – could he rely on Gareth to produce another scintillating display on the back of the one that had brought the young Welshman to international renown? Would Gareth give the previously infallible Maicon another humbling, or would he crack under the pressure?

Bale had certainly made a worldwide name for himself with the hat-trick in Milan. But could he live up to it as the teams came out at White Hart Lane for round two in London a fortnight later?

Chapter 8

RED ALERT

As we have said, Gareth is not one for nerves. He is a confident lad with a positive attitude and an optimistic outlook on life. He does not believe in getting panicky about foreboding situations – but even he admitted to the odd butterfly as the return encounter with the European champions drew ever nearer.

Inter would arrive at the Lane on November 2 eager to prove that Bale's hat-trick at the San Siro was a flash in the pan; a late flurry after they had eased their feet off the pedals. And the Brazilian full-back Maicon would travel to London determined to put the humbling he had suffered at Gareth's feet behind him. He would breeze into the Lane confident that he would have enough in the tank to stop Gareth in his tracks – and reclaim what he believed was his rightful claim to being the best full-back on the planet.

But all that would have to wait. First Gareth and his Spurs team-mates had to negotiate two extremely tricky Premier League matches. Everton at home and Manchester United away. Harry Redknapp looked at the two fixtures and set his team the target of four points; in the event, they would end up with a miserly one.

In hindsight, it was maybe inevitable.

Such was the massive high after the late comeback via Gareth's hat-trick in Milan that a low would follow as surely as night follows day. And that was the case: Spurs struggled in those two Premier League matches and Gareth's form temporarily deserted him, too.

If the team was functioning at full strength, you would probably have expected Harry's demand for four points to be achieved – three against Everton and, hopefully, one at Old Trafford. Even the omens were good: after their four previous Champions League games – two in the play-offs and two in Group A – Spurs had won three and lost one.

Everton arrived with only two away goals all season, both at Birmingham in their previous game on the road when they secured their first win of the season. So it was all looking hopeful but, like a bottle of champagne that had lost its fizz, Tottenham then went and struggled against the Toffees and United.

There was even a suggestion in the Press Box before the match that Redknapp had noticed how tired and deflated his men looked as they prepared for Everton. He told one close associate that 'they seemed like a balloon that had been popped' – and that even Gareth was struggling to get his impetus back. 'Harry asked them for four points from the two matches in the hope that it might lift their spirits and give them something to aim for,' a Spurs source said. 'It was his way of psyching them up – he knew they had hit a wall and was hoping that he could help them back over it.'

As the Everton match loomed, the boss appeared to become more resigned to the likelihood that it might be a struggle – and admitted he was thinking about 'freshening things up' in an attempt to beat the problem. He said: 'It's a difficult one. We're still without people like Ledley [King], and a group of players that are not available. But Rafael van der Vaart is available and Sandro could come into midfield. It's been difficult lately with a lot of travelling, internationals as well. We got back at 3.30am on Thursday, so I'll look to freshen it up tomorrow a little bit. We have players desperate to play.

'Everton are a good side, they had a dodgy start like they did last year but every year David Moyes gets them pushing. They will be up there pushing to get into Europe.'

Harry was spot on in his assessment. Moyes and Everton made life hard for their hosts on Saturday October 23. In particular, Phil Neville 'did a job' on Baley. The veteran full-back kept close to Gareth for the 90 minutes, hardly giving him room to breathe. Given that Gareth was still mentally and physically exhausted after his exploits in Milan, it was really no surprise that he struggled to get the better of Neville. The intent was there; the energy was not.

Gareth's day was made all the tougher by the fact that the canny Moyes also employed winger Seamus Coleman to double up with Neville to halt his progress. Coleman's natural defensive abilities – like Gareth he is a winger converted from full-back – and massive energy levels meant a worn-down Gareth never really stood a chance on the day.

It was an uphill battle and Everton nearly took all three points after taking a 17th-minute lead through Leighton Baines' free kick. Fortunately, a blunder by Toffees keeper Tim Howard just three minutes later allowed Rafael van der Vaart to level and earn a point for Spurs.

Redknapp accepted that the point was better than none and declared himself reasonably happy – a sure sign that he had, privately at least, anticipated that the Everton match might be a match too far for his tired troops. It is fair to say that he was now certainly not unhappy that Spurs were already out of the Carling Cup – at least they would have a week off as other clubs battled it out in the competition during the following midweek.

Afterwards he said: 'Everton are a good side and you'll never get an easy game against them. I thought we had the better chances but it didn't quite drop for us. You want to win every game, but what is important – when you're not going to win – is not getting caught out late on with the sucker-punch and end up getting beat. Sometimes we have done that in the past, like at Wigan. 'But we stayed solid and the centre backs were top class. We've always showed good spirit and a never-say-die attitude.'

Gareth could be reasonably happy with his contribution on a difficult day. No, he had not lit up the skies but he had tried his best when he was still tired out after his late exploits in Milan. And at least he avoided the treatment meted out to Peter Crouch by some disgruntled home fans – they chanted for him to be replaced by Roman Pavyluchenko when he missed a couple of easy chances. Redknapp defended the big man, who had not scored a Premier League goal since the previous May, pointing out he had set up three of Van der Vaart's four goals so far and saying: 'He gives you something else. You take Crouchy out of there and you've got to play perfect football to break teams down.'

Bale had no such problems with the crowd. As usual, he did

his superstitious little jig in front of them before kick off and earned a rapturous applause as reward for his endeavours in the San Siro. He applauded them back and did his best in trying circumstances. By the end, he was exhausted and almost slumped to his seat in the dressing room afterwards. 'I'm shot,' he told his team-mates. 'Absolutely knackered!'

Redknapp had seen the warning signs and now showed what an astute manipulator of players he is – and how good a man manager he is. He told Gareth to take a few days off – forget training, forget Tottenham, go on holiday somewhere and have a good time.

'It will do Gareth good to take a couple of days extra off,' Redknapp said later. 'The kid needs it, he's probably going to go away for three or four days and it'll do him the world of good. He's tired. The kid runs miles every game. He does unbelievable stats and takes some beating most days.

'He gallops up and down. He's got everything really. All the players look after themselves now and go to the gym in the morning and work after training with the fitness coaches. Gareth's got stronger and stronger and has that physique that can take knocks, but I thought Phil Neville did a decent job on him.

'Gareth has had two tough games with Wales and some tough games with us and needs a few days' rest now.

'He's such a nice lad. I walked off the plane and said, "I bet you never dreamt of scoring a hat-trick at the San Siro". What a thing for the rest of your life.'

Harry was definitely right about one thing: Gareth is 'such a nice lad'. Imagine what the more big-headed 'stars' of the Premier League would have done if handed a couple of days' extra break by their boss – gone to Dubai in a £5,000 a night seven-star hotel or maybe headed somewhere more raucous like Ibiza.

Gareth Bale made an altogether more measured choice. He headed home to Wales to see his mum and dad – much to Redknapp's obvious delight and pride. 'He had a few days off and went abroad – to Cardiff!' the boss purred when his boy had returned by the end of the week. 'He could have gone away but he wanted to spend a bit of time with his family.'

Harry obviously admired his player for being so level-headed and grounded and, down in Wales, Gareth's uncle Chris Pike, spoke of the family's pride – and joy – at his growing reputation and how he was handling suddenly being thrust into the limelight. Pike, the former Cardiff City player, told the BBC: 'His parents are very salt of the earth and have brought him up really well and have done everything for him in the sense of giving him time and love. I'm sure he will not change. It's the cliché that they all do change but I'm sure Gareth won't.

'I spoke to him on the Wednesday [after the hat-trick in Milan] and congratulated him on his performance at the San Siro and he was just going out with a couple of friends, very low key. He's just a smashing lad. I've known him for 21 years and I know exactly how grounded he is.

'He just loves playing football – he's not motivated by money, he's not motivated by fame, he's just motivated by football and he loves it.'

Gareth enjoyed his mum's home cooking, met up with a few old school pals and talked football with his dad. Then it was time to return to the Lane for the next match – a trip to Old Trafford for a Saturday evening kick-off against United.

The day before the match Redknapp admitted that he was considering giving Gareth an even longer extended rest by leaving him out of the team to face Sir Alex Ferguson's outfit. By doing so, he was admitting that, at this stage of the season anyway, the Inter return was more important than United away. Which, of course, it was. Lose at United and there was still time to play catch-up in the league...but if Spurs went down to Inter at home, it could put qualifying for the next stage of the Champions League in real jeopardy.

So Harry's thinking made sense. He explained it in this way: 'Gareth Bale is fine but we've got two big games and I'll look at it. He's had a real hard spell of playing game after game and internationals.'

And the boss bristled when it was suggested to him that he might have get used to selecting his team without Gareth – if Spurs accepted a mega bid for him. He said: This is the place for him to be. People say is he for sale – no, he isn't. The chairman wouldn't sell him I wouldn't want to sell him. I think he needs to keep progressing here. He's had one great year and has made unbelievable strides. This is where he needs to stay and keep improving and take Tottenham to where we want to go.'

It was then pointed out to Harry that Bale would have been just five months old when Spurs last won a League game at Old Trafford in 1989. But he said he wasn't bothered by that depressing run of 20 matches without a win: He added: 'I wouldn't take the blame for what happened in all those other years. It's a hard place for anyone. How many have gone there and won? They lose one or two there a season at the most. 'And it's different players here now. They wouldn't know about that record or anything else about them. It's a new experience for some of them, Rafael van der Vaart is looking forward to going there in a Premier League game and it will be a good experience for those players.'

It was hard to see how Harry could *not* play Gareth at Old Trafford given the injury list of major stars still hindering the club's season. Huddlestone, King, Corluka, Defoe, Dawson, O'Hara and Woodgate were still missing and Gareth's pace, cunning and poise could be vital if Spurs were to get anything at the Theatre of Dreams.

Bale did play – but Spurs did not return to North London with anything, save some criticism from some of their fans. They lost 2-0 and it could have been worse – although Redknapp claimed it should have been better. He based that claim around a controversial goal by Luis Nani in the final minutes. Heurelho Gomes rolled the ball out for a free-kick after Nani had clearly handled it – but ref Mark Clattenburg had not called play back and awarded the free kick. The Portuguese winger realised what had happened and mischievously smashed the ball into the net. Nemanja Vidić had put United 1-0 up when he latched on to a free kick from Nani on the half hour – but Redknapp and his men were furious that the Nani goal was allowed to stand.

'The whole thing was a farce,' Harry raged. 'It was handball. Nani put his hand on it and dragged it down. Mark Clattenburg is a top referee but he has had a nightmare with that. In the end Clattenburg will come up with some excuse as to why he didn't see it – he couldn't see, he let play go on – well if he did that he should have been saying to Gomes "play on, play on".

'I haven't spoken to the referee, he's not going to change his decision and he's made a mess of it all now anyway. They'll go in and come up with a story that will make it all look right, that's what happens.'

Even United boss Ferguson conceded that goal was 'bizarre'.

He said: 'No one knew at the time what was wrong. One minute the goalkeeper had the ball in his hands and next it's in his net. Nani looked back and looked at the referee and the referee said "play on", so what can he do but put the ball in the net?

'You can look at the referee and look at the linesmen and blame them, but the goalkeeper should know better. He's an experienced goalkeeper. I thought he made a mess of it.'

Some Spurs fans felt that Redknapp was hiding behind the Nani goal as an excuse – because he had messed up tactically. One lifelong supporter told me: 'It's Harry's fault we lost – not Nani's nor the ref's. Harry didn't get his game plan right. We were too defensive; we should have pushed up more on them and got the ball out to Baley so that he could use his pace and get some balls into the box for Keane and Modric to latch on to.

'It's all right moaning that the Nani goal cost us but it was 1-0 anyway, and that goal only came in the last few minutes of normal time, so we would have lost anyway. Harry always seems to lose his bottle when we go to places like Old Trafford. We should have attacked them more – and put them under more pressure, like we did in Milan with Inter.'

I can certainly sympathise with the fans who felt let down – but let's not forget that Redknapp did have to also take into account that looming return match with Inter, and that certain of his men were still showing signs of physical and mental fatigue. All in all, it was surely an acceptable team he put out – and acceptable tactics – if the end result was a win over Inter?

The match in Manchester certainly wasn't Gareth's finest moment. Again, he looked drained at times...maybe he was saving himself for the Inter return, or maybe he was working himself slowly back to form. It didn't help that wily old United boss Ferguson pulled a tactical masterstroke on him.

In the first half Gareth found himself up against the willing legs and pace of Brazilian full back Rafael da Silva. The youngster pushed Gareth's energy levels to the limit, so that by the second half Baley was almost all puffed out. OK, there was one moment of thrilling skill and excitement as Gareth skipped past three United players and sped towards goal – only to see his shot go just wide of Edwin van der Sar's far post on the hour.

But Ferguson then completed his master class in tactical awareness by substituting Rafael for the veteran Wes Brown four minutes later.

Brown is no sprinter – but he didn't need to be. By the time he was introduced in the fray in the 64th minute, Bale looked drained and Brown was able to compete with the wonder boy at a much more leisurely pace; certainly a pace that he preferred. At full steam, Gareth would have taken him to the cleaners; luckily for Brown, the train was still in the sidings this particular evening.

Gareth admitted he was glad to get out of Manchester as he slumped in his seat on the three-hour-plus coach journey back to London. 'That was a tough match,' he told a team-mate. 'I'm glad it's over and we can concentrate now on the Inter game.' Yes, he was tired and weary – but as he rested his aching body he instinctively knew that he would be OK for the clash that really mattered: the return against the Italian giants three days later. He would be ready for that – and he would show the world once again that he was the Lane's latest legend.

Chapter 9

TAXI FOR
MAICON

The Tottenham fans were in fine voice as they filed down towards White Hart Lane in their thousands. This was the kind of night the older fans had dreamed of for decades and one that the younger ones would be able to regale future generations with about how their team had advanced so dramatically during 2009 and 2010. Assuming the boys did the business for them, of course.

Gareth was confident but had a rare bout of minor nerves as kick off loomed. A Spurs source said: 'He wasn't his usual devil-may-care self but he always thought we could beat Inter. Harry had a special word with him – I think he could tell he was a bit more nervous than normal. The thing is with Harry, he can tell if someone's a bit quieter than usual and needs a reassuring arm around the shoulder.

'Baley is one of his favourites – him, Crouchy and Jermain

are probably his biggest favourites – so he took time out to help make sure Gareth was totally focused for what was probably our biggest match for nearly 40 years.'

One man certainly focused was Inter's Maicon. He arrived at the Lane laughing and joking and looked supremely confident. He had apparently laughed off comments about his humbling by Gareth in the San Siro, saying that it had been a one-off and would not happen again. He told the Italian press that his poor performance could probably be attributed to a '24-hour virus' he had picked up the night before the match. He had failed to shake it off before kick-off and it had affected his tackling and pace. Of course, Mr Maicon now had to prove it had been down to this 'illness' by getting the better of Gareth in the match.

Before kick off a timely boost for Gareth came from a most unusual and unexpected source...the boss of Arsenal. Arsène Wenger predicted that Inter could well struggle again to keep the Welsh rocket at bay. Wenger told Yahoo Eurosport: 'Many people in Europe discovered Bale because of his hat-trick in Milan, but the English all saw him finish last season as a cannonball.

'He was exceptional against us and then against Chelsea in the space of just three days. He made the difference in those games. I'm not surprised, he's an exceptional player. Also, he has exceptional physical qualities; you can see how he is able to run back and forth as much as anyone else out there.'

Harry Redknapp knew that Inter planned to double up on Gareth to try to negate his impact – as Everton had done by putting Coleman and Neville on him. But he revealed that the coaches at the Lane had been working on that with Gareth – to find ways to beat the shackling. In fact, the

Spurs boss said he felt that the experiences Gareth was now having as a winger would eventually stand him in good stead if or when he returned to being a left-back. Redknapp said: 'We've been working on that with him. That's why I said all along that long-term he'll be the best left-back around. When he plays there he come forward on to the ball and has no one getting tight to him. He's running from deep positions.

'We went to Benfica and I've never seen a left-back performance like it. He kept running the length of the field. He's got everything to be a great left-back. His defending is getting better – it's just at the moment Benoit Assou-Ekotto is a great left-back.'

I know many Spurs fans wouldn't mind a bit if Gareth never returned to left-back duties – and I can empathise with them. He is the ultimate modern-day left midfielder/winger, given his pace and dribbling skills and it's not surprising that many believe putting Gareth back in defence would be a waste of Spurs' most potent weapon. Gareth himself apparently prefers the freer role than being constrained at left-back – although being the professional he is, he is prepared to work where the boss tells him, for the good of the team.

At least Tottenham were boosted by the return to fitness of playmaker Rafael van der Vaart who, along with Gareth and Jermain Defoe (when fit again), was becoming one of the key men in the team. A relieved Redknapp said: 'He came through training OK. He trained and that was a bonus. He came down with a hamstring but he was probably fatigued in all honesty. He was probably tired and maybe it was cramp rather than a hamstring. There was no reaction so he could be OK.' At just £8 million from Real Madrid the Dutchman was undoubtedly the transfer bargain of the season. The day before he signed for Spurs he had been all lined up to move to Bayern Munich in Germany for £18 million – so full credit to White Hart Lane chairman Daniel Levy on this occasion for pulling off a fabulous coup in getting his man for £10 million less than the going rate.

Certainly Van der Vaart looked an £18 million player as he quickly settled in at Tottenham – it was a rare blunder in the transfer market by Jose Mourinho, by now boss at the Bernabeu, to let such a remarkable player escape for such relative peanuts.

The Dutchman was convinced his new team could beat Inter and advance to the later stages of the Champions League. He said: 'These are the games when the spotlight is on you as individuals to produce and it is on this stage that we must show our entitlement to be there. Big players love big games and we have to show we have that quality.

'Inter have many good players but we have to make them worry about us and ensure that this game is dictated by what we do. We showed Inter what we're about in the second half at the San Siro and now we have to believe that we can do it again. It won't be easy, how can it be? This is Inter Milan in the Champions League. But we have shown our fighting spirit and that anything in football is possible.'

He pointed to how Bale had inspired Spurs towards that unbelievable comeback at the San Siro as proof that anything was indeed possible. He said he considered Gareth already a world class star and added: 'We proved that point [about anything being possible] with 10 men against a very good Inter side when, had we played another five or so minutes, we might have got it back to 4-4. We had the momentum towards the end and we have to maintain that outlook from the start in front of our own fans.'

However, despite the return of Van der Vaart and his confidence, plus the excitement generated by Bale v Maicon round two, Spurs did not go into the match as favourites as their form had dipped since the match in the San Siro – while Inter had prospered. As Gareth and Co were going down at Old Trafford, Inter were beating Genoa thanks to a goal from Sulley Muntari, whom Redknapp had coached at Portsmouth. And while Inter were second in Serie A, Spurs were fifth in the Premier League and facing a real battle for that all-important fourth spot from Manchester City.

If anything, the pressure was more on Spurs than Inter as they needed at least a draw to keep alive their hopes of qualifying for the knockout stages. Defeat would have allowed FC Twente or Werder Bremen to take the initiative in the fight for second place in the group behind Inter.

But Gareth was convinced Spurs could keep their dream alive by beating Inter – and nostalgic boss Redknapp said he believed history was on their side. He said: 'Inter aren't just the champions of Europe but the champions of Italy. But tell you what, we'd win if we had those three playing for us – Danny Blanchflower, Jimmy Greaves and Bobby Smith. Did you know Danny Blanchflower invented the defensive wall? Northern Ireland were playing Italy in the 1950s and they had someone who could take a mean free-kick. So Blanchflower suggested a wall to stop him.

'At first, because he was Irish, they thought he was talking about building one. But, no, he was talking about players standing together. It had never been done before.'

Harry also believed destiny favoured his team when it was

revealed that Inter would have a stand-in between the posts – Luca Castellazzi – as first choice, and arguably the world's No. 1 keeper Julio Cesar, was injured. He was sure that if Gareth and his marauding talents attacked from the kick off, they would do serious damage. Harry added: 'There is a feeling that attack is the best form of defence for us. We are an open team and I don't have any options other than to pick an attacking team. We are an attacking team. Look at my midfield. We have Huddlestone, Modric, Bale, Lennon, Van der Vaart and then a front man, Crouchy.

'Unless I leave out Modric and play Wilson Palacios I can't thicken it up. I have two wingers who have to play and for me there is not a team that I can pick which is defensive. But then I like attacking teams. We are at home and we have to have a go. We need to get something after losing in Milan. Even over there I decided to have the two wingers on. It is the place we can hurt them.

'Their two wide men do not really defend. They attack with three forwards and Wesley Sneijder behind, and they have two holding midfield players and attack with six. The key tomorrow will be ripping into them on the flanks. We need Gareth Bale to again get the better of Maicon. Then you have Aaron Lennon on the other side; I think they can be the key.'

Harry had already told Bale that he would be in for a tough night: that Inter would double up with Zanetti likely to help out Maicon. He said he was ready for the rearguard action and showed his confidence by adding that he still expected to come out on top – that it was his job to find a way past them whatever they throw at him, if he were to be considered a world-class star.

Gareth said: 'Obviously teams are trying to stop me, so I've got to think of other ways to get past them. I'm going to have to keep learning in training and in games and try things and hopefully improve as a player which will allow me to do that. Against the world-class players, the likes of Ronaldo, teams double up all the time. Ronaldo still finds a way. And you've got to keep trying to improve your game and make it an all-round game, to kind of be unstoppable.'

Rather mischievously, it was suggested by one of the press corps that Gareth might be auditioning for a future role in the Inter team. He swiftly and emphatically kicked that idea into touch, much to the relief of the Spurs fans among the mass of reporters! 'I don't take much notice of what speculation's going on in the media,' he said. 'I just want to keep playing for Tottenham and working on my game. I'm learning every day, week in, week out.'

You could have cut a knife with the tension as the teams finally lined up for kick off. Both Bale and Maicon were there, with the Brazilian looking decidedly the more nervous and edgy. The teams played out the match like this:

TOTTENHAM: Cudicini, Hutton, Gallas, Kaboul, Assou-Ekotto, Lennon, Huddlestone, Van der Vaart, Modric, Bale, Crouch. Subs: Jenas (Van der Vaart), Pavlyuchenko (Crouch), Palacios (Lennon). Not used: Pletikosa, Keane, Bassong, Kranjcar.
INTER MILAN: Castellazzi; Maicon, Lucio, Samuel, Chivu; Biabiany (Coutinho), Zanetti, Muntari (Nwankwo), Pandev (Milito); Sneijder; Eto'o. Subs not used: Orlandoni, Cordoba, Materazzi, Santon. Booked: Samuel, Chivu, Lucio.

With a performance that will live forever in the memories of

Spurs fans, their team triumphed 3-1 over the European champions – and Gareth Bale was again Man of the Match. Once again, the man considered to be the best right-back in the world could not live with his lightning pace and skill. Once again Maicon was reduced to a stuttering, slightly pathetic, sad figure as he struggled to match the Welsh wizard.

Indeed, his night was best summed up by the mischievous taunts of the home fans as he was left for dead yet again midway through the second half. 'Taxi for Maicon!' they chanted, much to the merriment of many on the Spurs bench – although Inter boss Benitez did not enjoy the big joke one little bit.

He knew that he was constantly being compared to predecessor Mourinho and that defeat in London was another nail in his ever-closing coffin lid at the San Siro.

Gareth was understandably delighted. He made two of the goals with another superlative performance. Inter had panicked every time Gareth got the ball and that meant spaces opened up for Tottenham's other creative players, particularly Modric and Van der Vaart.

It was the Dutchman who put the hosts 1-0 up on 18 minutes. Then Gareth set up Crouch for No 2 just after the hour. Samuel Eto'o pulled one back 20 minutes later and it looked as if Tottenham might be in for a nerve-wracking finale.

But, just as in Milan, Gareth Bale once again emerged as the superhero. He killed off any dreams of Benitez and Inter may have had of going home with a point when he once again left Inter's defence in his wake as he crossed for substitute Roman Pavlyuchenko to make it 3-1.

Brilliant.

Afterwards the normally measured Bale was, unsurprisingly

given the result and what it meant, was bubbly and on a high. The incredible win moved Spurs above Inter at the top of Group A.

And Gareth said: 'It was great, so special beating the European champions. It will be a night that will never be forgotten. The fans were unbelievable. They acted as a 12th man. They have been fantastic all season and we capped it off for them tonight. It was a special night.'

Typically, he refused to accept all the plaudits that were coming his way, insisting that it had been a team result. He said: 'I'm just trying to keep my feet on the ground, work hard in training and do well in games and enjoy my football. We all had the belief that we could hurt Inter and we showed that. We were unlucky to go down to 10 in the San Siro. With 11 men on the pitch, we know what we can do. We know what we are capable of. We just have to produce it and we have. Hopefully, we will have shown people what we can do and hopefully we can go far in this competition now.'

Boss Redknapp had thrown a grateful arm around Gareth at the final whistle and he was as excited as anyone about his star man. He revealed that Portuguese legend Luis Figo, now working in an ambassadorial role for Inter, had told him he loved Gareth. Harry said: 'He said that Bale is just amazing, just amazing. When Figo says that he has to be good because he was such a fantastic footballer himself. He said, "He killed us twice". He didn't ask about buying him, he just said Bale was fantastic.

'As for selling him, Tottenham is a well-run club and not one that needs to sell. Bale was outstanding and he was playing against a right-back rated by many as the best in the world and he's given him a chasing. It's like you're a boxer knocking everybody out, but it's only when you do it against the top people that it counts. Well, he was coming up against the champions tonight – and he's done it again.

'No disrespect to Maicon but he's given him the most torrid time you will ever wish to see. It was amazing...what confidence you must have to go and do that to a player like Maicon, people who are so highly-rated.

'It's amazing really and he's done it in both games. This kid is just improving and improving and getting better and better... he's just a great left-sided player. It's probably a year now that he has shown this form. 'Getting the monkey off his back of never being on a winning team at Tottenham was amazing for him. I don't think he needs to go anywhere else to play his football. He needs to stay.

'We've got a good chance now to get out of this group, which would be what we aimed to do. We're playing well but we've got to keep it going.'

The Italians had already dubbed Gareth 'Incredi-Bale' after his hat-trick in the San Siro and now the likes of Inter were even more determined to land him one day soon – despite Redknapp's protestations. His team-mate Van der Vaart summed up the situation succinctly when he said: 'Everyone is scared of Gareth. Maicon is the best right-back in the world – and he killed him.'

The plaudits kept on coming. Former Liverpool star and TV pundit Jamie Redknapp told how his only regret was that Gareth was not English. He said: 'I wish Gareth Bale was available to Fabio Capello. The kid is so gifted. Now he has the confidence to support his ability and is an example of a young player taking an opportunity when it comes his way at Tottenham. He's been like a new signing in the second half of the season. With that sweet left foot, he could be world class.'

Gareth admitted he was aware of the fans' 'Taxi for Maicon' chant. He said: 'A few of the lads were on about it after the match, it was a bit of fun on the part of the fans. The atmosphere throughout the match was fantastic; I have never known an atmosphere like it before.'

Predictably, the next day's papers were full of Baley and his wonderful performance. Shaun Custis, writing in the *Sun*, typified the adulation in the English press: 'Hey! Can this bloke Bale play or what? It did not need a straw poll to decide that the sensational Gareth Bale was Tottenham's Man of the Match. On a glorious and historic night at White Hart Lane, he was clearly the shining star. The Welsh wing wizard has set his sights on emulating Cristiano Ronaldo and says his aim is to be unstoppable.

'In Milan a fortnight ago, he was unstoppable in the second half and hit a hat-trick in the Londoners' 4-3 defeat. Last night he was unstoppable for the entire game, as Inter's Brazilian full-back Maicon would testify. Maicon is supposedly the best right-back in the world but Bale has reduced him to a nervous wreck.'

But it wasn't just in England that the fourth estate were paying homage. The Italian press were also making the most of Bale's second wonder show against Inter, even though it was at the expense of their own champion team. Corriere dello Sport's headline was: 'Bale flattens Inter.' Turin sports newspaper *Tuttosport* had a front-page picture of the Spurs man under the headline: 'Frightening Bale sweeps away Inter.' And *La Repubblica*'s front page read: 'Nightmare Bale, Inter crashes.'

Yes, young Gareth had become headline news across the whole of Europe, and he was still only 21. The only problem now would surely be keeping his own feet on the ground – and for Redknapp to keep the team from getting carried away. They would all need to stay down-to-earth and focused as one of the two biggest domestic matches of the season now loomed ominously on the horizon...Arsenal...away at The Emirates.

Chapter 10

I'M ONLY HUMAN

You'd have to be not human to walk off that pitch after beating the European champions 3-1 and not be on a high. To not let it go to your head just a little bit. To think you couldn't now beat whoever was put in front of you in the Premier League.

Just as after the 4-3 defeat at the San Siro which, when you look at it after the stunning hat-trick by Gareth seemed almost like a victory, Harry Redknapp would have his work cut out keeping his men grounded as four league games now came thick and fast before Spurs once again launched into their dizzying European adventure.

The fourth match in the line would be no problem – what motivation did Gareth and the boys need with the prospect of playing their bitterest rivals, Arsenal?

But the three before that could be tricky if the team were not playing at full blast – Bolton away, then Sunderland and Blackburn at home.

It hadn't escaped Redknapp's notice that Spurs had struggled after playing in Milan. Indeed, as we have noted, they huffed and puffed to a 1-1 home draw with Everton and then lost 2-0 at Manchester United. Harry was worried that this anti-climax, and run of poor results, might be a regular occurrence if their European run of glory continued.

Of course, he wasn't the first boss to realise that European competition could leave your team fatigued both mentally and physically. Sir Alex Ferguson has complained about the same situation over the years – even in 2010 when United had also played in Milan. On February 16 2010, United won 3-2 in the San Siro against AC Milan (who share the stadium with Inter). Yet four days later, after the high of beating one of Europe's crack outfits in their own backyard, United crashed 3-1 at Everton in the Premier League.

That was the result that had Sir Alex bemoaning the fragile state of his boys after their European adventure. He said at the time: 'We left something in Milan and there was tiredness in the team. We played like garbage and got deservedly beat.'

But he added that he expected the problem to have resolved itself for the following game, a few days later, when United hosted West Ham, and they would have had time to readjust to domestic football and would have left their fatigue behind them. But he added: 'It is difficult to think that when you go through all the emotions and the pace and intensity and atmosphere of a game like the Milan one, you don't lose something.'

Harry Redknapp could certainly identify with those words of his close friend. It was now his job to make sure his men didn't mess up in the league; after all, they didn't want to miss out on the Champions League the following campaign after getting a real taste for the competition. And they would do – unless they finished in the Premier League's top four, or won the competition outright in their first campaign.

Gareth was confident he and his team-mates would be up to doing the business in the Prem. He saw no reason why there should be a blip. 'He is such a professional and can cope with massive wins or massive defeats in much the same way,' said a Spurs source. 'He's not one for getting carried away or getting depressed. He is such a level-headed individual. Nothing much fazes him; he is a great guy, really well liked by his team-mates and someone who is very much a team player – despite his undeniable individual skills. Truly an inspired and inspiring guy, and footballer.'

Certainly, Gareth had inspired many people by his tremendous showings against Inter Milan. One of them was Sam Warburton, his former school mate, who now told the world that he wanted to be 'the Gareth Bale of Welsh rugby'. A few days after Gareth's second demolition of Inter, Warburton said he hoped to emulate those heroics when he played for Wales against the mighty Australians in an autumn rugby union Test.

'I don't think I'll score a hat-trick of tries against the Wallabies, but a little bit of his inspiration would help,' said Warburton after Wales head coach Warren Gatland announced his surprise decision to give the Cardiff Blues flanker his eighth cap ahead of Wales' most capped forward Martyn Williams.

Warburton, 22, had been a school pal of Gareth at Whitchurch High School in Cardiff a few years earlier. As a Spurs fan, he was even more delighted at Gareth's world-stage success against Inter. He said: 'It is unbelievable. I always knew he was a good footballer when I played with him at school, no one ever touched him – he was head and shoulders above everyone else and it was obvious he was going to make it.

'He was always good at the sprints and long-distance running so he had all the attributes to get to the top. It gives me great confidence to see him doing well, another Whitchurch boy on the world scene taking them all on.'

After the glitter and glitz of the 3-1 win over Inter, Bolton Wanderers were first up for Baley and Co. Traditionally a resolute, dour, battling team under the inspiration of Sam Allardyce, they had taken on something of a new life under the more refined tutelage of former Burnley boss, Owen Coyle. The Scotsman enjoys his football being played on the ground rather than in the air, but even he admitted he feared for his team's fortunes against Gareth.

He said he planned to pit tough full-back Gretar Steinsson against Bale. The Icelandic ace was the sort who took no prisoners – but Coyle was honest to admit he didn't know if that would be enough in the battle to keep Gareth at bay. Coyle said: 'How do you stop Bale? With difficulty. But it is the same every week in this league. If it is not Gareth Bale, it is Didier Drogba, Fernando Torres, Wayne Rooney or Dimitar Berbatov. You have to give credit as well to Harry Redknapp for pushing him on from full-back.'

Coyle's decision to keep Steinsson close on Gareth looked an inspired one as Spurs struggled for fluency and energy at the Reebok on Saturday November 6, 2010. He shackled the wonder boy, who, to be honest, did look a little tired out after his latest exploits against the Milanese, and Tottenham began the long journey home to London with the bitter taste of a 4-2 defeat in their mouths.

Gareth admitted on that journey that he felt 'a bit whacked out' after what had been a tough week, and said he was looking forward to putting his feet up for a few hours.

Meanwhile, the man who had made his afternoon in the north-west so difficult admitted that he had been spurred on by Gareth's exploits against Inter. Steinsson told the press, 'I did watch the match – and knew I could be in for a tough old afternoon.' But instead of dreading the examination against the Welsh wonder boy, the Icelandic defender decided to use it as an opportunity to show his own worth – especially as a number of friends had texted him, urging him to put Gareth in his place. Steinsson said: 'I have never received so many texts before a game, telling me to rest up. I have played against Gareth before and he is a fantastic player and he has got a bright future in front of him.

'But I tried not to analyse it too much because, if you do that, then it just gets in your head. I just had a really good chicken korma and relaxed on the eve of the game. That helped me.'

Let's be honest, here...he was also aided by Chung-Yong Lee, who doubled back from midfield to help turn the screw on Bale. In fact, the Bolton ploy was to smother Gareth whenever he got the ball – with any of their players going for him if he was near them.

Bolton's big central defender Zat Knight admitted as much when he said that he too had watched – and been stunned – by Bale's showing against Inter. Knight said: 'I watched both games against Inter and it was scary. They showed he is a world-class player. But against us it's obviously going to be a different game, we'll be a bit more physical. I think there is a lot of pressure on his shoulders, saying he's the best player in the world and better than Lionel Messi after a few games.

'Potentially, he can reach that but I just hope people don't pile too much on him and let him gradually build and get better.

'Gretar [Steinsson] knows what he has to do against Bale. He's dealt with some quality players down the years. But we'll all chip in when necessary.'

Gareth's best moment in the match came when he launched a brilliant free-kick which beat Jussi Jaaskelainen only to hit the bar. But it was not to be – the truth of it was that he and his team-mates were too knackered after the Inter clash. This was simply a game too many.

But they kept coming: three days after the defeat at Bolton, Sunderland were heading to White Hart Lane for a Premier League encounter. The Black Cats arrived after a painful 5-1 thrashing at their biggest rivals Newcastle – and were determined to get back on track. It meant they battled hard, and came away with a 1-1 draw. The cobwebs of the Inter match had still not been fully blown away for Gareth and Co, even though they had enough chances to win the match. A top-notch performance by keeper Craig Gordon and some bizarre decisions by referee Howard Webb played a significant part as Steve Bruce's men clung on for a point as a goal from Ghanaian striker Asamoah Gyan cancelled out Van der Vaart's opener.

Gareth had played a part in the Dutchman's goal, sending in a long cross that Crouch nodded down for Van der Vaart to convert. But once again he found it tough going as Sunderland – and especially the aggressive Lee Cattermole - clamped down on him immediately if he got wind of the ball, and also stationed the resolute, and classy, defender Nedum Onouha on his heels for the 90 minutes.

The *Daily Telegraph*'s John Ley appeared to believe that Bale had been 'found out'. He wrote: 'Where Maicon failed, Nedum Onuoha succeeded, negating the threat of Bale just as Phil Neville and Gretar Steinsson had frustrated the winger for Everton and Bolton respectively.

'Bale did not play badly, the undoubted talents and trickery still on show, even if there was also the odd misplaced pass. But English clubs are learning how to cope with the player. Bale's rise to stardom was confirmed with his stunning hat-trick in the San Siro and a match-winning display in the return leg. Suddenly, the quietly-spoken 21-year-old was the man of the moment.

'Neville was the first to show how to play Bale, sitting back when necessary but pushing him inside when possible. Even Harry Redknapp, the Spurs manager, admitted that Neville handled him expertly. Steinsson followed suit in last Saturday's 4-2 win, albeit over a team still recovering from their European exertions and, on Tuesday night, Onuoha sat off Bale. Lee Cattermole was always in attendance – not always legally – and the visitors negated the flow of balls to his feet.'

And Karl Sears, writing on footballfancast.com, also felt teams had worked out how to thwart Gareth. At the same time, he suggested one answer would be for Harry Redknapp to make Gareth a left-back again: 'Tuesday night's game against Sunderland served only to reinforce this theory – Premier League teams have realised that Gareth Bale struggles to make an impact if he is marked tightly and not allowed room to build up speed. Much like Everton's Phil Neville and

Bolton's Gretar Steinsson, Sunderland's Nedum Onouha was able to mark the young Welshman out of the game for long periods, with Michael Turner helping out whenever required. As long as Bale keeps the left midfield role he will continue to be tightly marked or double teamed, meaning that one of Tottenham's best assets is going to waste. At the business end of last season Bale was still relatively unknown and was left alone to terrorise defences, but a lot has happened since April and now Bale is fixed firmly on the radar of every team in England.

'It is arguable that Bale's attacking threat would increase if he were to move back into defence. You can't double team a defender and it would be more difficult for opposition to pick up and track Bale's runs if he were coming from left-back.'

Some teams had done the inevitable and put two men on Gareth to stultify him and, yes, it had worked to an extent. But Gareth was still suffering from the inevitable mental and physical burnout from the Inter games. He would recover and resume his brilliant form, however many men teams put on him.

And, let's not forget, even by taking an extra man out of the game, he was already causing problems for the opposition – as it meant other Spurs players could now move into the space the defender, or midfielder, told to police Gareth had consequently abdicated.

Finally, eleven days after the 3-1 triumph over Inter Milan, Gareth and Tottenham returned to winning ways, having taken only one point from six against Bolton and Sunderland. The much-needed victory came as they beat Blackburn 4-2 at the Lane – it was the timeliest of tonics, setting them up for the grudge match against Arsenal the following week, and the vital Champions League meeting with Werder Bremen four days after that.

Gareth had certainly seemed much more relaxed in the build-up to the Blackburn match. He even spoke a little more about his personal life – revealing that he was 'not much into big nights out' and that he preferred staying and watching TV talent show *The X Factor* on Saturday and Sunday nights. Gareth also admitted he was hopeful that a Spurs fan, Matt Cardle, would win the show (he did!)

Cardle even trained with Gareth and the lads as they finalised their preparations for the game against Blackburn – making his way to the club's training ground in Chigwell. But by Friday, the fun was over as the team set off for the north-west.

Blackburn boss Sam Allardyce was in no doubt about the damage Bale could cause his team. Big Sam took the debate about Gareth's potential up to its highest notch yet – by declaring that he was already the best player on the planet. Allardyce said: 'With pace you have to have the ability and have a football brain. There's not a better player in the world than Gareth Bale at the moment for me. He's producing, and his delivery is fantastic. He has the potential to be a great player not a very good one. That final ball gives him the potential to be a great player, not just very good.'

Allardyce had been generous in his praise – and, unfortunately for him, Gareth proved him to be spot on as the Rovers match kicked off.

It was clear from the start that both Gareth and his team-mates had put their post-European blues behind them as they swamped Rovers from the very start. It was 2-0 at half-time and 4-0 within 75 minutes. Bale was back to his normal self, tormenting Rovers full-back Michel Salgado and grabbing two of the four goals, the opener on 16 minutes and the fourth on 75.

Gareth's first goal was a brilliant header after he was set up by Van der Vaart from a corner, his second was a finely placed shot from 15 yards. In between Pavlyuchenko and Crouchy killed off the visitors.

The only downside to an otherwise impressive performance came when Spurs eased off after going 4-0 up, allowing Ryan Nelsen and Gael Givet to score.

After the match, Sam Allardyce wore a wry smile as he was asked what he thought of Bale now – given that he had praised him to the heavens before the match. Big Sam said: 'Bale is almost unstoppable at the moment. He's an outstanding player, and punished us severely. We looked to double up on him, but good players are difficult to stop whether you double up on them or not.'

Gareth was named the man of the match and afterwards admitted his form had maybe dipped a little as he came to terms with the superstardom thrust upon him by the media and the fans after his double destruction of Inter Milan. He had also found he had to adapt to having two men on him all the time instead of one – at a time when he was more than a little mentally and physically drained.

Gareth, whose two goals against Rovers now made him joint top scorer at the club with Pavlyuchenko, admitted: 'It has been difficult for me recently when teams have had two players marking me. In a way I've got to try to find another way to get past them. I did that against Blackburn and I was delighted.'

Tottenham assistant coach Joe Jordan, standing in for the

under-the-weather Redknapp for the Rovers game, was just as delighted with Gareth's reinvigorated showing, pointing out that he had also made the second goal for Pavyluchenko.

Jordan said: 'Some of the football we played in the first half, the openings and opportunities Gareth created, were terrific, especially against a team who did well against Newcastle in midweek. I thought we played exceptionally well and should have been further ahead in the first half.

'Harry is a very positive guy. He wants to play on the front foot. We picked the team to win the game.

'We are disappointed we conceded two goals. But if you do drop your concentration level that is what will happen. At 4-0 up I thought we failed to pick up the second balls. I don't think it should take anything away from the result and the football we played. The way we played the game was fantastic. We played some great football.'

Peter Crouch was also in a much better frame of mind – after scoring his first league goal since he got the winner at Manchester City on May 5...the win that propelled Spurs into the Champions League.

Crouch said: 'I have scored six goals this season and I have been part of another five maybe – that is 11 goals. Everyone loves scoring, don't get me wrong, and I am no different. When you are a striker you get judged on that. I have been scoring in the Champions League and my last goal was against Inter Milan – which was only a couple of games ago.

'So, yes, I feel confident that I will score goals and it was pleasing to get one against Blackburn. I have been pleased with my performances and the manager would not play me if he did not think I was having an impact. We are looking forward to the game at Arsenal. We are not there yet, but we are certainly a lot closer to them than we have been for a long time.

'They are a top-quality side with a lot of young players. We changed our side around in the Carling Cup when Arsenal won 4-1 but they were fantastic. We know that they are a great side but I believe that on our day we can beat anyone. If you really want to have a proper impact on the league you have to go to places like Arsenal and pick up points. We have a lot of talent to do that.'

It was the first real public mention of the imminent clash with the Gunners – Redknapp had forbade talk of it until they had got the likes of Blackburn out of the way. Quite rightly, he had felt it could take the focus off the matches his team had to play before heading for the Emirates. But now Blackburn had been beaten and Crouchy had let the genie out of the bottle.

And it was some genie!

OK, the win over Inter Milan and the gallant fightback, courtesy of Gareth in the San Siro, had been two momentous occasions, but many Spurs fans would have taken beating Arsenal any day. Such was the level of animosity and rivalry between the two north London giants of top-class football.

The win over Blackburn was their first win in five league games and had put Tottenham within three points of fourth-placed Manchester City, and that vital Champions League spot. A win over Arsenal at their Emirates home – and yet more pressure on City – would put the gloss on a month that had already been unforgettable for the young man from Wales who was rapidly finding the world was at his feet.

Chapter 11

TOP GUN

The match at the Emirates was all it had been billed as – and more – for Gareth and Tottenham. Victory would bring further justification for the ever-growing belief that he was fast becoming one of the best players on the European stage, and also that the team were well on their way to becoming a regular fixture in the coveted 'top four' clubs in England.

That top four had, until the previous season, consisted almost exclusively of Manchester United, Chelsea, Arsenal and Liverpool. Now the Mersey giants had fallen by the wayside and Tottenham looked set for a regular battle with moneybags club, Manchester City, for that in-demand fourth spot.

But wasn't there even a chance that they could make third? Well, that would probably mean dethroning Arsenal...and were better to start than at the Gunners' own stadium on a cold November afternoon?

As the build-up began, so did the now regular plaudits for Gareth from the opposition. It was as if they wanted to get them in first before he destroyed them, as if to say to their own fans, 'Well, we told you so…we did warn you, you know.'

In the last league match, it had been Blackburn manager Sam Allardyce who had been all gushing about Baley. Now, Gunners boss Arsène Wenger led the chorus of approval, although it was, perhaps inevitably, in a more backhand manner. The Frenchman agreed that Bale was one of the most exciting new players, but argued that the Welshman's wonderful pace and control could be contained if the full-back was 'intelligent enough'. It would be a claim that would rebound back against him after his own right-back Bacary Sagna was destroyed by Gareth in the match itself! Wenger had said: 'You defend against him with your brain. If somebody has superior legs to you, you have still got resources. The main resource you can have is your brain and your intelligence. That's what you can do.

'You have slow defenders who defend very well against quick strikers. It doesn't take anything away from Gareth Bale who for me is a very promising and already a big player today. But when you give them room it is of course easier for them.'

Wenger added: 'It will certainly be important to keep Bale quiet. Many people in Europe discovered Bale because of his hat-trick in Milan but the English all saw him finish last season like a cannonball.

'He was exceptional against us and then against Chelsea in the space of three days. He made the difference in those games. I'm not surprised, he is an exceptional player. Also, he has exceptional physical qualities. You can see how he is able to run back and forth as much as anyone else out there.

'We watched him at the time he played left-back but we had Ashley Cole and Gael Clichy already so we did not go for him. But Tottenham also have Van der Vaart, Modric, Defoe, Pavlyuchenko. Tottenham have many good players in their team and for us it is important we produce a good team performance and not to focus on one player or single a player out in their team. We should just focus on our performance. If our performance is right, then we have a good chance to win. When you see inside the club everyone is focused on the next game and when the next game is Tottenham, is it a bit special.

'Tottenham have always had good teams, good players like Anderton and Ginola. It is the first time they have finished in the top four since I was here, so it means their achievement last season was better than before.'

Sagna himself added to the praise – and also pointed out that he and his team-mates would already be geed up for the match without the prospect of simply curtailing Baley. Forgetting the fact that victory would hand their fans gloating rights against their Spurs rivals, it would also put the Gunners on top of the Premier League.

Sagna said: 'He's doing very well at the moment but don't put pressure on him too early. At the moment, he's one of the most dangerous wingers. But we are all motivated to win. Everyone is ready, everyone is focused. A win would put us top of the league, now we have to do it.'

It had not gone unnoticed at the Emirates, or White Hart Lane for that matter, that Spurs had not beat the Gunners away since May 11, 1993 – when they had triumphed 3-1 – and that it had also been 68 league games since they last won away to one of the aforementioned 'big four'.

But Spurs legend David Ginola was convinced that the time

had now come to put that right. He told Goal.com: 'I'm very pleased how well Spurs have been doing for the last year but if they want to win the Premier League they have to beat Arsenal away. With players like Van der Vaart, Modric and Bale I don't see why Tottenham can't win the league, so let's wait for the game. They have got the players but are they mentally prepared to face some problems? They have to believe they can win, starting on Saturday. For many years, Spurs have played Arsenal and maybe not had the belief they can win three points but they have the talent now.'

Another former hero at the Lane, Darren Anderton, also believed that Spurs had now come of age as a top team – and he argued that Gareth was also now a much better talent than his former fellow Southampton protégé, Theo Walcott, now a star, of course, with the Gunners.

Anderton, who was part of that legendary team to beat Arsenal in '93, said: 'At the moment, I would rather have Bale as a winger ahead of Walcott. But I do think Theo will end up playing down the middle. I think Bale's delivery is spot on whereas Walcott's pace is more devastating.

'I think Arsenal will try and stop Tottenham getting the ball to him. But Arsenal are more of a European-style team who believe they are good enough to beat anyone, so that might give him more space. Bacary Sagna is very quick so that will be a key match up.'

Anderton accepted that there could well be bids for Bale, but said that they would not need to accept them if they could keep the player's ambitions satisfied...starting with playing every year in the Champions League. 'They have got to stay in that top four,' he told the *Daily Mirror*.

Arsène Wenger also made a point of mentioning that two of

the finest talents on display at the Emirates would be from Southampton. Naturally enough, he believed Walcott was just as good as Bale, but he also wanted to give Saints a pat on the back for producing such gifted footballers from their academy. He said: 'You have to pay tribute to Southampton because they had a good academy and they couldn't take advantage of it. At the time they were in the FA Youth Cup Final so they couldn't grow with this team. Unfortunately for them they became big players somewhere else.

'The fact is that a smaller club can't keep the good players for long enough to take advantage of it because they had to sell them too early. They had Walcott and Bale and they had some others.'

Walcott was also keen to get involved in the pre-match discussions – and to add his own praise for Gareth's remarkable rise to prominence. When asked who he though was the most exciting player in England, Walcott told FATV: 'In the Premier League? Gareth Bale for me. I am actually looking forward to playing against Gareth Bale because me and him grew up together at such a young age at Southampton and we've known each other since we were 10 or 11 years old.

'So it's going to be another nice little treat for us both.'

The final word, appropriately, before the match went to Gareth himself. He said he was confident Spurs could win, and boost their chances of even more glory that season. Gareth said: 'It will be a massive test obviously away at Arsenal but we'll be ready for it. We need to win every game we play at the moment. We're good enough to beat anybody and we've shown that in the past.'

He admitted he was ready for the match – that his confidence was sky high after he grabbed that brace in the destruction of Blackburn. He added: 'It was important we got that victory before the derby, just to get the winning feeling back after a recent poor run in the league. If we do get the first goal in matches, then we look quite comfortable.

'It was important to get ourselves kick-started again. The Champions League is coming around next week, so we want to build on that. It has been difficult for me recently when teams have had two players marking me. In a way I've got to try to find another way to get past them. I did that against Blackburn and I was delighted.

'There's been a lot of stuff said about me – but I try to keep myself away from that.'

Well, Gareth and the boys did translate their confidence on to the pitch at the Emirates – winning in dramatic style. It was becoming a feature of Spurs under Redknapp that they never seemed to take the easy way to glory. Much like Manchester United under Alex Ferguson – remember the Red Devils' 2-1 injury-time win over Bayern Munich in the 1999 Champions League final? – Tottenham were becoming winners the hard way.

Like United, that was also down to the way they were set up under the manager. Put simply, Redknapp liked his team to play attractive, entertaining football – like Ferguson, an undue reliance on defence was not his *raison d'être* – but it came at a price. It meant that you could win but you that you might experience a good few scares on the way as the opposition attacked you. It was great for neutral fans, but nervy for your own supporters.

And the game at the Emirates on Saturday November 20, 2010, was a full-blooded example of that. The Gunners roared into a 2-0 lead but Spurs fought back to win 3-2. Incredible...and totally heart stopping. And to ice the cake for Tottenham fans, their win meant that their bitterest rivals were also denied the opportunity of going to the top of the Premier League table!

Arsenal went in with that two-goal advantage at half-time thanks to Samir Nasri and Marouane Chamakh. Poor goalkeeping by Heurelho Gomes allowed Nasri in for the first and Chamakh smashed home a cross from Andrey Arshavin to make it 2-0.

To the neutral, it looked all over bar the shouting as the teams emerged for the second half. Surely Arsenal now had too much about them to forfeit a two-goal advantage – especially against their biggest rivals in front of their own passionate fans?

But that was discounting the fighting spirit of the side Redknapp had built – as we said, a team that was now being modelled in the fashion of Manchester United...magnificent attacking football, scary lapses and wonderful comebacks.

And who better to lead the fightback than Gareth Bale?

Yes, as in the San Siro, it would be Gareth who now stepped up to the plate and proved he has got what it takes to inspire a football team to great heights. At the tender age of 21.

Bale finished in style after a counter attack by Van der Vaart just five minutes after the break. He did his little jig of a dance, as per usual, to celebrate the goal, but he had other things on his mind. This was no time for fun; he knew that there was still a mountain to climb if Spurs fans were to avoid being teased by their Arsenal work colleagues on the Monday morning. That goal had made it 2-1 – but what if the Gunners now hit back with a third? It would surely all have been for nothing...

So after his goal he urged his team-mates on – as a team they battled and earned a glittering reward almost 20 minutes later when the ever-improving, ever-influential Van der Vaart grabbed a deserved equaliser. The Dutchman scored from the penalty spot on 67 minutes after Arsenal skipper Cesc Fabregas had foolishly handled his free kick.

A draw looked likely – and many Tottenham fans told me afterwards that they would have gladly settled for a point after being 2-0 down. One lifelong fan Nat McEwan told me: 'A draw would have been a good result after we had been so sloppy in the first-half. To come back from two goals down to pinch a point at Arsenal was nothing to be scoffed at. It would have kept those buggers from taking the mickey out of us and would have kept us in contention for a Champions League spot, so, yeah, I would certainly have taken it.

'But to get all three points and earn our first win away to Arsenal in donkeys years was fantastic, unbelievable, one of the greatest results for years! I tell you, we have got the makings of a good team under Redknapp – what with Baley, Van der Vaart, Modric, Lennon and Defoe. But they are all midfielders and forwards...that tells me something...if Harry can sort out the defence we will be a force to be reckoned with. Until he does, we will just be a little below the level of the really top teams like Chelsea and Man United.'

Ironically, it would be a defender who would earn Spurs all three points at the Emirates as Younes Kaboul headed home from another free-kick from Van der Vaart with just five minutes remaining.

As the whistle went for full-time, Gareth and his team-mates hugged each other and then went over to salute their jubilant fans. It was a moment none of them would forget: the moment they finally laid the ghost of not winning at Arsenal and also not being able to beat one of the big four.

Spurs midfielder Jermaine Jenas summed up the relief when he said: 'I think it was important because every time we went to Manchester United, Liverpool it just kept coming up. It is important we put that to bed now and I think it shows what we are made of – we have shown guts today.

'Arsenal are still a fantastic team but it was the first time I've come to the Emirates thinking we could win. The first-half wasn't great for us but I still look around and feel we have the players who can do anything. We have the creativity and the goals within us to do it.'

And although fans were critical of the backline, boss Redknapp felt they deserved a pat on the back, particularly William Gallas, who had had to endure a torrent of abuse from the Arsenal fans as he returned to his former club for the first time in the shirt of their most hated rivals. Harry had stirred things up a little more, in that inimitable way of his, by making Gallas skipper for the day. Afterwards, Harry said he was delighted with the man he had signed on a free transfer from the Gunners.

Redknapp said: 'No one wanted me to sign him – only me and William. I don't think anybody else really fancied it too much. He's been there and done it all but I had to fight my corner to get him. I went out on a limb with everybody – the fans, chairman and everybody else.

'I just thought it was a fantastic free transfer. I don't think anyone was mad about him coming to Tottenham because of Arsenal. I nearly took Patrick Vieira the year before and I don't think either of them have committed a crime just because they've played for Arsenal.

'Also, top players upset people – it works for great teams. They sort their problems out in the dressing room. Roy Keane, Steve Bruce, all these players. You talk to Joe Jordan about the Leeds players. Everybody needs that in their dressing room. Tony Adams would have done it at Arsenal, with the back four they had. You need people like that who want to win. They make your job easy. But William is a nice guy. I don't know him that well, he's a quiet person, I met him just before I signed him and came away and thought "What a smashing fella".

'People told me he is getting older and had a few injury problems and wouldn't play many games. But he's the one player who plays every game. I think he will be fine for Wednesday [in the Champions League] against Werder Bremen.'

Not all Spurs fan – by a long distance – shared their manager's view that Gallas was 'a smashing fella'. No, even after the win at the Emirates some would never find it within themselves to take him to their hearts. Supporter Nat McEwan added: 'Well, he's Arsenal, isn't he? Whatever he does, he is still one of them – and that doesn't just disappear overnight. He played for our biggest enemy for years and was their captain – against us and delighted in beating us when he was with them. So we're hardly gonna welcome him with open arms, are we? Still, he earned a good mark by leading us to victory at Arsenal for the first time in all those years.'

Redknapp added to the euphoria by later claiming that he believed Spurs could now win the league title for the first time since 1961. He said: 'You've got to aim for the top. We're not writing ourselves off. We can beat anybody and this has put us right back in the race again. It's wide open. If my players believe in themselves as much as I do, we can achieve anything.'

He also admitted he was delighted with the never-say-die

ove: Gareth Bale celebrates scoring against Slovakia on 7 October 2006. In
ng so, he became the youngest player ever to score for the Welsh national team.

ow: Bale in action for Southampton. He was the second-youngest player
r to turn out for the Championship side when he made his debut against
lwall in April 2006.

In training with the Wales team – Bale would have been eligible to play for England through his grandmother, but considers it an honour to play with the Welsh side.

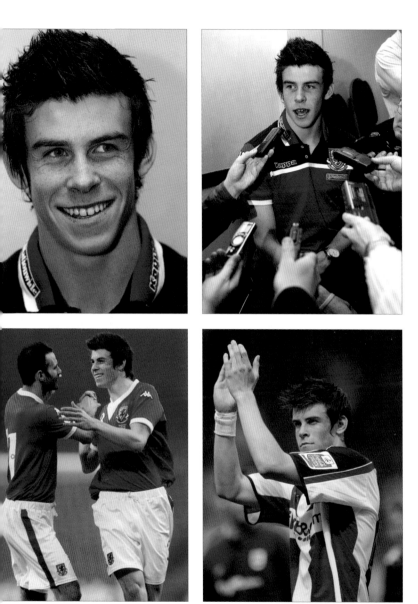

Above: A young Gareth Bale getting used to the media spotlight at a Wales press conference.

Below left: The old guard and the new – Bale with Welsh legend Ryan Giggs during their match against San Marino in 2007.

Below right: Bale shows his appreciation to the fans after one of his last games for Southampton.

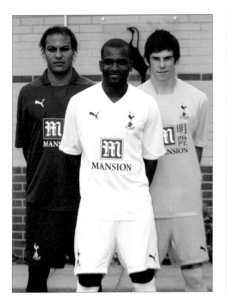

Above left: Spurs show off their new signings – Younes Kaboul, Darren Bent and Gareth Bale – in July 2007.

Above right: Bale in action during his first appearance for Tottenham, a pre-season friendly against St Patrick's Athletic.

Below: Taking a break with Spurs team-mate Younes Kaboul.

above left: Bale getting his first taste of European football in the 2007 UEFA
Cup first round.

above right and below: Getting stuck in for Spurs in training and on the pitch.

Above left: Showing off the Carling Cup with Chris Gunter after Spurs' 2008 victor

Above right: Bale in action for Spurs against Dinamo Zagreb.

Below: In the thick of it during another UEFA Cup match against Wisla Krako

ove left: Bale celebrates scoring his first Champions League goal for
*t*tenham, against FC Twente on 29 September 2010.

ove right: Challenging Real Madrid's Cristiano Ronaldo in the Champions
*t*ague quarter-final.

low: Bale shakes hands with Real manager Jose Mourinho.

Above: Bale looks on in anguish as his goal is disallowed during Spurs' Champions League quarter-final second leg clash with Real Madrid. Spurs went on to lose the match 1-0, going out of the competition 5-0 on aggregate.

Below left: Gareth Bale and Real Madrid president Florentino Pérez hold aloft the Welshman's No 11 shirt at Gareth's official unveiling in the Bernabéu.

Below right: Gareth laps up the acclaim of thousands of Madrid fans with a celebratory salute after finally signing for the Spanish giants from Tottenham showing – a la Manchester United as we have already mentioned – that his men had come up with after Gareth's goal had given them the belief that they could get back in the game. He said: 'To come back showed great character, it really was a fantastic second-half performance. I gave them a rollicking at half-time, and woke them up a bit. We took the game to them from the start of the second half. We had to go for broke. It wasn't a case of trying to stem the tide; it was a case of trying to get back into the game. We were either going to get beat 5-0, or have a go. That's what we did, because that's my nature.'

Gareth himself was just as delighted with the result – and the way he and the team had shown what they can do when their backs are up against the wall. He told Sky Sports: 'It's the one game everyone looks out for and to get the victory, especially at the Emirates, is something special. The gaffer said before the game we have got a great squad and a great team and we can match anybody. We didn't have the greatest first half but showed what we can do in the second half. The boss brought JD [Jermain Defoe] on for the second half and it paid off. The win was something special.'

Gareth then told the *Daily Mirror* that he desperately wanted to avoid any more injury setbacks. He said: 'What's important for me now, above everything, is to make sure I enjoy every second. I've been able to stay calm because, for a while when I wasn't getting in the team, I was taking it for granted I wouldn't be playing. 'When I came to Spurs and picked up an injury just after I arrived at the club it felt like the worst thing ever. Now I'm back playing I realise how much I just love the game and don't want to take it for granted. So now I am in the side I want to enjoy it.'

He added that the win over Arsenal was just the result they needed as they approached what could be a pivotal Champions League group encounter against Werder Bremen. Yes, it was a match they needed to win if they were to make the knockout stages...another vital match for Gareth. They just kept on coming as his and the team's success snowballed at the back end of 2010.

Chapter 12

JUST TWO GOOD

The return against Werder Bremen exploded into life at the Lane just four days after Harry's boys had won at the Emirates. There had been fears among the fans that Spurs might struggle after the mammoth shift they put in to beat Arsenal. Would they be too fatigued to raise their game – even though it was a crunch Champions League clash? Would they struggle against the Germans who had rested some of their players before the match?

There were even doubts if the two stars of the show at the Emirates – Bale and Van der Vaart – would even start the match. It was revealed that Gareth had suffered a hurt shoulder against the Gunners and Van der Vaart missed training the day before the Bremen game to have a scan on his ankle.

In the event, Gareth would make it and Van der Vaart would miss out through injury. Much to Redknapp's relief, Gareth reported fit on the day of the game and Spurs ran out worthy 3-0 winners over the team they had opened their Champions League group account with in Germany in September.

It was certainly another very eventful night for Bale. He missed a penalty and hit the woodwork twice, but could still afford to smile as his team moved smoothly and easily into the last 16 of the competition.

They advanced thanks to an opening goal from Younes Kaboul, a cracker by Modric and a late third from Peter Crouch. Gareth flunked his penalty just before the hour mark. Modric had been played into the box but found himself upended by defender Felix Kroos. But Gareth's subsequent penalty was well saved by keeper Tim Weise, who had represented the German national team and was one of Bremen's few successes on a torrid night in North London.

For Spurs, it represented more misery from the spot – it was their third miss of the season so far after Pavlyuchenko and Van der Vaart had also messed up.

The *Sun*'s Shaun Custis astutely summed up the evolution of this Tottenham team as their season now started to take shape: 'Tottenham have grown from Young Boys into men. Back in August, there were real fears Spurs' Champions League campaign would end in humiliation. They were 3-0 down to the Swiss side, Young Boys of Berne, inside the first half-hour and faced being knocked out of the competition in the preliminary round. 'But that tie was turned round in dramatic fashion and Harry Redknapp's side have not looked back to such an extent they have now cruised into the knockout phase with a game to spare.'

Redknapp was beaming after his team had marched into the next round. He was pleased that his backline had kept a clean sheet – their first for three months and 18 games. And he even managed a joke when asked about Gareth's penalty miss, saying: 'So Gareth missed a penalty – well, at least now we've found something he's not good at...he's only human after all!'

A Spurs source told me that Gareth also managed to see the funny side of it after the initial disappointment had sunk in. 'He did eventually smile and laugh about it in the dressing room when the other lads cheered him up. They told him not to worry about it, that it was nothing worth worrying about given the emphatic result. He's a perfectionist and hates getting things wrong. It was preying on his mind, but the lads soon brought him round, taking the mickey and slapping him on the back.

'Then, after they'd heard Harry say it showed Gareth was only human after all, they all started chanting, "Gareth's only human, Gareth's only human, Gareth's only human!" He can be a serious lad and it's good for him that there are a few jokers in the camp – like JD [Defoe] and Gomes.'

Gareth was confident that the team could now go into the last 16 with real hope. 'He would love to win it,' the source continued. 'It's what he got into football for in the first place, to play in the biggest competitions and to win silverware. He always knew the chances of winning anything with the Welsh national team was remote, so it is doubly important to him that he lifts trophies at club level.'

Harry Redknapp was also ebullient. A few days earlier he had tipped his team as potential Premier League champs – now he roared that they could lift the Champions League, too. He said: 'I'm trying not to get too carried away but I love Champions League football and every year I've always gone to watch games at Arsenal, Chelsea – but to be part of it is something else. 'We've played some great attacking football. We're a match for any team in this competition. I believe so much in what this squad can achieve. Once the players start believing how good they are, there's no limit to what they can do.'

And they were starting to believe how good they were. That was one of the beauties of Redknapp as a football manager – he instilled belief in his players, much in the same way as Sir Alex Ferguson did. Certainly, Gareth had improved under his tutelage and become a more confident person and player. 'Harry was constantly on at him that he could be one of the best players in the world,' says a Spurs source. 'He told him he had everything – all he had to do was harness it all together and he would make it. He was on at him for months and months and finally it all just seemed to start to click, with the results evident to everyone in the two games against Inter Milan.'

After beating Bremen, Harry once again boosted Gareth's burgeoning confidence levels by paying tribute to the way he had terrorised the Germans down that left flank. He purred: 'Gareth Bale could play anywhere along with Luka Modric and there are a few of them. Aaron [Lennon] is starting to go past people, which is want we want him to do, but some of the crosses Gareth put in tonight on the run were amazing. It was a bit like when we played Inter with their right-back.

'We had reports about how good Bremen's right-back was, how he likes to get forward and trouble people but Gareth gave him a torrid time again.' The poor victim, Bremen right-back Clemens Fritz, would certainly not disagree with that assessment.

The boss was also constantly nagging at Gareth and the

team as a unit to write their names in the history books. He kept telling them they were talented enough to make history as did the brilliant Spurs side of the early Sixties. His work as a Mr Motivator-style figure was paying dividends as the team now attacked the season on the top two fronts – the Premier League and the Champions League. He told his men that their triumphs could continue – reminding them that they had been without prolific scorer Defoe for the previous seven weeks because of his ankle injury. With Jermain back in the team, why should they now fall apart?

Harry said: 'He has been so keen to come back after his ankle operation. He has returned quicker than expected and, hopefully, will set White Hart Lane alight whether he starts or comes off the bench. I'm sure he will have a big impact.

'He is important for us. If he can come in now and go on a run for us, it would be fantastic. I would love him to get eight, nine, 10 goals in the next 15 games or so. That would be a result. The stage is set for him. Defoe looks as if he is back to his best. He can take us forward and could push us right into the title race and who knows what in Europe.

'I have never worked with a more single-minded goal-scorer than Defoe. He has always been like that. But then that's what great goalscorers do – focus. Greavsie did it. Lineker was like that. I can see a bit of Ian Wright in him as well.'

The fans hoped Harry was right – certainly they were right behind him, Gareth and the boys, all dreaming that they would eventually win one of the major trophies. Hopefully that season.

The team had the next day off to recover in anticipation of the home match against Liverpool the following Sunday (just four days after Bremen). The games were coming thick and fast and it was important they didn't get burnt out – rest was as vital as training.

It was revealed in the days in between the two matches that Harry might be chosen as the boss of the Great Britain team for the 2012 Olympics (in London) – and Gareth immediately made it clear that he would love to play for the gaffer if it came off. Gareth said: 'The Olympics would be a great opportunity for a young player like me to play in a major tournament as part of a Great Britain team. I'm Welsh and we all know Wales don't tend to qualify for too many of the big occasions.'

Also, Manchester United fans made it clear that, should Spurs ever want to cash in on their best player, that Gareth Bale would be the player they would most like to see at Old Trafford. A fans' poll revealed that 23 per cent wanted Baley with Wesley Sneijder of Inter Milan in second place on 18 per cent.

Then Gareth himself spoke out about his hopes for the campaign. He said he could see Spurs winning something if everything went to plan – and also made the incredible claim that he was not at his speed peak yet after it was revealed he had raced down the wing at 19mph as Spurs beat Inter Milan at White Hart Lane.

Gareth said: 'You work on things in training and, with confidence, it gives you that extra bit of zip, so yeah, I'm faster than I was before – and, with luck, I can get quicker.'

But he told the *Daily Mirror* that he did not want people to start comparing him to Ryan Giggs – despite the obvious similarities between the two Welsh geniuses. Gareth said: 'I don't want to be thought of as "the new Ryan Giggs". I want to be thought of as my own person. He's a great man and a great player, but everyone wants to be thought of as their own man and their own player. It's true that I always used to watch Ryan when I was younger – as he was Welsh and left-footed. He was someone I always used to look out for and used to watch when he played for Wales. Ryan's one of the best players playing in the Premier League.'

And he reiterated his belief that he did not need to leave White Hart Lane to achieve his ambitions: 'I don't think about anything like that, to be honest. I'm just happy playing at Tottenham. We've got a good squad and hopefully we can achieve a few things.

'The Champions League is important to everybody, including myself, I enjoy playing in it. I think we want to test ourselves against the best players and the best teams in the world.'

Just before the home clash with Liverpool, Gareth received a further double boost when it was disclosed that he had made the shortlist for the FIFA/FIFPro World XI – and another former Spurs hero, Gary Lineker used the occasion to say he believed Gareth was well on the way to becoming a legend himself at White Hart Lane. If he could make the team itself it would be some achievement. It wouldn't be easy: he was joined in the list by ten members of Spain's victorious World Cup squad and 16 of the best players from the Premier League. The list had been compiled from the votes of 50,000 professional footballers from across the world – which served to show just how revered the boy from Wales was on the planet as a whole, never mind England, Wales and Europe.

He would be competing for a place in defence – as an attacking fullback. This was the glittering list of defenders Gareth was among at the back end of 2010: Daniel Alves (Brazil,

Barcelona), Gareth Bale (Wales, Tottenham), Michel Bastos (Brazil, Lyon), Ashley Cole (England, Chelsea), Patrice Evra (France, Manchester United), Rio Ferdinand (England, Manchester United), Philipp Lahm (Germany, Bayern Munich), Lucio (Brazil, Inter), Maicon (Brazil, Inter), Marcelo (Brazil, Real Madrid), Alessandro Nesta (Italy, AC Milan), Pepe (Portugal, Real Madrid), Gerard Piqué (Spain, Barcelona), Carlos Puyol (Spain, Barcelona), Sergio Ramos (Spain, Real Madrid), Walter Samuel (Argentina, Inter), John Terry (England, Chelsea), Thiago Silva (Brazil, Milan), Nemanja Vidić (Serbia, Manchester United), Javier Zanetti (Argentina, Inter).

He would have to beat off the challenge of the likes of Evra, Cole and Lahm for the left-back role when the final FIFA/FIFPro World XI was confirmed at FIFA's Ballon d'Or gala in Zurich on January 10. But who would have seriously bet against him at that stage of the campaign?

Definitely not Gary Lineker. He said he was confident Gareth would become one of the greatest players in the world – and could that it as part of a 'great Spurs side.' Lineker, who spent three years at White Hart Lane as a striker, said of Spurs as a team: 'They are doing brilliantly. They need to be a bit more resilient and stronger but they have the potential to become one of the great Spurs sides if they can make themselves a little harder to penetrate.

'It's their first go in the Champions League and they have set the competition alight in their attitude and the way they've played. They have got a lot of qualities, they have a terrific squad and a big squad, a lot of good players and I think Harry [Redknapp] is right that they are two or three short of challenging for honours.'

Lineker, who was speaking at Wembley Stadium at the

launch of the venue for the Champions League final in May, then said of Gareth: 'Bale could be potentially a truly great player. He can do it all. He can run all day and he's quick, which is an unusual combination, he's powerful, his delivery is very precise, he takes all the dead balls, got a wonderful left foot, he's competitive, works hard - and seems to have a good head on his shoulders.

'If he's fortunate to avoid injury he could be one of the world's best.'

And after the plaudits, it was back to business, as Gareth and his team-mates prepared for the arrival of Liverpool at White Hart Lane on Sunday 28 November. Kop boss Roy Hodgson knew his team would have their work cut out. Before the match, he announced his admiration for the work Redknapp had done at the Lane – and for the talent of men like Baley and Modric. Hodgson said: 'Wins are hard to come by against the top teams and we have to admit that Tottenham are no longer the Tottenham of old. They are a top team. It is an expensively assembled side and we are not playing against mugs any more.

'One defeat in eight is a good run at any stage of the season. We have to be happy with that but we are not stupid. We know that if you go to Tottenham it could be two defeats in nine.'

Gareth would have agreed with that assessment. And with influential skipper Steven Gerrard missing for the visitors, he was confident Spurs would have enough in the tank to win. He said: 'I like to think if we are fully on our game, we can beat any team in the world. I think if we go into the game against Liverpool with the attitude we had in the second half against Arsenal, there's no reason we can't beat them.

'Gerrard missing is good for us because he's a great player.

Roy Hodgson hasn't been there long, but he's making his mark and they're improving as a team, so we know it's going to be difficult.'

It was a turnaround in fortunes: Spurs, on the back of a three-match winning run, were now expected to dispose of a team who, a couple of seasons earlier, had been universally recognised as one of the 'big four'. Now Tottenham had replaced them in the Premier League elite and Liverpool's rocky early form under Hodgson did not suggest they would pull off a shock at the Lane. Even the Merseysiders' traditional dominance – this would be the 135th league meeting between the clubs and Liverpool had 63 victories, compared to Tottenham's 37 – could not change the bookies' minds. No, Spurs were favourites and should take all three points.

On the day of the match Liverpool legend Kenny Dalglish joined in the debate about how to stop Gareth. He admitted it would be a big ask for Liverpool – but that it was essential if they were to get anything from the match. Writing in the *Mail on Sunday*, Dalglish said: 'To stop wingers, you try to show them the side which is your best and where they aren't as strong. Unfortunately for Liverpool, Gareth Bale hasn't got a weakness. Show him the inside and he'll sprint down the outside; and vice-versa. That is why teams double up against him and Liverpool do have the personnel to do that. Glen Johnson is one of the quickest defenders around and it'll be quite a sprint down the touchline between them. 'If Bale cuts inside, a workhorse like Dirk Kuyt will be there to try to block him. For Kuyt, Lucas and Christian Poulsen, if he plays at White Hart Lane today, it is also important to cut out the service to Bale in the first place.'

Dalglish had taken the place of Gary Lineker as the paper's

star guest columnist and was proving an inspired 'buy'. His words had much wisdom, but Liverpool were unable to translate them into action, much as they tried.

Bale drove forward throughout the match and at times left Glen Johnson dizzy. Even when the Kop boys doubled up on the Welsh winger it was to little effect – apart from ending up in the ref's notebook. Raul Meireles was booked midway through the half for bringing Gareth down as he headed for goal once again.

Yet it was Liverpool who had taken the lead just before the break when Martin Skrtel fired them ahead. The Slovakian centre-back then turned from hero to villain (at least in his fans' eyes) when he put through his own goal after 65 minutes.

Now it was all Tottenham and they should have sewn up the points before Aaron Lennon finally put the game to bed with his injury-time winner. Jermain Defoe missed from the spot after Gareth had won a penalty. Gareth's subsequent free kick was strong and accurate – maybe too accurate and worrying for David Ngog in the defensive wall…he blocked it with his hands. Unfortunately, Jermain was unable to end the continuing, depressing Spurs penalty jinx.

Lennon's winner was certainly welcome to him from a personal point of view: it was his first goal in a year, since the 9-1 demolition of Wigan the previous November. And the way the team fought back from behind – yet again Manchester United-style – brought words of praise from the boss. Redknapp said: 'That was a great comeback. We started slow then came into it. Roy Hodgson has got Liverpool playing well and they had good movement up front. But we got on top in the second half and had chances.

'We have the belief we can come from behind. We have

attacking players, so we'll get chances. You can't write us off. Whether it's Gareth Bale, Lennon, Modric or the front players, we've got attacking players all over the pitch. We're always in with a chance, even at 1-0 down. It's a case of sticking them away.'

And Defoe admitted there was some truth in my assertion that Spurs were becoming the new Manchester United with their never-say-die spirit. He conceded that he and the team were now happy to emulate United if it continued to bring results.

The striker had seen the determination and will-to-win mentality of the United players while on England duty, and said it had rubbed off on him. Defoe said: 'I remember when I first got into the England squad. All my mates would ask me what training was like.

'I used to say, "You know what, it's mad, because the Manchester United players, the likes of Rio, Phil Neville, Gary Neville, Becks, in little five-a-sides, they want to win every game. And if they don't win they are moaning".

'Gary Neville never stopped. It was amazing. We would train and in the evening they were still talking about it.

'It didn't matter what game they were playing in, they wanted to win. I think that's a great thing to have and it's important we have that. When you're a kid, you can find that funny because it's about development and not always about the result. I always want to win, though. I'm a forward, I'm a goalscorer and I always moan anyway.

'But it was interesting to see such a winning mentality.'

The boss was less pleased at the fact that Jermain had become the fourth Spurs player to miss a penalty in the season so far. He added: 'Jermain takes them in training and rattles them into the corners. I was hoping he'd score and I was happy with him taking it. Gareth took one and missed. Crouchy, not really. Aaron, no.

'Where do you find a penalty taker? It might be an idea for the ref just to give a goal-kick. You could do with someone just smashing it down the middle, putting their boot behind it.'

The win crowned a fab week for Gareth, pushing Spurs up to fifth in the table. I am told he celebrated that night by watching *The X Factor*, with his girlfriend and a Chinese takeaway. This was a boy who liked the simple life – a modern footballer who was living the dream, who lived and trained like a continental star rather than some of the beer-swilling, lecherous modern-day footballers who were staining the name of the British game.

The players now finally had a few days' break before the next match. Snow and bad weather cut short training and the lads worked in the gym and indoors. There were serious doubts whether the next match, the Premier League clash at Birmingham would even go ahead.

It did, which meant a rather scary trek on the team coach through the snow-hit roads from London to the Midlands for Gareth and Co.

Brum boss Alex McLeish promised to make things even tenser on the pitch for Bale – saying his very own 'beast' would be lying in wait for him. It was none other than former Spurs full-back Stephen Carr, whom McLeish had rescued from the scrapheap when he was freed by Newcastle. Carr had repaid him by turning in some fine performances – and McLeish was confident he would be able to deal with the threat of Bale.

The Brum boss said: 'Stevie trains like a beast, he plays like a beast. I like to see players training the way they play on a Saturday. We have that kind of ethic at this club and Stevie typifies that. He's been a revelation. 'Bale's a great player. You do try to deal with the supply, but also when Bale goes off on his runs, you can't leave one-on-one exposure. We saw the Inter Milan game and he ran from the halfway line and I saw a very naive defender fly in when he should've backed off – that was just pure bad defending. I'd like to think our defenders aren't as naive as the Inter Milan guy was.'

Carr had been a popular lad while at White Hart Lane. But could he stand up to Gareth's pace and dribbling skills? Now 34, he had featured in less than 80 games in four years. McLeish was convinced he was up to the task: 'He's looking like a young guy, he's like a sprinter. Sometimes you see a full-back going forward and they have to get a taxi to get back. But Stevie Carr is right back in as soon as he's mounted an attack. His recovery levels are fantastic.

'When you get players like that on free transfers then you're all doing the club a service. Guys like Stevie go through brick walls to win you games.'

And on the day itself, Carr did not disgrace himself. He even earned a cheer from the travelling Spurs fans, in tribute to his excellent 11 years' service at the club from 1993 to 2004. Gareth had a fairly quiet match – by his now massively high expectations – and that was partly down to the evergreen Carr.

The match ended 1-1 after Craig Gardner's late equaliser cancelled out Sebastien Bassong's early opener to earn a point for Brum. Gareth was instrumental in the goal, sending in a free kick that Brum keeper Ben Foster flapped at, allowing Bassong in for the headed goal.

Carr earned some accolades for his 'job' on Bale, but was typically modest when asked how it felt to have been the man who temporarily curbed the flying winger. Carr was keen to praise the men in front of him for their help – but also told the *Birmingham Mail* that Gareth reminded him of Ryan Giggs.

He said: 'It's what you get in front of you that helps you. I got help from the front and it helped. Bale's going to be an unbelievable player in the future and he's already having a great season. I've played against some great players and he's up there.

'It's his pace and the way he runs at you. He's like an old-school winger as well. Ryan Giggs used to always get the ball and run at you. Bale just goes at you too. I thought I did OK but I had a lot of help from in front.'

I was told Gareth was a little subdued on the journey back to London. He had a snooze and listened to his iPod as he contemplated his afternoon's work. It had not been his greatest day at the office, but he had done OK, being involved in the goal and working hard for the team.

Fortunately, there wasn't much time for Gareth to brood about a one-off average day. After a few days' break in between matches, the schedule would now liven up again, with the final match in their Champions League group on the Tuesday, followed by the Premier League crunch on the Sunday against Chelsea.

Victory in Holland against FC Twente – or even matching Inter Milan's result at Werder Bremen – would mean Tottenham had won the group in their first campaign in the competition. That would be a tremendous achievement for Harry, Gareth and the boys – and the boss promised that he would go all out with attack to try to do it.

Before the match, Gareth paid tribute to Harry, saying that he had helped toughen him up. He told how Harry had thrown down a gauntlet – 'prove you're good enough to be a first-team regular' – and that he had thrown himself into doing so. Gareth said: 'Looking back on some things, I think, "Wow". A year ago, I didn't think I would be doing stuff like that. But I don't think I ever thought my future lay elsewhere. When I wasn't playing, I went in to see the manager and to ask when was I going to be given my chance.

'There were a lot of things the manager wanted me to do and there were certain aspects of my game I needed to improve on. He wanted me to toughen up as I was still a young boy at the time. So I worked hard in training to prove to him that I was worthy of a spot in the team.

'He always said, "Be patient and keep working hard in training and you will get your chance". So I was always confident, I just had to be ready to give 100 per cent when the chance came and I got my chance and never looked back. I have always had the belief in my own ability, so I knew if I trained hard and was patient, things would happen for me. If someone had said to me a year ago that I would one day be described as one of the best players in the Premier League and best left-sided players in the world, I wouldn't have believed them.

'But I try to keep myself away from what is written and said about me. I know there was a lot going on after the Inter Milan games and there was a lot of talk – but I switched off to that and concentrated on training. I must keep my feet on the ground to continue progressing, I must keep working hard, because hard work is the reason why I've had a good year.'

The good year would continue as Gareth helped Spurs to a

3-3 draw in Holland against FC Twente – a result that also confirmed them as winners of Group A after Inter crashed 3-0 in Bremen, and meant they would avoid the biggest guns in the next round (particularly Barcelona and Real Madrid).

Redknapp had outlined that he wanted to stay clear of the two Spanish giants in his pre-match press briefing, saying: 'Yes, we want to finish top if we can. Inter Milan will go to Germany looking to win because that top position is important. Otherwise, it's Real Madrid, Barcelona, Bayern Munich.'

The match was feisty and certainly no walk in the park for the visitors – Twente were keen to avenge their 4-1 defeat at White Hart Lane back in September. They were also in form: since losing 1-0 at Inter Milan the previous month, Twente had won both of their Eredivisie fixtures, triumphing 4-2 at NEC before beating De Graafschap at home in the match before the arrival of Spurs.

The match was – and this was, of course, now becoming a typical feature of Spurs outings as Harry went for broke with wonderful attacking football – full of goals. It ended 3-3 and the visitors made the history books by becoming the first club to score two or more goals in every group game.

Luka Modric was missing through injury but Gareth and Defoe were supported by the impressive Jermaine Jenas in the creativity stakes. Three times Spurs forged ahead – with a crazy own goal and a brace from Defoe – and three times the determined Dutch drew level.

The first Tottenham goal was a freak, but welcome all the same. Keeper Sander Boschker misjudged a back pass and the ball dribbled cruelly past him into the net. It was reminiscent of Paul Robinson's howler for England when Gary Neville passed the ball back to him in Croatia in October 2006.

Gareth played his part in getting the all-important point; after his low-key show at Brum, he was now all action, speed and trickery once again. He set Defoe up with two fine first-half crosses that the striker would normally have buried. But it was his cross early after the interval that led to Defoe's first of the night. The Dutch defence failed to clear it, allowing Lennon in to take control and set up Jermain for his opener and Tottenham's second.

The result meant that Spurs had netted 18 goals in their group games – more than anyone else in the competition. Sure, there had been some heartstopping moments on the way, but Harry was determined that his team would continue to attack and play with flair.

After the match he said: 'We look to score and attack teams at every opportunity. We've got people who can hurt teams, that's how we've approached the games. 'We've gone for it, we have a go. At the end of the day, we've finished top of the group. You can't say "well, they've conceded goals"; we've scored more goals than anybody. If you want us to shut up shop, we can do that and come away and be difficult to beat and stick five across the midfield. But we don't; we come away and have a go. It's a great achievement from the players to finish top of what for me was the most difficult group of the lot.

'We've had a team near the top of the Dutch league, Werder Bremen, who are a good German side with lots of good players, and the holders Inter Milan. I think it was the toughest group and to top it is brilliant. We've got a good squad of players. We'll give anybody a game.'

The *Sun*'s Paul Jiggins summed up the achievement – and how it had been achieved with such style when he said: 'Tottenham lived up to their tag of "The Entertainers" as they roared into the last 16 as Group A winners. When it comes to goals, excitement and entertainment among Europe's elite, there is no team quite like Harry Redknapp's at the moment. In fact, you could say Spurs are just TWO good as they became the first club in the tournament's history to score at least two goals in each of their group games.'

Gareth was delighted with his improved performance, the result and Harry's statement of attacking intent as he boarded the flight back to England that night. 'Yes, Gareth was really on a high,' says a Spurs source. 'It had all come right and the match sort of ended a little chapter in his life. It had been the Inter away match in the group stage that had propelled him to worldwide fame and acclaim – and now he and the team had completed the first stage by winning the group. He couldn't stop beaming on the way home. He rang his parents and his girlfriend and told them it had been a great night – and that he was already dreaming of playing in the next round come next year.'

But the dreaming only lasted a day or two. Harry saw to that. Just as he had knocked Gareth into shape over the previous 12 months, he now brought him and his team-mates back down to earth during the next few days. There was no time for dreaming in the new, massively ambitious world of Tottenham Hotspur FC. Focus was what was needed now…especially with Premier League champions Chelsea due at the Lane the following Sunday. The result of that crunch match would go some way to gauging just how far Spurs had come – and how far Gareth had come. It was a showdown that he was anticipating with relish – another chance to show his worth against another of the giants of European football and one of Tottenham's bitterest domestic rivals.

But before we assess Gareth's input in that local 'classico' let's take a look at his exploits at international level, with the Welsh national team.

Chapter 13

THE PRINCE OF WALES

It's the section of his career – like Ryan Giggs and George Best's given their relative level of failure at international level – that will most likely always give some the stick with which to beat Gareth Bale. No doubt when he one day gets to hanging up his boots (unless there is a miraculous upturn in the fortunes of the Welsh national team) some pundits will try to put him down, saying say that, yes, OK, he was a Tottenham great – but he wasn't really a world great because he never lorded it on the international stage. That is, of course, patently a load of rubbish.

It is hardly Gareth's fault that he was eligible by birth to play for a country that if not among the world's minnows could certainly never be relied upon to even qualify for the World Cup finals...let alone win the darned thing. Early on in his career Gareth was realistic enough to know it was highly unlikely he would ever win anything with Wales. But that never diminished the joy and pride he felt at representing his country. It was never a chore or an imposition; he always presented himself fresh and available. Gareth was a Welshman and proud of it. 'He loves playing for his country,' says a Wales insider. 'He considers it a great honour and privilege and would never dream of hiding behind injury to avoid it.'

Of course, many media critics believe that was just what Ryan Giggs – the man to whom he will invariably be compared over the coming years given that they both came from Wales, both fly down that left wing and both are the top Welsh footballers of their relative generations – did during his international years.

Gareth made his first appearance for Wales at the age of 16 in 2006. Ryan was a year older at 17 when he started out on his international career in 1991.

Ryan had become the youngest player ever to appear for the seniors when he made his debut as sub in a European championship qualifier against Germany in Nuremberg on October 16, 1991. Ryan was 17 years, 332 days old. Wales lost 4-1. He had four more caps as a sub as the management team tried to break him in gently.

His first full appearance would be 18 months later – at home to Belgium in a World Cup qualifier on March 31, 1993. He scored his first goal in the 2-0 win. That was the beginning of Ryan's odyssey with the Welsh national team – from that game on he would always start if fit.

The critics claim Ryan could have done more for Wales – particularly that he should have turned out for his country in friendly matches. They point to him frequently pulling out of such games through injury and moan that he missed 18 consecutive friendlies (and did not play in one until nine years after his debut, in 2000) and 50 games in total through withdrawals, often blamed on hamstring trouble by his club boss Alex Ferguson.

That first friendly appearance would come on March 29, 2000, when Wales took on Finland in Cardiff. Ryan admitted he was upset by the constant jibes over the years, telling the *Guardian* the day before the match, 'When people say you don't want to play for your country it hurts. Then you find people having polls asking fans whether I should be picked to play for my country in future, and that's just stupid because I always give 100 per cent when I play for Wales.

'I hope that by playing on Wednesday it will finally kill off the thing about me not playing in friendlies for Wales.'

It didn't 'kill off the thing', but it helped sideline it. Ironically, Ryan would score Wales' goal in a historic match. The Welsh went down 2-1 in front of a crowd of 66,000 in the first football match at the Millennium Stadium.

The critics may have had a fair point over Ryan's friendlies record, but Wales still got excellent service from Giggs when you look at his efforts in competitive matches. He was their most consistent performer in the matches he did play in – and certainly their best hope to inspire victory in what were sometimes mediocre squads. He did his best, but like Georgie Best, would ultimately see his international career assessed as having been a failure because he did not reach a major finals.

The end for Giggs came in June 2007 when he was named Man of the Match in the Euro 2008 qualifier against the Czech Republic in Cardiff.

Ryan had paved the way for an emotional farewell by announcing his decision the previous Wednesday. He said he wanted to say goodbye in front of the Welsh fans, so he could thank them for all their support and encouragement over the years. He also admitted he hoped the decision would be beneficial to his club career – that it would allow him to extend his time at Manchester United. In retrospect, given that he was still going strong at Old Trafford by the time this book went to press in the summer of 2011, it was the right move at the right time.

Ryan said at the time, 'I feel this is a good time, the right time to retire and it's a difficult decision for me. I have loved playing for my country and I have loved captaining my country. It wasn't an easy decision.'

They hardly sounded like the comments of a man who 'found it a hassle' to turn out for his country, did it?

Gareth, of course, had been made aware of the inevitable comparisons between himself and Giggs and Best – how George had also never found success on the international stage because Northern Ireland never reached the finals of any major competitions. Like Ryan, George also made his international debut at 17, the first of his 37 Northern Ireland caps arrived in Northern Ireland's 3-2 victory, ironically, over Wales at Swansea in 1963.

Like Giggsy – and probably Gareth – his career at international level would never match the highs of his time at Manchester United, though there were highlights such as his superlative display against the Scots at Windsor Park in 1967 when he single-handedly destroyed the opposition with a performance of breathtaking skill, with Northern Ireland winning 1-0.

Yes, Gareth knew all about George and Ryan – and how they had seemingly been cursed at international level never to taste glory. But, like them both, he would always maintain he loved playing for his country – and wanted to gain as many caps as he could, irrespective of the lack of glory they might achieve. 'That was his big ambition with Wales,' a source confirmed. 'He knew he probably wouldn't win anything but there was always the chance of notching up the most caps. That would be a record to remember – something to show the grandchildren one day!'

Given an injury-free run over the next decade, Gareth would surely be in with a chance of becoming Wales' most-capped star. As this book went to the publishers, his international record read as follows: Full caps: 27 (3 goals); Under-21 caps: 4; Under-19 caps: 1; Under-17 caps: 7 (1 goal). Neville Southall still holds the proud record of most capped Welshman after amassing 92 caps from 1982–1998. As Gareth made his debut in 2006 and already has 27 caps, time is certainly on his side.

The first of those caps came on May 27 2006, when Gareth made his senior national team debut as a substitute in a 2-1 win over Trinidad and Tobago, making him the youngest ever player to play for Wales. He was just 16 years and 315 days – and the day was even more memorable as he played his part by setting up the winning goal scored by Robert Earnshaw.

Afterwards Gareth told BBC Wales Sport: 'I wasn't expecting all this this year. I'm proud and so are my parents obviously. I just want to build on it from here. I enjoyed every minute. It's a great feeling to have an assist on my debut. Thankfully the match was going alright for us and it wasn't too quick a pass so I got my chance to come on.

'It was exciting just warming up on side and I was just

wishing I could get on. Thankfully I came on and I managed to set one up. It's been a new experience for me being around all the big players. It feels like a dream come true.'

Wales boss John Toshack was the man who made the dream come true. He decided to send Gareth on as the match looked like ending 1-1. He had seen enough of Gareth in training to know that he had a wonderkid on his hands. 'I just thought, "hell, give the boy a run out, you never know, he might supply a flash of inspiration and win us the game" – and he did just that!' purred Toshack.

Gareth and Earnshaw exchanged a couple of one-twos before Gareth set him up for the goal. 'The boy's a natural,' Norwich striker Earnshaw said. 'He's destined for great things, I'm sure of it.'

Before the game, Wales' stand-in captain Danny Gabbidon said he saw much of Wayne Rooney in the way nothing seemed to faze him – and in how he was such a naturally gifted footballer. Gareth had played just 180 minutes of pro football for Southampton, but was not nervous as he entered the fray for Wales. As we have noted before, he is not the type to suffer major nerves, and his debut for Wales did not cause him to have a sleepless night – although he hardly had time to become anxious when Tosh tossed him on towards the end of the match.

Neither was he fazed that he had just set a new record for the youngest player to win a Wales cap – breaking Lewin Nyatanga's record. In fact, Gareth had only made his Wales U21 debut in their 1-0 friendly win over Cyprus in Port Talbot 11 days before his first cap against Trinidad. After that match, Gareth said: 'It's good to get some experience at under-21s level. I was moved around a bit in the match against Cyprus from out on the left wing to left-back. We were trying a few things with Estonia in mind next week.'

Gareth was referring to the second leg of the U21 Euro qualifier in Wrexham. Wales had won the first leg 2-0 and Gareth added: 'It will be a difficult match – they will come at us because they are 2-0 down from the first leg and we have to be ready. It is not going to be easy and we know just how important it is to win this qualifier to get into the UEFA championships next season.

'They will have looked at us now and worked out how we play, so it was important we were able to experiment in the Cyprus friendly to give ourselves some different options. They will not have given this tie up. We know we have to stand up to them. But we have been together a few days now, it's good for us and it helps us gel as a side.'

But Gareth needn't have worried – Wales won the second match 5-1, for a 7-1 aggregate.

After his national team debut against Trinidad and Tobago, Gareth was asked if he was worried that he was being left behind by former fellow Southampton protégé Theo Walcott. At 17, Walcott had signed for Arsenal and had been picked by Sven Goran Eriksson for England's World Cup squad of 2006.

Gareth said: 'I'm not envious of him; he is my friend so I am just so happy for him and just want him to do well in the World Cup. He will cope, he takes everything in his stride as we've all seen these past days. I just hope he can get on in the matches and show people what he can do.

'We've had a few chats and Theo is coping fine. It's been a big change for him but he is trying to take each day as normal. Going to the World Cup is a big thing, obviously, for him, but I feel he will take it in his stride. He can't avoid the spotlight now, but he just wants to focus on his game and his life and get on with things.'

They were generous words – and typically of the gentleman Gareth Bale had always been. A truly nice guy in a tough, unforgiving industry, even from the tender age of 16. Wales assistant manager Roy Evans, former boss of Liverpool, was convinced Gareth would become just as big a star as Walcott looked like being. Before the Trinidad match he said: 'We are getting them young this time. We have got virtually the squad we want and it's ironic we will be looking to add maybe one more youngster of Walcott's age, and he should also have come from Southampton.

'There's always the chance that, like Walcott, we've got someone similar and from the same club. Now we've got to get the balance right between young and experienced players.'

Gareth missed out on his country's first Euro 2008 qualifier in the Czech Republic on Saturday September 1 2006. The boys went down 2-1 after looking as though they might sneak a point – a double by David Lafata killing them off after Martin Jiranek's own goal had given them hope.

But Gareth was back in the side for the 'fantasy match' against the mighty Brazilians at, ironically enough, White Hart Lane the following Tuesday.

Boss Toshack decided it was time to give him another taste of international football because he 'always believed he would become a great one day' and it was 'important to test him against the best'. Well, they don't come much better than the Brazilians.

Gareth came back in the team at the expense of Sam Ricketts and made an immediate impact. He may have only turned 17 on July 16, but he showed no sign of nerves.

Indeed his first touch left the Brazilians complaining after he went in hard on one of their players. More irony in that the player at the wrong end of Gareth's strong but fair tackle was none other than Maicon...the man he would destroy against Inter Milan in that Champions League double header in 2010! The bald Brazilian went down as though he had been shot, but got back on his feet when he realised the ref was none too impressed.

This was the first meeting between Bale and Maicon, who had celebrated his 25th birthday just 10 days after Gareth turned 17. 'It's incredible really when you think that Maicon would be the making of Gareth in 2010, and was the first big name he clashed with on the international stage back in that 2006 friendly,' says lifelong Spurs fan Nat McEwan. 'I must admit I didn't know they had played against each other before and I'm sure I'm not alone among Tottenham fans. It's good to know that Gareth left his mark on Maicon even when he was 17!'

For reasons of posterity – and because Gareth will probably never face the Brazilians again unless there is another friendly – let's record the teams that night in North London. They lined up like this:

WALES: Jones, Duffy, Bale, Gabbidon, Collins, Nyatanga, Bellamy, Earnshaw, Robinson, Davies, Giggs.
BRAZIL: Gomes, Maicon, Luisao, Alex, Edmilson, Marcelo, Cearense, Kaka, Vagner Love, Ronaldinho, Julio Baptista.

Gareth would last 46 minutes before being replaced by Ricketts while Maicon would also drop to the bench close to the hour mark, Cicinho replacing him. It would be the latter who would set up the second, decisive goal, putting in a fine cross that Wagner Love headed home on the three-quarter-hour mark. Marcelo had opened the scoring on the hour with a brilliant left-foot shot as Brazil ran out worthy 2-0 winners. The match was a 'good learning curve' for Gareth and his team-mates according to Toshack. The manager had feared his side might 'take a hiding' and was pleased with their commitment and endeavour. He had also taken star man Ryan Giggs off at the same time as Gareth, saying: 'It was in our interests and Manchester United's.' He went on to explain that the winger was now 32 and needed to be used sparingly if he were to feature in more games for the national side.

Brazilian boss Dunga scratched his head when he heard that...saying he would love to have Ryan in his team any time! He said: 'Everyone would like to have a player like him, but he is not Brazilian.'

Giggs was coming to the back end of his career as Gareth was just seeing his open up – and four years later, after his exploits against Maicon and Inter, it would be Gareth the Brazilians would label 'the new Giggs'.

The fantasy was now over for Bale and Wales. They had to put the Brazil match to the back of their minds as they headed into three key Euro 2008 qualifiers that could well determine whether they would be in contention for the actual tournament...or not. After losing to the Czech Republic in the first group match, they could ill afford any more slip-ups.

But slip up they did – and big-time against Slovakia at home on October 7, crashing 5-1. The only consolation for Gareth was that he scored the goal for the hosts, notching a place in the record books virtue of him becoming the youngest footballer to score a goal for the full Welsh national team.

Jason Koumas had been fouled just outside the box and Gareth guided his subsequent free kick into the top corner of the net.

But by then the Welsh were two down – with goals from Dusan Svento and Marek Mintal, the latter coming after keeper Paul Jones made a hash of a clearance. It would be a nightmare afternoon for Jones – hardly the way he would have hoped to have celebrated his 50th cap for his country. Mintal grabbed his brace a minute after Gareth's goal and further goals from Miroslav Karhan and Robert Vittek put the boot in on Jones and Wales.

Gareth was delighted by his goal – 'it was a great feeling, I was jumping for joy when it went in' he would tell friends later – but his ecstasy turned to agony as Wales ended up on the wrong end of a thrashing.

There were, quite rightly, grumblings a many in the Principality about Toshack being the wrong man for Wales, but BBC pundit and former Wales star Kevin Ratcliffe urged caution, pointing to Gareth's display as one of the pluses from the shambolic showing. He said: 'Sometimes you have to suffer defeats like against Slovakia to find out what's best for the team. Toshack's squad is very young, but someone like Gareth Bale looks a terrific prospect, he scored a memorable goal.

'Only two players in that team are playing regular football in the Premiership, the rest of the side is made up of kids – and they are not getting regular games either! The team simply doesn't have the legs for 90 minutes. But those youngsters are going to be good players when they come through these tough experiences and learn their trade.'

New skipper Craig Bellamy admitted the defeat was

'disastrous' but said everyone – the players, the management team and the fans – needed to rally round or it would get even worse. They now had to get their heads right for another fixture – four days later – the make-or-break clash against Cyprus at home. Another defeat would be catastrophic – almost certainly ending their already diminishing hopes of qualifying and almost certainly bringing the curtain down on Toshack's reign. Just how could he survive a loss against football's perennial also-rans; minnows who they should beat comfortably?

Bellamy said: 'We've a few days to lift ourselves for Cyprus, we have to do that quickly. We've always lacked depth as a small nation, but a lot of players out there aren't getting regular club games. You could see that, it's a hard ask to step up to international football.'

The 5-1 thrashing b Slovakia at the Millennium Stadium would go down in the history books as Wales' worst home defeat since England beat them 7-1 in Wrexham in 1908. Toshack praised Bale for his goal but added to the comments being put forward by Ratcliffe and Bellamy, pleading for patience as he tried to build a team around young players.

He said: 'Slovakia looked a lot better than they are and we looked a lot worse. We were sleeping for the first goal and the second was a bad mistake.

'Gareth Bale got one back, but the third and fourth goals were very poor. I know where the problems are. We had only two people out there who are playing in the Premiership and no outfield men over the age of 30. But it was a poor result. It's just as well we have another game on Wednesday, I wouldn't want to go for a long time on the back of that.'

But just as everyone was dismissing the threat of Cyprus –

and agreeing that Wales should easily beat them – the news filtered through that the minnows had crushed the Republic of Ireland 5-2 in Nicosia! The Irish had been at half strength and had suffered after big centre-back Richard Dunne was sent off, but every pundit I had spoken to had expected them to walk it against the Cypriots. It was a warning shot across the bows of the Welsh – suddenly the easy-looking tie at the Millennium seemed more like a potentially disastrous banana skin.

Toshack stuck with Gareth for the crunch match in Cardiff, but – perhaps seeing the potential he had to be much more than just a left-back, even at 17 – moved him up to left midfield, as part of a five man shield across the centre of the park. Toshack also defied logic by bringing in two more youngsters. He dropped calamity keeper Jones for Lewis Price, 22, of Ipswich, and MK Dons' Craig Morgan, 21, took over from Robbie Edwards at the heart of the defence.

The gamble paid off against a Cyprus side still buzzing – and unchanged – after their win over the Irish.

Gareth played his part in the victory, bolstering that left side and pushing forward when he could.

Goals from Koumas, Robert Earnshaw and Bellamy secured the vital win that finally got the Welsh off the mark in their qualifying campaign.

It was a gutsy performance, best summed up by the *Mail*'s Ian Ladyman in this way: 'If the true test of a footballer's character is how he responds to a setback then perhaps John Toshack has good reason to have such faith in his young Wales squad after all.

'As he continues to resist the temptation to call on some of his country's more experienced – and currently retired –

players, Toshack knows he must deliver some results to justify his policy.

'And after the 5-1 defeat at the hands of Slovakia in Cardiff, Toshack was delighted to see his team produce a performance of courage and stature to earn their first win in three qualifying attempts last night.'

Toshack, who would surely have been sacked if Bale and Co had blown it, was understandably purring with delight after the match. He said: 'It was almost perfect tonight and a great response from the players. I thought 3-1 flattered Cyprus and it could have been more.

'Some of these players were playing for the Under-21s 12 months ago and I can't believe how much they have been criticised since the weekend. I have never known anything like it and I have worked in six different countries. They just dusted themselves down and they were terrific. People said that the young players were struggling but we put two more in today and they did very well. They should be very proud.'

Wales had just one more fixture to complete their programme for 2006 – it was the friendly match against a team ranked even lower than Cyprus, the woeful minnows from Lichtenstein. Gareth missed the match but was happy as his team-mates chalked up a comfortable 4-0 win at Wrexham.

Toshack had insisted on playing the team made up predominantly of part-timers as he reckoned they were a similar obstacle to the one fellow minnows San Marino would pose in Euro 2008 qualifying the following March. To that degree, it was a good night, boosted also by the return of talisman Ryan Giggs, who took back the skipper's armband from Bellamy.

Toshack said afterwards: 'We can be pleased. We scored

four goals which is always pleasing and they were good quality goals as well. Three local lads came on and our first half in particular I was pleased with. 'Maybe at the back there were two or three sloppy balls, but some of our football was very pleasing.'

Wales' next match was another friendly, this time at Belfast's Windsor Park against Northern Ireland on February 6 2007. Gareth was an unused sub as the match petered out to a 0-0 draw.

Then it was back to business in Euro 2008, with two key games – the Republic of Ireland away and San Marino at home. The trip to Ireland was historic; the first match at the nation's new stadium, Croke Park, but the result was not one Gareth and Wales would want to remember. Stephen Ireland grabbed the winner six minutes before the interval after Robbie Keane set him up.

It was a sickener. The lads knew the odds were now truly stacked against them in the qualifying stakes: they had lost three of their four opening matches. Wales could have done with more experience in the back five – instead it was like feeding a group of cubs to the wolves, it was just asking too much of the kids. Toshack hauled Gareth off on the three quarter mark, sending on 26-year-old Danny Collins to beef things up. But it was to no avail.

Afterwards Toshack admitted that the defeat had been a killer, saying: 'As far as qualification is concerned, it looks over for us now.' It was an honest assessment, but did not go down well with the public...many people felt Toshack should have been more upbeat and insisted in public at least that anything was still possible. How was he supposed to motivate the young players like Gareth – who was now low after being subbed and losing – when he was at the same time telling them they were out of Euro 2008?

The manager argued that his team had shown promise in the second half: 'I thought the first half in particular was as bad as it has been. At times I could not believe what I was seeing, the Republic were far the better side and thoroughly deserved their goal, there were no complaints. In the second half we pushed them back and controlled things, but we lacked that bit necessary in the last third.'

Now his demoralised boys had four days in which to recover for the home match with minnows San Marino – and Toshack admitted that even that could be a tougher encounter than expected. He said: 'We must pick ourselves up quickly. People will think the next game is a simple one for us. The Irish found that was not the case and they were probably a bit fortunate to have won when they played San Marino recently, it was a very late goal that saved them.'

It says a lot for Gareth that, at the tender age of 17, he had the nerve and talent to not only recover quickly from the devastating setback in Ireland – but also emerge as one of Wales' star players just a few days later. After being taken off in Dublin, you might have expected his confidence to have taken a knock. Not at all – there he was, back in Cardiff, defending well, attacking when he got the chance and being in the right place at the right time to grab Wales' second goal in the 3-0 triumph over San Marino.

The crowd of 18,700 at the 74,500-capacity Millennium Stadium reflected the mood of apathy among the Welsh public. They were sick of Toshack and agreed with his downbeat belief that there was nothing more to play for in qualifying Group D.

But the lack of support did not dampen Gareth's enthusiasm as he notched his second goal for his country. He curled the ball home after 20 minutes, his goal adding to the one drilled home in the third minute by skipper Giggs. Jason Koumas completed the scoring after David Cotterill was fouled in the box just after the hour mark.

'Gareth was on a high after scoring,' I was told. 'But he's the sort of lad who doesn't get that down, even after the loss against Ireland he picked himself up fairly quickly. He's a boy who is naturally bright and positive. He's a natural born winner.'

Even Toshack seemed a mite more optimistic after the win, suggesting that there may be a glimmer of hope in the qualification stakes. He said: 'At least we were back to the game we are trying to develop. We lost it completely in Dublin, so a win is a win. It's difficult to talk about improvement because there is such a difference in playing Ireland away and San Marino at home.

'We're happy with the result but it still doesn't make up for the result on Saturday. Up until that game we had been going well - even in the Slovakia game we lost at home we played the way I wanted. We just have to look at the Czech Republic game now on 2 June because it's a game we have to win otherwise it will be goodnight for this campaign.'

It wasn't goodnight for Toshack – but it wasn't far off as Toshack's team could only manage a 0-0 draw. Before the Czech Republic, Wales drew 2-2 with an extremely poor showing against New Zealand at home. Gareth missed that match and the Czech Republic clash. The latter saw – as we mentioned earlier in this chapter – superstar Giggs sign off for good from the international stage, waving goodbye to his adoring public for the final time in the red shirt of the country he loved. It was his 64th cap for his country and he had netted 12 times.

By missing the match, Gareth also missed the fans' disappointment mixed with anger that Wales had now almost certainly missed out on another finals. The websites were full of invective and demands that Toshack should be sacked, but one fan, Niall, perhaps best summed up the true nature of the situation: 'It's easy to say get rid of Toshack but what else can he do? He's coaching a group of average Premier League players, who think they're a lot better than they are, i.e. Savage, Cotterill and many others.

'Toshack is blooding youngsters now, who with these games versus very good teams will mature quickly and will become better players. Koumas, Nyatanga, Bale, Eastwood, Collins, Gabbidon, Hennessey, Bellamy, Earnshaw, Price, Duffy, all these players have great potential, and I feel that a push for World Cup 2010 or Euro 2012 is not unrealistic.

'But I also feel Toshack will not be there to reap the benefits of his hard work. When he took over he realised it was an ageing squad, he ripped it up and started again, we can only get better! As for Giggs without a doubt a legend, but for Wales, he never quite did it for us did he?'

Gareth was back for the national team as they prepared for more Euro 2008 qualifiers by taking on Bulgaria in a friendly in Bourgas on August 22, 2007. But the Tottenham backroom staff were none too happy that he played. He has been suffering with knee and thigh injuries and had missed out on making his first competitive start for Spurs in the first three Premier League games of the season. Even Toshack admitted he had had doubts about even taking him in the travelling squad. The Wales boss said: 'I'm aware that he is a major doubt, but I can wait until the weekend to see how he recovers. Maybe Spurs would want him to have 45 minutes with us, but I can understand them being concerned.'

Well, he would play a part in the Bulgaria match – for those first 45 minutes before he was replaced by Neal Eardley – and then make his competitive debut for Spurs four days later, in the highly-charged atmosphere of Old Trafford, against Manchester United!

Coincidentally, just before the matches against Bulgaria and United, Gareth would explain why he had chosen Spurs over the Red Devils – and why he had also chosen Wales over England. He revealed that he could indeed have been an England star, courtesy of eligibility through his English grandmother.

Gareth admitted United had been after him but said of Spurs: 'This club has a lot of potential and young players. They showed a lot of interest in me and I wanted to come here. Now I just want to concentrate on my football and try and get a regular place in the side.'

And of the England situation, he added: 'It is an honour to play for Wales. I could have played for England because my grandmother is English. She never tried to put any pressure on me though. Nobody ever got in touch with me personally from England, only through my agent.

'But I wanted to play for Wales and my hero as a kid was Ryan Giggs. I play on the left as well so I have tried to take certain elements from his game and adapt them into mine. I have never played against him before so I am looking forward to that this season.'

The showing in Bulgaria by the Welsh was much more like it – a much improved team performance and a winning goal from Freddie Eastwood meant a happy flight home for Gareth. But they were also indebted to a fine show from keeper Wayne Hennessey, who kept the likes of the Petrovs, Stilyan and Martin, at bay on several occasions.

Eastwood scored in first-half injury time and Toshack admitted the goal had brought Gareth and the boys in to the dressing room 'buzzing' as they sat down for their half-time cuppa (and in Gareth's case, a shower and change of clothes as he was told he would not be needed for the second half. He was to rest up after his recent injuries).

Toshack said after the game: 'The goal, when it came at that point, gave everybody a real lift. When you have been battling away like that, to have someone at the sharp end give you a lift like that is very important. Our boys came in at the break really buzzing, and it gave them all confidence to go out and finish the job. It also deflated Bulgaria, they struggled in the second half until they managed a late onslaught.'

Next up, the following month, were two vital Euro 2008 qualifiers – the results of which would either bury Welsh hopes for the finals, or miraculously resurrect them. Gareth would play in both games – at home to Germany on September 8 and away in Slovakia five days later.

The Slovakian result would live long in the memory for Gareth as Wales pulled off an unlikely and convincing victory. But the earlier match would spell the end of his dreams of qualifying for a major international finals – for 2008 at least. There had been fears voiced in the press that Gareth might struggle against the Germans as he still strove to get back to full fitness after his injuries – but Roy Evans, assistant to Toshack in the Welsh set-up, brushed aside such worries, saying he felt Gareth would show his star quality in the clash at the Millennium Stadium: 'Gareth looks a fantastic player. He has been magnificent already for us and can only get better and better.'

They were kind words but the result was a killer blow – as the Germans left Cardiff with a 2-0 win courtesy of a double strike from Miroslav Klose. And for once, Gareth was culpable – allowing Roberto Hilbert to nick the ball off him and cross for Klose to head the ball home.

The win guaranteed the Germans early qualification and ended Welsh dreams. They were now 10 points behind the second-placed Czech Republic, with five games to play. Toshack refused to single any players out for errors afterwards, instead concentrating on the overall class and strength of the Germans: 'We can't have any complaints about the score, they were superior to us in nearly every aspect of the game. We were up against a stronger side physically, and that made a huge difference. They were first-class and we were never in the running. They were fitter and faster and deserved their victory.'

Gareth was understandably apologetic to his team-mates for his blunder in losing the ball to Hilbert, but he didn't let it destroy him. He was 18 and still learning the game: he would have mostly good days, but some bad ones. This was one of the latter, but to Toshack's credit he took him to one side and told him to forget it. There was no disgrace in losing to one of the best international teams in the world – and they would have lost irrespective of the momentary lapse of concentration by Gareth.

Toshack now had the unenviable task of raising Welsh spirits for the next of those remaining five qualifiers, four days later in Slovakia. Remarkably, Wales would run out 5-2 winners against the team who had crushed them 5-1 the previous year. Craig Bellamy grabbed a brace as the Welsh went to town – and Gareth particularly enjoyed the match, relishing the freedom down the left side of the pitch, switching positions from left midfield to left wing with Joe Ledley and bombing up and down the field. 'It was as if the shackles had finally come off,' says a source with the Welsh national team. 'OK, they were now out of the running for the Euro 2008 finals, so the lads seemed to say, "Well, let's give it our best shot, then, we have nothing to lose". It was refreshing to see kids like Gareth and Joe enjoying themselves – and gave us all a glimpse of a hopefully better, more exciting future.'

The win was Wales' biggest since they crushed San Marino 5-0 11 years earlier and Toshack was quite rightly in an ebullient mood. He paid tribute to the wonder show from Bellamy, but was also quick to point out the significance of the team performance. Toshack said: 'Craig gave us that result. His pace and willingness to run was stunning. The goals were very special and came after the team had gone behind early on. But that was an equally outstanding team performance. Overall I was very pleased with the outcome.

'Coming after a very disappointing display and defeat by Germany on Saturday, in which we had plenty of problems against a very good side, that was the perfect response.'

Indeed it was. But after the euphoria of that win, Wales and Gareth would now crash to one of their lowest lows in their next match. A low that would see Toshack question his position as Wales manager – and leave the usually bubbly, positive Gareth Bale really down in the dumps.

Chapter 14

IN THE FOOTSTEPS OF LEGENDS

It wouldn't get much lower for Gareth on the international scene than it did on the dark autumn Saturday of October 13 2007. He and his Welsh team-mates slumped disconsolately in their seats on the jet home from Cyprus after they had crashed to a demoralising 3-1 defeat in Nicosia. 'Yes, it was a real downer,' a Welsh national team source said. 'Gareth didn't much want to talk to anyone on the plane back to the UK – in fact, none of the players were in the mood for even a game of cards. They just wanted to get home, sleep and put the nightmare behind them.'

Yet the afternoon had started oh so optimistically, particularly for Gareth. It was he who set up the first goal; his fine free kick curling into the goalmouth, leaving James Collins with one of the easiest opportunities to drill the ball home for the opener.

It was Collins's first goal for his country and hopes were high on the Welsh bench that the team, led by the determined figure of Craig Bellamy, could now press on and make a statement of intent for the future. OK, they might be out of the Euros, but a big win would give them a real boost for the World Cup qualifiers and would stamp the seal of approval on Toshack's methods and reign.

But Wales always seem to do things the hard way and, lo and behold, this would be no exception to the rule. After that bright beginning, they would collapse in the second-half, conceding three times inside 20 minutes; two goals from Yiannis Okkas, and one from Konstantinos Charalampidis crushing Welsh spirits.

Toshack was also quiet on the plane on the way home. He had two years of his contract to run and, inevitably, there were, many calls for him to call it a day and walk away after a performance he himself described as 'shocking'.

After the match he said: 'I was bitterly disappointed by the performance and want to apologise to our fans who made the trip out here to watch this debacle. Cyprus were worthy winners and we were fortunate to be 1-0 up at the break. We tried to make some changes at the break but went from bad to worse.

'It was a shocking performance and we did not compete in any areas of the pitch. We were second best everywhere. It was very, very disappointing to watch that.'

He added that he was aware that, as the manager, he was ultimately responsible for the result – and said he would examine his own preparation work for the match: 'I will have to have a long hard look at myself and what I am doing here. After what I have seen in this match I am obviously doing something wrong... we were second best everywhere.'

Tosh would now have to raise the spirits of Gareth and his team-mates for another Group D away match four days later against minnows – this time San Marino. They desperately needed a good result if Wales themselves were to avoid being dubbed small fish in world football.

As Bellamy admitted: 'There is something seriously wrong with Welsh football if we now fail to beat San Marino on Wednesday. We know we did not deserve to win the game – we were that poor. The way we have been playing lately and our tactics, we do run a fine line that can punish us. And Cyprus did just that.'

Fortunately, they would come through against San Marino – but only just. Wales came away with a 2-1 win thanks to goals by Earnshaw and Ledley, but Gareth would pick up a booking and it was another mighty unimpressive performance from Toshack and his side.

The Welsh had gone in 2-0 up at the interval, but then allowed San Marino to score via a shot from Andy Selva – which ensured Toshack would be biting his fingernails right up to the final whistle. Afterwards he admitted: 'I still feel we have a lot of work and talking to do if we are going to change some players' attitude. I still want to push younger players in. Some of these lads have had a rollicking, but these days you don't seem to be able to do that to young players. They think they know it all.

'I hope the next 10 days we are together will be better than this one was. OK, so this was a win, but that's all. We set about the first half in the right way, scored two and could have had more. But in the second period we had to make a change because David Vaughan was struggling with a groin injury and we didn't really get started after that. We gave away a needless free-kick for them to score. From then on, we were biting our nails and calling for the whistle. That was a pity because it should not have been that close. But it was difficult against a defence that did not come out. But to concede like that, with us not marking properly and generally being sloppy disappointed me.'

He was far from alone in his disappointment. The website message boards were flooded with angry comments from fans, most agreeing that the football was of 'a non-league level' and demanding Toshack's head be served up on a plate.

It was all unedifying, depressing stuff for the many young players within the squad like Gareth. Some were downhearted and found it hard to pick themselves up although Gareth, as we have already mentioned many times in this book, did not suffer the blues for long. He was a naturally optimistic, happy lad who took all football had to offer in his stride – both the good times and the bad.

Some fans who had made the trip to San Marino had made their feelings known on the terraces about the quality of the performance on the pitch, verbally abusing the team from early in the game. It all flew over Gareth's head, but Bellamy was not as tolerant. Indeed the Wales skipper was furious after the match, saying: 'I have played for Wales for a number of years and that's one of the worst atmospheres I have been involved in. Some of the chanting early on was vicious. I am proud to play for my country but that was one of the most difficult games I have been involved in.'

Wales had two more fixtures in 2007 – and Gareth would miss both because of injury problems. The home match against the Republic of Ireland and the away fixture in Germany would also wrap up their Euro 2008 qualifying campaign. Given that the Welsh emerged from both with creditable draws – 2-2 at home against the Irish and 0-0 in Germany – the future looked a deal brighter than it had done after the double nightmare against Cyprus and San Marino.

Gareth would suffer another injury in December 2007 – and this time it would be a bad one...bad enough to sideline him for eight months and seriously hinder what had been a most promising start to his international career. Gareth had damaged the ligaments in his right ankle and the injury would require two operations and the insertion of a metal pin (which has since been removed).

It was a career threatening setback, but Gareth was made of strong stuff. He kept up his spirits and worked damned hard to get back to fitness – his single-minded determination not to meet the knacker's yard just as he was breaking through into the big-time was the turning point.

The injury meant he missed Wales' first five fixtures of 2008 but finally returned to the team for the opening World Cup qualifier against Azerbaijan on Saturday September 6 2008. It was a disappointing display by the team as a whole – a 1-0 win courtesy of a late goal by Sam Vokes hardly being what the fans at the Millennium Stadium had anticipated against another group of world footballing minnows – but Gareth could at least be pleased with his Man of the Match contribution.

He did well on his return to the international fray, setting up the goal on 83 minutes and pushing his team-mates forward with confidence in an early foray. Indeed that early excursion into the visitors' backline, which saw Gareth bundled over in the box, could have resulted in a penalty from a more vigilant ref than Aleksandar Stavrev of Macedonia.

But Bale earned karmic retribution seven minutes from time when he sent in a pinpoint corner that Vokes swept home with a conviction defying his 18 years. 'We expected a difficult game and they were tough opposition,' said Toshack. 'I'm satisfied with the result and I don't think anyone could begrudge us the points. We dominated the match and heads could easily have dropped after the penalty was missed. They were bouncing and our lot were deflated. But we kept going, refused to let it bother us for long, and fully deserved the winner. We were easily the better team.'

But a much tougher task awaited Gareth and the boys four days later – in Russia. It would be a match Gareth would not forget in a hurry…he missed a penalty but then made amends by setting up a goal!

The penalty miss came after just 15 minutes as ref Damir Skomina pointed to the spot after Bale, rampaging forward from left-back, was tripped by Sergei Semak. Gareth took the kick and smashed it to the right of Igor Akinfeev, but the brilliant Russian stopper pulled off a fine save. It was Gareth's only blunder in a match in which he was 'simply outstanding' according to his boss, Toshack.

But the miss did temporarily slow up the early momentum of the Welsh team while at the same time giving the Russians a fillip. So it was no surprise when they went ahead seven minutes later – although the manner of the goal was unsurprising, and unacceptable. Just as Gareth blotted his copybook with the penalty, so keeper Wayne Hennessey would now wreck his own otherwise outstanding night's work by fumbling a Craig Morgan header into the path of the

Russians. Konstantin Zyrianov collared the ball, darted forwards and was duly brought down by Carl Robinson. Roman Pavlyuchenko scored from the spot, putting the hosts 1-0 ahead.

Wales equalised when Joe Ledley lifted the ball home just after the hour mark, but substitute Pavel Pogrebnyak killed off Welsh hopes with just nine minutes remaining. It was a sickener for Gareth and his team-mates who had matched the Russian team of Guus Hiddink.

Toshack had confounded his critics and had shown he was really beginning to appreciate the contribution – and effect Gareth Bale could have on a match – by pushing the youngster forward from his left-back slot in the second half. The move freed up Gareth to attack the hosts – and left the Russians nervous every time he darted forwards.

Toshack said: 'I am disappointed for the players because there were a lot of young lads out there and I thought we worked very hard. In the second half we were the better side. I can understand the Russians thinking they just about shaded it but I thought we deserved a point. A draw would have been a great result in the circumstances. They are one of Europe's top four sides and we've got an injury list as long as your arm.

'If this had been a boxing match, we would have lost on a split decision. Gareth Bale, Chris Gunter, Ched Evans, Sam Vokes, Ledley etc are all young boys who will now know, against the best teams, he who hesitates has lost.

'After Bale's penalty miss, we dropped our heads a little because we are still an inexperienced side but otherwise Bale was outstanding again.

'We didn't get tight to them often enough and they hit us hard. There's no disgrace to lose 2-1 to a side like Russia, particularly in the circumstances, but to come so close and lose the way we did is obviously bitterly disappointing. Overall I am satisfied – but if we are going to have any chance of qualifying we have to get 12 points by the end of March.'

That was an optimistic aim and would take a lot of achieving by the youngsters Toshack was entrusting with the nation's fortunes. There were three more fixtures to round off 2008 and Gareth appeared in all three – Liechtenstein at home and Germany away in World Cup qualifiers and Denmark away in a friendly.

The match against minnows Liechtenstein – the seventh smallest country in the world at the time – brought the expected three points while the match in Germany garnered none, also as expected.

Wales beat Liechtenstein 2-0 on Saturday October 11 in front of a lowly 13,500 crowd, but it was no walkover. In fact, it was almost half-time when David Edwards finally put them ahead – just what was it with Toshack's Wales and the struggles they had against teams they should have monstered? A minute after the goal Bale earned a penalty when he was bundled over in the box by Martin Buchel. But Bellamy missed from the penalty spot.

Luckily sub Ched Evans wrapped up the all-important three points with the winner 10 minutes from time, and Wales were looking down from second place in the group. 'Gareth and the younger lads have done well,' said Toshack after the game. 'But maybe a few of the older ones can step up to the plate and do a bit more for us.'

They would certainly need to if they were to get anything from the tough-looking encounter in Mönchengladbach the following Wednesday. Bellamy, especially, would need to find his shooting boots again after missing chance after chance (including the penalty) against Liechtenstein – following on from Gareth's miss from the spot against the Russians. Toshack added: 'Craig came off wondering why he didn't have a hat-trick and the match ball. But these things happen to strikers. I missed one myself for Wales in Hungary 30 years ago. So I don't know whether Gareth and Craig are in good company being with me or if I'm in good company being with them.'

Toshack could afford a joke then, but he wasn't laughing four days later when his team lost to the Germans, although they did put in a battling, creditable night shift. Wales, with Gareth outstanding at left-back, held out to almost the three-quarter hour mark when a rasping, unstoppable shot from Piotr Trochowski broke Welsh hearts. The loss meant Wales slipped a place in qualifying Group Four to third. 'Gareth and the boys felt they had done enough to earn a point and were a bit disappointed,' a Welsh national team source said. 'He played well and showed he could hold his head high against world-class players – which is what the Germans are.'

Toshack agreed that his players had given their best and done well: 'The fact all the players are disappointed in the dressing room is a good sign. Germany are a top side and we did very well against them. I couldn't fault the lads at all.'

But Tosh spelled out his uncomfortable belief that Wales would now needed to win all their remaining games to make the World Cup finals – including the two home games against the Germans and Finland the following March. He said: 'March is not quite last-chance saloon but we need to win both those games if we want to qualify. I want to be on 12 points then and see where it takes us. We've had the two toughest games and we need to win the rest.'

Craig Bellamy was much of the same opinion, telling BBC Sport: 'If you look at the table we've probably played the two toughest games, Russia and Germany away from home, and we can take heart from that but we have lost twice and that is disappointing. I just don't know how to start turning glorious failure into glorious success, if we knew that it wouldn't have taken us 50 years to qualify for a major tournament.

'There have been better Welsh teams than this one who haven't done it. But we are a decent side as I've been in Wales teams who've struggled to get anything together away from home whereas we are turning up and having a good go. No one wants to feel the hurt and we're not too far away, I just hope the experience the younger players are gaining from these tough results might do us good in the long term.'

Bellamy himself struck the winner in the next match, the friendly in Copenhagen – a fine 1-0 win over Denmark. Gareth played well but was subbed for Neal Eardley with three minutes of normal time remaining.

Gareth found himself on the left wing – rather than back in defence – for the first international of 2009, a 1-0 friendly loss in Portugal against Poland. Then it was on to the big two – Finland and Germany at home in the World Cup qualifiers and two matches the Welsh just had to win if they were to turn their finals dream into anything approaching reality.

The good news was that Gareth added another two caps to his growing tally. The bad news was that he probably wished he hadn't bothered as Wales crashed in both matches.

Before the encounters, Gareth said he was enjoying his time in the Welsh side. He said: 'I love to get forward and attack and with Wales there is more licence for me to get forward as I play wing-back. But I need to improve my defensive side. I've been working hard on it and hopefully it will pay off. Spurs assistant boss Kevin Bond takes a group of us and I am learning.'

He also admitted that it was vital Wales won both matches, adding: 'The Finland game is must-win. If we can do that, it'll give us a kick-start for Germany.'

With those comments in mind, the loss to the Finns was a particular blow: Gareth and the boys knew the Germans would be tough, but had fancied their luck against the lesser talents of what Bellamy would later dub 'a bad team' (Finland). Goals from Jonatan Johansson and Shefki Kuqi destroyed Wales and the team and their manager were very low afterwards.

Toshack said: 'As hard as we tried, I couldn't see a way through. The players found it difficult and, if I'm honest, I did as well. It's very difficult. You look at the young lads, like Sam Vokes, Ched Evans and Gareth Bale. They come through and then some of them hit the brick wall and they're not getting the game-time you would like. If we win our last five games I don't think it will be enough. It hurts and it's frustrating but that's the truth of it.'

Bellamy was desolate, also writing off any hopes of qualification as he said: 'This isn't a nice feeling and maybe you could say I should concentrate on club football. But no. I'm Welsh and that is how I am. Getting knocks like this is part and parcel of what I have grown up with, disappointments like this have always been there. We have never done anything, we are not going to do anything – certainly with this campaign – so wipe yourself down and get on with it again.

'I don't want to sound bitter but I think it is over for both us and Finland. Russia and Germany have far too much quality, which means it's the same situation we've been through before. Try to get as many points as you can, play for pride, play loads of games. It's just so disappointing.'

Gareth and Co went down 2-0 to the Germans in Cardiff – the same scoreline they had lost to the Finns. A scorching shot from Michael Ballack and an Ashley Williams own-goal condemned Wales to another defeat in Group Four. But it was a much improved showing from Wales, without Bellamy, who cried off with a late injury. Toshack blamed the ref for the loss, saying he failed to spot a first-half handball by Serdar Tasci that would have given Wales a penalty and changed the outcome. He was also angry about the throw-in that led to Ballack's opener in the 11th minute, saying: 'You wouldn't see decisions like that down at the local playing fields. We are disappointed with the first goal. It was a ridiculous decision to not give a throw-in for Wales.

'The linesman pointed our way, Aaron Ramsey was heading towards the touchline and Ballack went into that area where Aaron is expected to be. Then we feel we should have had a penalty for the handball and a sending-off. It was a penalty and red card. It is tough enough against one of the best sides in the world without those decisions going against you. It's very disappointing from a top referee.'

Complaining, unfortunately, would not change the outcome. It was another defeat and hopes of making the 2010 World Cup were fast disappearing for Gareth. Eight weeks later he was part of the youngest ever Wales team that chalked up a 1-0 friendly international victory over Estonia in Llanelli, but missed another win by the same scoreline in the World Cup qualifier in Azerbaijan a week after that. Injury also ruled him out of the friendly loss in Montenegro in August and the September World Cup qualifier defeat (3-1 at home) by Russia.

But he finally returned for the qualifier in Finland, which would decide whether Wales finished third in the group. Gareth played his now usual wing-back role, which meant some defending and some attacking. But to his credit, Toshack had encouraged him to go with his instincts – which meant he tended to attack more than he defended.

Indeed, it was Gareth who helped set up Bellamy for the Welsh goal in what turned out to be a disappointing 2-1 defeat. Bale pushed the ball out to David Vaughan who, in turn, sent Bellamy on his way. He also set up Simon Church 10 minutes before the break for an opportunity the Blackpool man should really have buried, but instead nodded wide.

Roni Porokara had put the Finns ahead within the first five minutes and Nicklas Moisander killed off Welsh hopes when he stabbed home the winner with 13 minutes remaining on the clock. The defeat meant Wales had now sacrificed third place in the group to the Finns – another letdown in another big international tournament for Gareth. Yes, he could certainly sympathise with Ryan Giggs when the veteran spoke about his own feelings of disappointment at never reaching a major tournament with his country. It was a heartbreaker that men of such world-class talent as Gareth and Ryan would never grace the biggest international arenas. 'Gareth had hoped that he and the lads would at least clinch that third spot,' says a Wales source. 'At least if they had done that it would have showed they were on the right track. To lose out to the Finns was a real blow. The young lads were all a bit low on the way home to the UK.'

Toshack was also upset that they had not secured third spot.

He admitted: 'We are bitterly disappointed by the result. We wanted to finish in third spot and that is now beyond us. We conceded two very sloppy goals with mistakes from experienced defenders.

'We had a poor start, scored a super goal but then things just petered out. With the amount of injury problems we have had, we were only able to name four players on the bench. That in the end denied us any options to be able to change the game. The goals we let in were sloppy although I felt we deserved a draw.'

Skipper Bellamy was disillusioned at his country's sixth loss in nine World Cup qualifiers. He said: 'We keep saying the youngsters will blossom but what plusses can we take from the campaign? It's familiar territory for me with Wales. This hurts.'

Wales were guaranteed to finish fourth in their group whatever the result in Liechtenstein the following week – but that was not good enough for Bellamy, or Gareth Bale for that matter. Was Toshack the right man to take them on to glory in the qualifiers for Euro 2012? He believed he was, and bemoaned what he considered bad luck for the losses that had cost him and his players any hope of making the World Cup finals in South Africa in the summer of 2010.

He said: 'This group has been very frustrating and we have had one problem after another. We have lost twice to Finland while doing OK against the two big sides, Germany and Russia. I won't be glad to see the back of this group, only glad one day to see us able to put out our best side without injuries, withdrawals and retirements to disrupt our plans.'

Wales duly triumphed in Liechtenstein, beating the minnows 2-0 with goals from Vaughan and Aaron Ramsey.

Gareth lasted 80 minutes before he was taken off and replaced by Lewin Nyatanga.

Before that he twisted and tormented the minnows' defence, leading them a merry dance with his darting runs and skilful teasing. Gareth set up Vaughan for the first goal on 16 minutes and indirectly the clincher – after he was fouled on the edge of the box. Ramsey lashed the ball home from the resultant free kick.

The *Guardian* summed up Gareth's contribution, headlining their report: 'Gareth makes hay as Wales take consolation win in Liechtenstein' and declaring him to be the Man of the Match. Gareth was certainly pleased with his own performance – he declared it to be one of his best so far in a Wales shirt – and that the team had finished the campaign on a winning note.

Toshack was also happy to sign off with a win in what had been a topsy-turvy, mostly disappointing campaign. He said: 'I think we deserved to win and maybe we could have had a couple of goals more. I'm pleased with the result. We created six or seven good chances, took two and overall I think it was a well-deserved result. I thought we gave the ball away at times when we shouldn't have done. Quality-wise we weren't as good as we should have been but I thought we set about our task well.'

There now remained just one match in Wales' international remit for 2009 – and the winner would clinch local bragging rights. Yes, a month after the win over Liechtenstein, Scotland would arrive in Cardiff and, with Gareth in fine form yet again, Wales would secure a 3-0 win that took some of the pressure off under-fire boss Toshack while also raising hopes that better times maybe, finally, did lie ahead in 2010, especially when you took into account the fact that the average age of the Welsh side that started was just 22.

The Scots had not beaten Wales since 1984 and that 25-year jinx never looked like coming to an end. The result meant that Scotland boss George Burley was now the target of the snipers, giving Toshack a (temporary) reprieve.

Wales overran the Scots, with all three goals coming in the first 35 minutes from Dave Edwards, Simon Church and Aaron Ramsey. For once, Gareth was overshadowed by one of his fellow young team-mates...Ramsey, who had a belter of a game. Not that it worried him – Gareth would always put the team performance and result first. He was just delighted to see off the Scots.

To his credit, Ramsey also saw it that way, telling BBC Sport: 'I was quite fortunate as I played a part in the goals but that win wasn't just me. The movement of our players was good and the whole team played very well.'

Three months later Gareth was back in Cardiff for Wales' first international of 2010, the friendly against Sweden. The Tottenham wonder boy was singled out as the biggest threat by the Swedes – and so it proved, as he launched the brunt of Wales' most dangerous attacking moves. But a goal by Johan Elmander before the break settled the match, leaving Toshack rueing his decision to take Gareth off just after the hour. Without his inspiration, Wales never looked like breaking through.

After the win over Scotland the previous November, Gareth and Wales now looked to be back to square one again. Which meant the pressure was now back on Toshack, although he professed himself relatively happy. He said: 'I don't think we can have too many complaints about the result. We came up against a very well-drilled side, very experienced at international level, were too good for us and maybe the result was a bit kind to us.'

Gareth missed the next two matches – two friendlies to prepare for their next major international campaign, the qualifiers for Euro 2012. Wales lost away to Croatia in the first of those friendlies, in May 2010, and then thrashed Luxembourg at home in August.

Three weeks later, on September 3, it was down to business as qualifying began in earnest in Montenegro. Yet again, it was a letdown as Gareth, now back in the fold, and his team-mates crashed 1-0. Gareth played a marauding role down the left-wing and set up a few good chances. Bellamy should have scored from one of them, in the final 10 minutes, but lashed his shot wide.

Montenegro skipper Mirko Vucinic grabbed the decisive goal on the half-hour mark, and Gareth, Bellamy and the rest of the boys were left with that now familiar feeling of déjà vu. They seemed on the road to nowhere fast – and with games due against England and Bulgaria the fans were starting to rebel against the Toshack regime. Just how long could he last?

Bellamy urged patience, saying: 'Everyone wants to get off to a good start but Montenegro are a very good team. It isn't over for us but I do believe it would be much easier with a positive result. We have to be realistic now and do something about qualifying. So often we've been out of the group early, so it's about time we did something and got into that major tournament.'

But was that just wishful thinking?

Toshack would be judged on results – and results only, even if he was still contending he was building a team full of brilliant kids for the future. To give him his due, the Wales boss then admitted that the next match – the home game against the Bulgarians the following month was a likely make-or-break fixture for him. He said: 'To be honest we're already looking at the Bulgaria game as one we must win or we could be out virtually already. We lacked quality in midfield and our performance in the opening period was not good enough really. After that game we face the two tougher sides in the group, England and Switzerland, so we really have to win that one.'

They say that a week is a long time in politics – well, it is in football, too. Six days after the Montenegro game, the Welsh FA decided they had enough of promises and hope and dispensed with Toshack's services. The 61-year-old manager admitted he had considered resigning after Wales' 1-0 loss in Montenegro but had then decided against it, instead travelling to Bulgaria to watch their Group G game against Montenegro in a scouting mission.

Soon after the Welsh FA pulled the plug on his reign, even though he offered to remain in charge to face Bulgaria at the Cardiff City Stadium on October 8 and Switzerland in Basle on October 12.

Toshack said: 'I spoke to the [Welsh FA] president Phil Pritchard after the friendly in Croatia in May about reviewing it after the first three matches of this group. Even after the disappointment of the game in Montenegro that was still the way I felt. I discussed things after the game and each of us put our point of view over a few things and really we have come to the agreement that it may be better for everybody concerned if a change was made now.'

Toshack, after a brief spell in charge in 1994, had returned to the Welsh helm in 2004 to succeed Mark Hughes. But his reign was a disappointment – Wales managed just 10 competitive wins in 29 qualifiers, losing 16, since his first game in March 2005.

Brian Flynn would be the man the Welsh FA turned to as a temporary replacement as Toshack headed for the exit door. And Gareth was one of the first to lay out the welcome mat for the man who had introduced him to international football when he was boss of the Welsh Under-21 side. Flynn had once described him as a 'Rolls-Royce of a left-back'. And Gareth now said, 'I remember Brian saying that. It's always good to hear things like that, but hopefully I've started to live up to some of the things Brian has said about me. But it's not just me. Brian has shown faith in pretty much all the squad at different stages and that's why we're here now. I know the lads here are good enough to perform at international level, he's backed us and now we have to repay him.'

Flynn's first game in charge was the Euro qualifier against the Bulgarians in Cardiff. Unfortunately, it was just as dismal an outcome as the days under big Tosh. Ivelin Popov scored the only goal of the match to condemn Gareth and Co to another sickening defeat – one that meant they had now lost their opening two games in Group G, and suggested even at this early stage they would need a miracle to progress.

It could have been worse but for a series of top-notch saves by Wales keeper Wayne Hennessey. They also had left-back Chris Gunter sent off in the closing stages.

But there was little time for reflection or an inquest – Gareth and his team-mates had to prepare themselves for a quick turnaround as they headed to Switzerland for their third qualifier in the group the following Tuesday, with Flynn once again at the helm.

Flynn had been told he must impress in Basel if he were to have any hope of getting the job on a permanent basis – and he, in turn, now turned the screw on Gareth. He told him via his pre-match press conference that he was effectively carrying the hopes of the Welsh nation, as well as those for his job prospects!

Flynn said, 'Gareth is one of our most experienced players. And he has the tag of being a match-winner, which he carries on his shoulders as well. It is a big responsibility, but he's capable of that, be it from a free kick, a pass, a dribble to create something. He's got a lot of responsibility. I told him when he was 15, "you are going to be extra-special" and he can get better as well. Gareth will get man-marked and tactically he has to work it out himself. He has to be clever. He's has got pace, but he can't rely on it just to get out of the situation.'

So no pressure there for Gareth to deliver against the Swiss.

New Wales skipper Ashley Williams also upped the ante for Gareth, seconding Flynn's assertion that he could be the difference between the two teams. Williams said, 'Everyone knows how good a player he is. He's probably going to find it tough when he plays for Wales especially if we don't have Craig Bellamy and Aaron Ramsey playing. He's our biggest attacking threat and teams are going to pay special attention to him. But I think he's a good enough player to deal with that.

'They will have a lot of the ball and hopefully we can get it to him on the break and let him do his stuff. I think he really gave it a go against Bulgaria, he did make things happen, and if he plays in an advanced role, that's the way he plays.'

Williams was right in his predictions – the Swiss did have

a lot of the ball, and Bale did make things happen. Unfortunately, the Welsh would be at the wrong end of a 4-1 thrashing that left their qualifying hopes in tatters. True, Gareth would take some consolation from the disastrous result by grabbing their goal, but it was little consolation given that it meant another qualifying campaign was all but over before it had really begun. The depressing fact that truly summed up how bad the situation was – and how difficult it would now be to qualify – was this...it was the first time ever that Wales had lost their opening three qualifying matches in the Euros.

The Swiss had taken the lead on eight minutes when Marco Streller headed them in front. But Gareth raised Welsh hopes just five minutes later when he scored a fine equaliser. Andrew Crofts put Gareth through and he made no mistake as he dispatched the ball home into the corner. But it would prove a false dawn as the hosts scored three more goals to kill off Welsh dreams, leaving them rooted at the bottom of the group, with no points.

The *Daily Mirror* summed up Gareth's contribution in this way: 'Gareth Bale put his heart and soul into trying to nail down the Wales job for caretaker Brian Flynn. The Tottenham gem, who threatens to become the outstanding Welsh star of his generation, slammed in an equaliser – before celebrating by making the shape of a heart with his fingers. But love, comfort and joy were in painfully short supply for acting boss Flynn last night in Basel, where a heavy defeat undermined his claims to follow John Toshack into the hot seat on a permanent basis. Wales' Euro 2012 qualifying hopes lay in tatters, too.'

Flynn still wanted the job on a full-time basis despite two

poor results out of two. On a disappointing night to mark his 55th birthday, he said, 'The two defeats haven't improved my position, but perversely, I want the job even more than I did before. It's been a joy. I think I'm the man for the job and have no doubt about my credentials. You can see an improvement but there is more to come.'

Gareth led the chorus of players who said they would be happy for Flynn to become boss on a permanent basis – despite his two defeats. Gareth told BBC Sport Wales, 'Personally I hope he does get the job on a permanent basis. I think Brian has done very well since he's come in. He's made the training a lot more lively and it's good to work with him.'

But the Welsh FA did not back Gareth and his team-mates when push came to shove. It was Flynn who got the shove in mid December 2010...and another former Wales hero Gary Speed who was called up to take the job on a full-time basis.

Speed was Wales' most capped outfield player after making 85 appearances for his country and he signed on for three and a half years – which meant he had a chance to turn around Welsh fortunes in the current Euro campaign and in the qualifiers for the 2014 World Cup in Brazil.

The 41-year-old, who left his job as manager of Sheffield United to take over, said, 'It's something that's very difficult to turn down when your country comes calling. I am a very proud man to be asked to be manager of Wales. I'm just thankful I've got the opportunity to come and try to make Wales successful. It's an opportunity I'm really looking forward to.'

But was Speed too young to turn around a young team in dire need of inspiration and maybe a wise old head to settle them and inspire them? Only time would tell - their next

Group G qualifier was the biggie, against England in Cardiff on March 26, 2011.

Gareth told *Sport* magazine that he felt Speed could be a success – and at the same time stressed just what playing for Wales meant to him. Gareth said, 'Most players who play for Wales are passionate about it, and I'm exactly the same. I think Euro 2012 is out of our reach now, but Gary Speed has the whole of this qualifying campaign to build, make us a better team, and hopefully he can do that. We want to start being in contention to qualify for tournaments, and I want to be involved in that future – hopefully it'll be a bright one.'

Gareth had thrown his full support behind the new man but knew it would be a long hard slog if they were to get a result against England – let alone achieve that dream of ever qualifying for a major international tournament. Still, Bale was managing to make a name for himself as an international player of stature even while playing for what could at best could generously be termed as an up-and-coming Welsh national team as the end of 2010 loomed.

Paul Hayward, the *Observer*'s fine chief sports writer, summed up Gareth's growing place of honour in the pantheon of Welsh wonders in this way: 'Bale has marched through this critical minefield to become the latest in a distinguished lineage of Welsh wingers, from Cliff Jones to Ryan Giggs. Jones, a touchline terror for Spurs from 1957–68, says: 'He is without doubt one of the best in the world and I have no doubt he will become the first Welsh player to win 100 caps. He's only 21 and he's got so much in front of him. In fact he'll only get better and better.' Well put, sir...

Chapter 15

THE DALGLISH SEAL OF APPROVAL

Kenny Dalglish is one of the greatest footballers and footballer managers ever. No need to discuss...it is a fact, pure and simple. So when, at the end of 2010, he put on his critic's hat and assessed the year just gone, his word counted for rather more than your average Fleet Street footie scribbler. This was, after all, the man who had been there, done it and got the T-shirt to prove it.

Writing in his weekly *Mail on Sunday* column on Boxing Day, he pinpointed Gareth Bale's arrival on the scene under the appropriate heading 'The Discovery of the Season'. Dalglish then said of Bale: 'He really came of age in 2010. The Spurs man showed glimpses towards the end of last season of what he was capable of, and this term he has been virtually unplayable. The way the young Welshman twice took Inter Milan apart won't be forgotten in a hurry. His big test is to try to reproduce that form consistently over years, not months. Then he will be a genuine world-beater.'

You could also argue that the last two sentences summed up the Tottenham team as a whole – and the 'big test' boss Redknapp faced if he was to keep the likes of Bale and Van der Vaart happy. They would certainly need to reproduce the form they had shown so brilliantly from August 2010 if they were to progress and win trophies: the essential prerequisite for both Gareth and Rafael if they were to commit to the Lane for the long-term.

After the thrill of winning their Champions League group, Tottenham and Gareth were rightly looking forward to 2011 with optimism and relish. But they still had three games to play before the old year would be gone for good: Chelsea at home, Aston Villa away and Newcastle at home. In the old days, you would probably have agreed that Spurs could expect five points out of nine – a draw with Chelsea and Villa at best and a win over Newcastle. In the event, they would amass seven points, much more to the form of title contenders or, at the very least, contenders for that fourth Champions League spot.

The big match among the three was, of course, the one with London rivals, Chelsea. The Blues were the reigning Premier League champions and would provide a reliable yardstick of just how far Gareth and the team had truly come on.

Gareth himself upped the ante for the game when he spoke to Ian Wright on Absolute Radio a few days before the match. He proclaimed he was confident Spurs could win the title – which meant, of course, he was confident they could see off the challenge of Chelsea at the Lane.

Gareth said: 'I think we are a lot more confident now,

obviously qualifying for the Champions League and a string of good results in the league. I think we've all got more belief that we can compete up there with the best teams and we will be working our hardest to do that.

'I definitely feel like all of the lads feel like we've got the kind of squad that is capable of being up in the mix and you never know hopefully we can be in there with a shot. We go into every game looking to get at win and especially at home. We are all confident of beating anybody at home as we showed last season against Arsenal and Chelsea and this year of the likes of Inter Milan so we're all confident that we can win games.'

In another interview Gareth admitted that the three straight wins against top opposition – Arsenal, Bremen and Liverpool at the back end of November – had convinced him that Spurs were now a team with sufficient class, character and strength to mount a credible challenge on all fronts. He said: That was a massive week for the club. We had two unbelievable results in the league and to qualify for the knockout stages of the Champions League was something special. We just want to build on this now. The lads are full of confidence, the team's playing well and there's no better feeling. It's a great team to play in.

'We've got a close squad, everyone gets along well and I think that shows in the game. We work for each other and that's why we're getting results. A lot of our points this season have come from being behind...but it's not nice going behind, even though we seem to do well from that position. We definitely want to keep more clean sheets now and keep winning.'

And in an interview with the official Tottenham club website,

Gareth outlined just why he thought his form had been so brilliant this season. He said: 'In the past I've had injuries and coming back from them hasn't been too easy. I had to be patient not being in the team for a long time and you've got to be ready to take the opportunity when you get it. There was a lot of talk about me going on loan and I don't know if anything was ever going to happen. Benoit Assou-Ekotto got injured, I got my chance and I've been prepared for a while, doing a lot of running after training just to get ready. My chance came and I was there to take it.'

He said he had put in a lot of extra hours on the training pitch so that he was fit and ready; that he had been determined to nail down a place in the starting XI. When asked why he kept such a low profile, and did so few interviews, he replied: 'I just want to keep it low key and concentrate on my football.'

Gareth's profile was also boosted before the Chelsea match by Barcelona's 5-0 thrashing of Real Madrid in Spain. It emerged that after the crushing loss Real boss Jose Mourinho confronted his board of directors and blamed them for the defeat – saying that if they had given him the money to buy Gareth, it wouldn't have happened. Football writer Steve Featherstone summed it up in this way: 'Mourinho shocked his employers after the 5-0 capitulation at Barcelona, by insisting that to reach the heights of the Catalan opponents they need one thing. Gareth Bale. Bale, 21, has had a meteoric rise to fame this season in a Spurs side that are turning heads at every stage in the Champions League.

'Bale himself has been the catalyst for many of their top performances and his single-handed destruction on Mourinho's former employers Inter Milan has done enough to convince the 'Special One' Bale is the final piece of his Madrid jigsaw. Of course, many believe that Mourinho was trying to divert attention away from the fact Barcelona had just crucified his side in front of one of the biggest audiences in the world. The Spanish press were immediately throwing about figures of up to £80 million for the Welsh wonder, a far cry from just over a year ago when he was used primarily as a squad player at the Lane.'

There was also the little matter of winning the 2010 BBC Wales Sports Personality of the Year. Gareth succeeded Ryan Giggs and was presented with the award by Spurs great Clive Allen at Tottenham's training ground. He beat Commonwealth champion bowler Robert Weale into second and 400m hurdles champion Dai Greene to third. Gareth told BBC Wales: 'It was a great honour just to be put up for the award so to win it is something special. I remember when I was a younger I was up for the young sports personality award and to be up for this now, shows how much I have come in the last couple of years.

'It has been a great year for me playing week in, week out, I've scored a few goals and the team qualified for the Champions League so there have been a lot of highlights but I'm just concentrating now and building for the future.' Typical of the boy, always humble, always more interested in getting back to work than playing 'the big I am'.

And he would do just that with the visit of Chelsea to the Lane on December 12. Gareth and his team-mates were convinced now was as good a time as any to get a result...the Blues had won just one of their five previous matches and, in an unusually nervy, unsteady patch, had lost two of them.

It was a stark contrast to the thrilling football Carlo

Ancelotti's team had exhibited at the start of the season with goals now hard to come by and defensive deficiencies clear to see. Club captain John Terry had been hit by injuries and looked a yard short of pace and it would be down to Portuguese fullback Paulo Ferreira to halt the runaway train that was Gareth Bale. Ferreira lasted just 45 minutes in the corresponding fixture the previous season as Bale gave him a merry runaround, scoring the second in a 2-1 win for Spurs.

Even bookies William Hill felt pity on Chelsea and the prospect of facing Gareth, highlighting that he was the man most likely to destroy them. Their spokesman said: 'The focal point remains Bale as he continues to impress everyone with his storming performances from the left wing. Already this season he has made two of the best right backs in the game in Maicon and Bacary Sagna look average, it could be Jose Bosingwa is added to that list by the Sunday night. His pace, strength and determination are a defender's worst nightmare and even with John Terry back in the fold and Petr Cech in top form you'd be mad to think they can silence him from start to finish.

'The Welsh wideman doesn't just turn on the style against the chaff either, in fact his best performances have come when the cameras are paying particularly close attention – which they will be on Sunday. The best bit is that he's a whopping 10/3 to score anytime – it's an absolute steal given Chelsea's recent wobbles. Their trip to Marseille on Wednesday said a lot about their recent issues as a toothless attack failed to breach the French side's defence as they fell to a 1-0 loss.'

Finally, Chelsea got a warning shot from Spurs themselves, or more specifically, full-back Benoit Assou-Ekotto, who said: 'Bale is one of the best players in Europe at the moment. We have to keep him for a long time if we want to be successful. I'm just glad I am a left-back and he's left midfield as it means I don't even have to face him in training. He can cause so many problems, so whoever has to face him will worry.

'If Spurs want to be a very big club one day, like Chelsea or Manchester United, we have to keep him. We don't want to try and sell him to the other big clubs.

'We have started well this season. We are new in the Champions League and we have had to get used to playing twice a week, which is not easy. But we have to get on with it if we want to finish fourth. We want to finish higher than that and I think we can.

'It's an open league this year but we need to keep going and make sure we beat the likes of Chelsea, United and Arsenal. We're good enough and have proved it but the key is to keep going and not lose focus.'

Well, this – against the reigning champions – was his and Tottenham's chance to show they did have what it takes to make a genuine title challenge.

Gareth wouldn't come up against Bosingwa – but his replacement Paulo Ferreira would have nightmares about the game for some time to come.

Before the match, Ferreira had sounded confident he could tame Bale, saying: 'If I have to play against Gareth Bale again, I will be ready. I will try to give everything. He did very well against me last April [when Gareth scored as Tottenham beat Chelsea 2-1 at White Hart Lane] but let's see what he will do this time. He is in great shape and it will be difficult to mark him but Spurs are not just about Bale. They have a good team as well. He is a very quick player and it is hard to keep up with him. Even Maicon struggled against him earlier in the season for Inter and he is one of the best right-backs in the world but I will do everything to stop him.'

That everything Ferreira spoke about would, unfortunately for him, turn out to be not quite enough. OK, by his own exacting standards, Gareth would have one of his quieter days at the office – although he did leave Ferreira for dead on several occasions.

Tottenham had gone ahead in the 15th minute with a goal from Roman Pavlyuchenko, but spurned the chance of closing the gap on the top four as the match ended 1-1. An angry Didier Drogba, depressed because Ancelotti had started him on the bench, earned Chelsea a point in the 70th minute. Keeper Gomes allowed the Ivory Coast striker's shot to slip through his hands.

Indeed, Drogba should have won it for the Blues but Gomes saved his penalty after the keeper had upended Ramires in the penalty area.

A sign of Bale's increasing fame came when Michael Essien went in on him studs showing, bruising his ankle. Gareth was predictably angry but Essien did not even receive a yellow card. As Gareth's reputation grew, so did the attention – legitimate or otherwise – that he received from the opposition.

Tottenham had left Chelsea gasping for breath early on, but finished holding on for a point – so the outcome was probably a fair reflection. But those early marauding attacks showed that Gareth and Co had come a long way; from now on, they had earned the right to be seen as equals to the reigning champions. At least.

The *Daily Telegraph*'s Henry Winter summed up that changed state of affairs when he revealed that Spurs were not at all pleased by the 1-1 draw: 'Tottenham's disappointment last night spoke of their heightened expectations. Harry Redknapp has engendered a belief in his players that they can compete for the major honours. If Gareth Bale has shone all term, the eye-catching return of Michael Dawson from ligament surgery added further credibility to their ambitions.'

Winter was right. A Spurs source added: 'It's true, no way were the lads pleased to have got one point. They thought they could have beaten Chelsea – in no way did they feel less than against them. Gareth and the lads were hardly celebrating; they were down in the dumps. It was an opportunity missed to throw down a real marker – to prove that they could beat the reigning champions and could, therefore, be considered realistic contenders for the title. Harry was also down, but was brilliant – he told the lads to go away and keep their chins up, that they would have better days, and that they were good enough to challenge for the title.'

Harry was just as defiant in his press conference after the match, confirming his belief that his team were worthy to be seen as potential champions. He said: 'The title race is very open. I saw Manchester City and they're strong. United, Arsenal, Chelsea, Tottenham. It's open. It's tightened up a lot, and lots of games have become tougher to win. Maybe in all honesty the top teams are not as good as they used to be.

'United aren't as good as they were with Ronaldo and Tevez. Chelsea have had injuries. Against Sunderland, who did fantastic, their back four was not there, they had no Lampard or Essien, no Terry. When they get them back they will be strong. Maybe the top teams aren't quite as strong as they were a year or two ago.'

Harry was in a slightly mischievous mood as exemplified by his final comment when he said that if Frank Lampard had taken the penalty instead of Drogba, he would 'definitely' have scored!

That was about the only moment of fun after the match in the Spurs camp. 'The lads had a few days off from the next match, but it wasn't time spent relaxing,' says a Spurs source. 'No, Harry had them out training hard. He and they all believed they had missed a great chance of showing they should be seen as a real threat in the title race – Gareth and the lads knew they would have put down a real marker if they had beaten Chelsea. OK, a draw was not the end of the world, but they all felt they had enough in the tank to have beaten them.'

The next match in the Christmas schedule looked a tricky one; away at Aston Villa the following Sunday, December 26. Fortunately, the hard work of the previous week, on the training ground and in the gym when the weather turned too snowy and icy, paid dividends. The boys came away from Birmingham with a precious 2-1 win. A brace from the ever-impressive Van der Vaart killed off the Villa, who had only a late Marc Albrighton consolation goal to lift their spirits. Ironically, it had been the young Villa right-winger who had claimed before the game that he felt he could help negate the effect of Gareth down his side of the field. He had said: 'It will be a tough afternoon with the likes of Gareth, who is up there as one of the best in the world at the moment – but that's part of my job. All the top wingers get back to help their full-back out, it's vital. He is having a fantastic season and is showing himself to be an unbelievable player – I rate him massively.

'He's shown that on the Premier League stage and in the Champions League. He tore world-class defenders apart like they weren't there. Just look at his performance against Maicon of Inter Milan. It was sensational. He'll be tough to cope with but I'm confident we have the players to do that. If we keep him quiet, hopefully that means we keep Tottenham quiet and get a good result.'

It didn't quite work that way, but you can't fault the young man for his confidence. Another irony was that the result had been exactly the same when the teams had met at the Lane on October 2 in the same competition (the Premier League), with the same scorers. Yes, it had been 2-1 to Tottenham thanks to goals from Van der Vaart, although Albrighton had put Villa ahead that day.

The match at Villa Park almost three months later, in the grip of bitterly cold winter weather, also served as a reminder of just how far Gareth had come since the start of the season. He had scored 10 goals already during the campaign and, before kick off, was being lauded by Harry Redknapp for providing the most crosses in the Premier League so far that season – a total of 136.

Peter Crouch also spoke out about how much of a joy it was to play up front when he had Gareth on one wing and Lennon on the other, constantly supplying him with fine crosses. 'He [Bale] was great last year, but now in the Champions League it's more high profile,' Crouch told the *People*. 'As a striker, it's a dream to have him on the left and Aaron Lennon on the right. You just have to get yourself in the box and you know nine times out of ten, they will get the right cross in for you.'

Crouch also said that Gareth was always 'brilliant' in training when the striker first joined the club, adding that the Welshman and Arsenal winger Theo Walcott were always touted as potential world-beaters when they were with him at Southampton. He said: 'Gareth was in the youth set-up when

I was at Southampton, and I used to hear people talking about him and Walcott all the time. When I first signed for Spurs, Gareth was in and out of the side – but in training he was brilliant. It was just a case of when he started doing it more consistently and now he is doing it week in, week out against some of the best players in the world.'

As against Chelsea, Gareth was not at his scintillating best at Villa Park. But he didn't need to be. Villa had gone backwards under new boss Gerard Houllier, who appeared determined to rip up the blueprint for success drawn up by previous incumbent Martin O'Neill. Spurs fans were taunting their opposite numbers in the Holte End long before the final whistle; two chants proving particularly galling for the Brummies...'We only had ten men' and 'You're not very good'. Galling in the sense that, well, yes, they were true.

Jermain Defoe's controversial sending-off midway through the first half for elbowing James Collins looked like putting a spanner in the works for Redknapp's game plan (which was basically to outplay and outfox Villa in the midfield battle zone and then hit them fast and hard). But that was not the case; in fact, the sending off merely seemed to spur Spurs on and the win moved them to within one point of the top four.

Gareth had played a key part in the second goal, running from deep in his own half before passing to Lennon, who then set up Van der Vaart for his second goal of the afternoon (and his 10th of the season in all competitions).

Afterwards Redknapp was delighted with the character his team had shown in triumphing with ten men. He told BBC Sport: 'We fight to the end. Playing like this it should be a great season for us. Losing Jermain made it difficult, but we kept the ball well. At half-time I said to the lads I felt there was another goal for us. In the second half they pressed us better but we hit them with a fantastic goal.

'When you can win away with 10 men I think we did a great job. The second one was really important and then I had the feeling we would win the game.'

And so it was on to the club's final match of an eventful 2010 – the home clash with Newcastle United.

But first Gareth would carry out a Christmas charity visit close to his heart. He and team-mate Jonathan Woodgate met parents and children at Whipps Cross University Hospital in Leytonstone, east London, as part of the club's annual visit to the hospital. Gareth said: 'It's always an emotional time. We come to see the kids and it's nice to pay a visit. It's nice to be able to give something back, especially around Christmas time.'

And the staff at the hospital certainly enjoyed seeing Gareth and Jonathan. Whipps Cross head of nursing Eileen Elms said: 'We are extremely grateful to Spurs for this annual visit – they are always very co-operative, spend genuine time talking to the children and parents on the ward and really do make a difference to the environment over the Christmas period, which is a difficult time for anyone to be in hospital.

'The club is very generous with their gifts and make sure all the children get the right present – for this we would like to thank them.'

Then it was back to business for Gareth, with the visit of the Toon Army, who had proved something of a surprise package since coming up from the Championship at the start of the campaign. In big, raw centre-forward Andy Carroll, they had a man who was frightening defenders all over the country – and a man who could well turn out to be the English national team's centre-forward for the next decade if he did not implode through a variety of personal demons.

Certainly Harry Redknapp appreciated the young man's burgeoning talent and had him on his transfer radar, although the big striker would eventually end up at Liverpool for a remarkable record fee for a British player of £35 million at the end of the January transfer window in 2011.

But Harry knew he already had some world beaters in his current squad – and he did little to disguise the fact that he recognised Gareth was chief among them. Before the match, he told reporters: 'For me, at this particular time, he's got to be the footballer of the year in this country. I can't think of anyone who's done as well as him. He's not a player that we would really want to sell. You've got to hang onto your best players.'

One wag of a journo asked Harry if there was any truth in the rumours circulating about a possible swap deal for Manchester City's Emmanuel Adebayor and Gareth Bale. Ridiculous query really given that Adebayor was worth about £15 million – and a month later would be siphoned off to Real Madrid on loan by his unimpressed City boss Roberto Mancini – while the bidding for Bale would surely only start at £45 million plus.

Harry joked: 'Yeah I thought we'd have a straight swap. I thought it sounds like a good deal. It's not April 1st is it? I've never made any inquiries regarding him. I keep reading in the papers that we're after him but that's nothing but a big lie. Gareth Bale is going nowhere right now, as I'm not planning to put him on sale but my decision wouldn't be final.'

The *News of the World* put the story into a slightly more realistic perspective when it said that City had actually offered

Adebayor and £50 million for Bale – a total of around £65 million. But even that made Harry laugh; he had no intention of selling his star man.

Andy Carroll and Newcastle would put up a spirited fight on Boxing Day, but would still go down 2-0 at the Lane, despite facing 10 men for the last 35 minutes. The Sun's Pat Sheehan best summed up the importance of a gritty win by Gareth and the boys when he wrote: 'Make no mistake, this was not a victory over a flaky Newcastle side but a heart-pumping, edge-of-the-seat thriller over Alan Pardew's battling, organised team who were undone by Luka Modric's brilliance.

'For the first time in years, Tottenham are taking the field expecting to win rather than simply believe they are in with a chance. The north Londoners have gatecrashed the top four with a fair share of drama, a large dollop of class and now a touch of steel that underpins every great side.

'Okay, maybe great is too strong a word to describe Tottenham's season just yet but they have emerged from the pack of hopefuls to become genuine contenders.'

It is easy to see what Pat meant when you look at the stirring performance and the undoubted quality of the second goal, the final one of Tottenham's amazing 2010 – a classic scored, inevitably enough, by Gareth himself.

Aaron Lennon had put Spurs ahead just before the hour mark, jinking in from the right and smashing a lovely shot pat the hapless Tim Krul in the Toon goal.

But Gareth's goal was something else – a microcosm of the macrocosm that was his fantastic season so far. It had all the ingredients that had propelled him to worldwide fame in the two Milan games. Namely his speed, skill and deadly finishing.

Luka Modric sent Gareth on his way down that left wing

and the Welshman seemed to pick up even more speed as he zoomed in on the goal and the figure of Krul, who looked like the proverbial rabbit caught in car headlights.

The keeper had absolutely no chance as Gareth then pulled the trigger, unleashing a mighty shot past him and into the corner of the net with just nine minutes remaining. Redknapp commented later on the goal, saying: 'Gareth's done that all season. He went on the outside of Newcastle defender Steven Taylor and smashed it in. Ten goals is an amazing stat for Gareth. You want your central midfield player to get six or seven and your front men to get a few more, but he's scored his goals as a winger.'

Soccer365.com also provided a fine description of Gareth's goal, saying it showed they should now be taken seriously as a real top four outfit: 'Bale scored another magical goal, as he and Tottenham continue to act like the real deal. Spurs' 2-0 victory over Newcastle came as a result of two goals of the highest quality. Aaron Lennon showed world-class technique when he took a simple touch into space, then sent the ball flying into the far corner.

'Bale's goal typified the daring of his play this year. After receiving the ball on the left he cut outside, then inside to lose his defender, before firing a bullet of a shot into the bottom corner from a difficult angle. With Tottenham's stars playing like true stars, there are few that would rule out Spurs' contention for Europe next year.'

The win over the Geordies was due reward for the player of the season so far – and for he and his team-mates efforts in the match after Younes Kaboul was sent off for stupidly butting Cheik Tioté. It was also only Spurs' second clean sheet of the campaign – the first coming in the opening match against

Manchester City – and Gareth used his post-match comments to gave a much-needed verbal fillip to the regularly under-fire keeper Gomes.

He said: 'Gomes has been outstanding all season making unbelievable saves. I think Gomes is THE best, he pulls out saves from nowhere because he is so lanky. 'It's great for the team, it gives us confidence at the back and we keep scoring goals at the other end. He has shown for a long while what a high class keeper he is. 'He has pulled off some fantastic saves this season, week in and week out and hopefully he can carry on keeping a lot more clean sheets in the future.

'The criticism is unfair on him if you have watched him this season he is the best keeper I have ever seen in my life. He has been an outstanding keeper since I have been here and hopefully he can keep getting better and better.'

He then told Sky Sports he was delighted with his goal, saying: 'It was nice to get on the scoresheet. I've got a few goals this season and I want to keep working hard, scoring goals and most importantly helping the team. 'We've had a good couple of days and a good Christmas. We'll be going into a big London derby looking for three points and there's no reason why we can't.'

Gareth also told the official Spurs website he was delighted at the way the festive period had seen the team earn maximum points from the victories over Villa and now Newcastle. He said he felt the way Spurs battled to victory despite being down to ten men in both games showed their character and desire to win was stronger than ever.

And he said he hoped the holiday period run would end in style with a win over Fulham on New Year's Day. Gareth said: 'It was a great win over Newcastle and it's been a good

Christmas period for us. Now we want to take this into the New Year, keep plugging away and get the maximum points like we know we can.

'It's been difficult. Playing two games in three days is difficult enough with 11 men, but playing most of the game at Villa with 10 men is much harder work and the last half hour against Newcastle was a lot of hard work. But we showed the character we've got, the work ethic we've got and we came away with maximum points from the two games and hopefully we can take that into the New Year now.'

He added that he and Spurs' other creative players were enjoying the opportunity to counter attack: 'Sometimes when the opposition attacks it gives the opportunity for me, Aaron, Luka and Rafa to get forward and counter attack them like we did against Villa and Newcastle.

'We showed what we can do. Hopefully we can take that into the second half of the season where it counts and push on.'

Boss Redknapp was also delighted with the result and the character his men had shown. He said: 'It's been a great run and a good start to the Christmas period. Six points is a good start. Three more on Saturday [against Fulham] would be fantastic. But it's going to be hard staying in the top four this season, tougher than the last. United are certainties. City and Arsenal are strong and I think Chelsea will come back strong. I wouldn't rule them out of the title yet. They've had a bad run, but when Frank Lampard and Michael Essien get back fit, you'll see a different Chelsea. I wouldn't write them off.

'City have improved a lot since last year with the money they've spent, so it's going to be close, very tight. If we can make it again this year, it'll be great. Who knows where we'll finish if we can get in there.'

As 2010 shuddered to its inexorable end, December ended much as it had begun. With more accolades – to add to the one from Dalglish – pouring forth for Gareth and the dramatic advances he had made during the year. On Boxing Day, the *Observer*'s Paul Hayward decided Bale was the Player of the Season (so far). Crowning him, Hayward said: 'None of the other names advanced as player-of-the-year-so-far can beat the revelatory force of Bale's presence in an improving Tottenham side. His emergence at outside-left offers proof that young, potential-rich players tend to need a buoyant working atmosphere to fulfil their own promise.'

Could Gareth win the PFA Player of the Year award? The bookies, Betfair, suggested it was unlikely but that it was not impossible. Dan 'The Betting Man' Fitch explained: 'The Premier League season may be at its rough halfway point, but there is another hotly contested title that is already on its back straight. Due to the fact that the votes for the PFA Player of the Year awards are cast well in advance of the end of the season, the race for that individual title is now approaching a climax.

'The favourite to win the title is Gareth Bale. Having only broken into Tottenham's first team last season, Bale has been brilliant this campaign, destroying both domestic defences and those in the Champions League. If Bale were to win the award, he would probably have to break a longstanding voting pattern amongst his peers. In the Premier League era, only one man has ever been voted as Player of the Year, without playing for a side that finished within the top three.'

Maybe it was a mere coincidence...or maybe a good omen, but that player who broke the mould was none other than

David Ginola, in 1993 and, of course, he was playing for Tottenham at the time.

In the *Daily Telegraph*, Andrew Fifield commented on how Gareth and Spurs had taken the Champions League by storm, saying: 'Watching Spurs in Europe is rather akin to seeing a teenager drive a Ferrari: they don't quite know how they got their hands on it and it's probably all going to end in tears, but they are sure going to enjoy the ride while it lasts. Their six games delivered 31 goals – by far the highest aggregate in the competition – and saw them top a supposed group of death, while making a world star out of Gareth Bale.'

He said the high point was Tottenham's 3-1 win over Inter Milan when the 'reigning champions were flattered to lose 3-1 on a night when Bale left Maicon, supposedly the world's best right-back, looking like he belonged on Hackney Marshes.' Fifield argued that Tottenham could go further in the competition and do well the following season 'provided they can keep Bale and Harry Redknapp…'

The *Independent*'s Sam Wallace also picked out Gareth's demolition of Maicon as his footballing moment of 2010, saying: 'My moment of the year, for sheer, rip-roaring, up-and-at-them excitement is Bale's performance against Internazionale in the home game at White Hart Lane on 2 November. I could have picked the second half of the game at San Siro when, after all, he scored a hat-trick in a 4-3 defeat were it not for the fact that there was something mesmerising about his performance in north London.

'Every great performance requires talent, self-belief and determination – of which Bale had all. Great performances are also measured by the stature of the opponent who is overcome and in the Inter full-back Maicon there was no greater test for Bale.'

Soccer magazine offered some controversy – by refusing to pick Gareth for the left midfield/wing role, saying it should go to Andreas Iniesta of Barcelona. They wrote: 'We could put Gareth Bale as left midfielder but that place is reserved for Iniesta. But because of Bale's very powerful left foot and his speed, we simply had to find him the place in the "Best Eleven", so he is our left fullback. Although he didn't win anything last year, he thrilled the soccer world with his performances against Inter in Champions League...he scored a hat-trick in the first game and in the second he caused major problems for Inter's defenders.'

Goal's Ewan MacDonald argued that Gareth was certainly one, if not the, best young player in the Champions League so far. He said: 'Perhaps the best youngster of all in the group stages – and certainly the only one to make Carlo Garganese's [editor of Goal.com] Team of the Group Stage – Gareth Bale had fans worldwide glued to their screens as he ran riot in Spurs' famous win over Inter. Maicon, once almost invulnerable at right-back, was made to look ponderous and irresponsible by the Welshman, who has inevitably found himself linked with no small number of clubs, ranging from Manchester United to Real Madrid.'

Respected Sky Sports pundit Chris Kamara also pointed to Gareth being the star of the season so far, although he also emphasised he felt Arsenal's Samir Nasri was in the same class. Kamara told Skysport.com: 'Arsenal have always had someone special in their team - from Thierry Henry to Dennis Bergkamp – and they've been looking for someone to step forward this year. Samir Nasri has done that and he was wonderful against Fulham. On *Goals On Sunday* this weekend, I discussed the Player of the Season so far with Ben Shephard and Ian Holloway and we decided it was between Nasri and Gareth Bale. Ben said the best performance was Bale's against Inter, but the more consistent player was Nasri. 'Personally, I think it's hard to compare them because Bale has a more regulated position on the left wing and will be tightly marked some weeks. Nasri is more of a floating player and he can go about his business a lot more easily. What I would say is that they're two outstanding individuals and they've lit up the Premier League for the first half of the season.'

Another Sky pundit and *Daily Mail* columnist, Jamie Redknapp, also had kind words for Gareth, saying in his *Mail* column: 'We've all gone Gareth Bale crazy, but I picked him out as one of my players to watch for the season - I was hearing so many good things from the training pitch. He can now be the best left-sided player in the world. And he can do that playing for Tottenham...

'With Gareth and Ryan Giggs, the two best left-sided players of the last 20 years have both been Welsh. It's a weak position in the England team and we have all had to look jealously towards Wales.'

Then Gareth earned an accolade from abroad when he was been included in the team of the year chosen by the readers of the respected and influential Madrid-based sports newspaper Marca. The poll received more than 125,000 votes and Gareth was in exulted company in the line-up. The team lined up like this: Casillas (Real Madrid); Maicon (Inter Milan), Pique (Barcelona), Puyol (Barcelona), Bale (Spurs); Xabi Alonso (Real Madrid), Xavi (Barcelona), Iniesta (Barcelona); Ronaldo (Real Madrid), Villa (Barcelona), Messi (Barcelona).

Gareth was the only British player selected, making the side at left-back in a team containing seven of Spain's World Cup-winning side, and only one other player outside that country…ironically, it was Maicon, the man whose reputation he wrecked while at the same time as establishing his own in the two Champions League group encounters against Inter Milan.

Finally, the fans back in the UK had their say. Of course, in the UK, many had openly embraced Gareth as their Player of the 2010/11 Season (so far), but even abroad Tottenham fans were hailing him as simply the best.

A typical example was from the Tottenham Hotspur Canadian Supporters' Club, who declared on their website, spurscanada.ca, on Boxing Day: 'Nobody can deny how great Gareth Bale is. He is fast, two footed and strong. He can go inside and out, play defensive and attacking but most of all his main virtue is in his mind. He has great desire and this desire propels him to go forward and make things happen – even sometimes when there seems there is no hope. We all know what he did to Maicon in Milan and then back at Tottenham. No team can feel comfortable playing against him or Tottenham today. When they double and triple mark him, it opens the door for great runs by Lennon on the other side. When they stop Lennon it all went through Modric. Gareth Bale sets the tone for the team and the pace and he can win games alone and open the door for all of our attacking weapons.'

There is a saying in football that the fan always knows best: I think those comments from Canada prove it is correct. I particularly agree with the idea that 'his main virtue is in his mind'. It is an analysis that few pundits have made but, when you think about it, is massively appropriate. After all, this was the boy who had the strength of mind to come back after several injury layoffs determined to reach the very top – and who worked doggedly hard to do just that.

In 2010 Gareth had been named BBC Wales Sports Personality of the Year, shortlisted for the FIFA/FIFpro and UEFA.com Teams of the Year, named BBC London Footballer of the Year and was third in World Soccer magazine's Young Player of the Year.

And as we rang in the new year of 2011, there was no doubt that he had certainly earned all the plaudits and accolades. And just to ram home the fact that Tottenham viewed him as their key man for the future, Daniel Levy added to the constant denials from Harry Redknapp that Gareth would not be sold in the January transfer window. The Spurs chairman told the club's AGM: 'I've never deemed us to be a selling club. Both [Dimitar] Berbatov and Michael Carrick had two years left on their contract, both players wanted to go and that was the reason they were sold.

'But in the case of Gareth, he's got a long contract and I can assure you he will not be sold.'

So that was that. Gareth Bale would be going nowhere and he certainly had enough ambitions to keep him happy at the Lane for the foreseeable future.

As 2011 loomed, he revealed to friends that he had a new aim…a new year's resolution he was determined he would keep: he wanted to do even better in the second half of the season and, hopefully, pick up even more honours and awards. This was not a boy who would be happy to simply rest on his laurels…

Chapter 16

RING IN
THE NEW

Gareth Bale would begin 2011 in the same style as he ended 2010. He had said a fond farewell to the old year by scoring Tottenham's final goal – and would ring in the new by scoring their first goal in the 1-0 win over Fulham at the Lane.

Cottagers boss Mark Hughes, another former boss of the Welsh national team, had predicted before the match that Gareth was going to be a world-class star. Hughes said, 'Gareth has come on in leaps and bounds. Everyone was aware of the talent he had as a kid but at times he looked awkward because of his style. Now he has filled out and with every step of his progression he is accomplished and it doesn't faze him. If he keeps going then there is no saying what level he could reach.'

Gareth's winner extended Tottenham's perfect Christmas

and sent them back into the top four. And he had extra reason to celebrate his 11th goal of the campaign…for it was a rare headed goal. It came just before the interval as he met Van der Vaart's free kick, nodding the ball past Mark Schwarzer. A Spurs source said: 'Gareth was on cloud nine after getting that goal with his head. He doesn't score many with his head so he was delighted to put that one away. Harry is always encouraging him to get in there with his head, he's a big lad, a bit like Cristiano Ronaldo in size and stature and skill – and everyone knows how brilliant Ronaldo is in the air. There's no reason why Gareth can't build on it and create a name for himself as a fantastic header of the ball, too. His aim is to be an all-round great, so don't be surprised if he works on that aspect of his game more in training over the next few months – and adds to that New Year's Day headed goal with a good few more!'

Many pundits wondered aloud whether the headed goal was pure luck. Gareth cleared that one up with Tottenham's official club website when asked if it was indeed a fluke – or whether he meant to score. 'Yes, I did mean it!' he said. 'Just before Rafa was going to take the free-kick, he said to run towards the near post, I did that and reacted to the free-kick. The ball was right in front of me and I had to direct it as best I could towards goal and thankfully it went in.

'It's great to get on the scoresheet as often as possible and I just hope to keep doing that to help out the team.'

Gareth Messenger, of football website A Different League, summed up the importance of Bale to Spurs when he said of the Fulham match: 'Gareth Bale has excelled and it was Bale's 11th goal of the season that gave his side victory over Mark Hughes' Fulham side at White Hart Lane on New Year's Day.

An insipid first half display from both sides created little in chances but Bale rose highest to direct Rafael van der Vaart's fiercely struck free-kick to give his side all three points and take Spurs into the Champions League places.

'The combination of Van der Vaart and Bale proved to be vital yet again for the home side. In what was a lacklustre display by Tottenham, the performances of the Dutchman and the young Welshman proved key in the London side's victory.'

And Peter Berlin of Inside Soccer made the point that Bale was more than capable of overcoming the double marking and tough tactics of stubborn defences as teams wised up to his speed and skills. Berlin said: '2010 was a breakthrough year for Tottenham's left-sided Welsh lightning bolt. But Premier League defences, helped by the permissive attitude of English referees, have quickly found ways to neutralise his thrusts – chiefly by thumping him at every opportunity. On Saturday, John Pantsil of Fulham, quickly earned a yellow card for hacking down Bale...

'[But] one mark of a great player is that when one door is shut, he will find another way through. In a tight game, Bale made the difference. When Spurs won a free kick after 42 minutes, Bale had a brief chat with Rafael van der Vaart, then trotted forward, leaving the kick to the Dutchman. Van der Vaart smashed the ball toward the far post. Bale, standing near the penalty spot, flicked his head at the flying ball and deflected it past the wrong-footed Mark Schwarzer. It was an impressive flash of courage, reflexes and fast thinking.'

Gareth's winner extended Tottenham's unbeaten run to eight games and lifted them back into the top four at Chelsea's expense. It was a great start to the New Year and boss Redknapp praised his men – a virtually unchanged side that had played its third match in seven days…and won the lot!

He said: 'It was a tough game and credit to Fulham, they played very well and put us under pressure. You could see an equaliser coming. But there are no easy games. We looked like one of two were running on empty. But you're in a no-win situation, aren't you?

'If you go and make seven or eight changes, like Arsenal did [at Wigan], everybody goes, "Why did he change his team?", if you don't get the result. I stuck with the ones who have played. That's what I consider the best team for today and we clawed a result out. I thought [Michael] Dawson and [William] Gallas were outstanding when we were under pressure. We played with 10 men Sunday and Tuesday but nine points from the week is fantastic. Any team that achieves something don't play well every week but they win.'

Redknapp added to the speculation that former England skipper David Beckham was about to join the club on loan from LA Galaxy when he added: 'He could've come on when we were under pressure. He might've kept the ball for us.' Former Wimbledon boss Dave Bassett would almost immediately argue against Beckham's arrival at the Lane – contending that it would be bad news for the likes of Gareth Bale. He said: 'You'd have the Beckham circus that comes to London. Let's face it Gareth Bale's getting plenty of publicity now, as is [Rafael] van der Vaart, and all of a sudden it's all going to be about Beckham. If he doesn't play you're all going to be asking why, if he does play you're going to be asking why are they leaving Aaron Lennon or Gareth Bale out?

'I think you've got a system with Tottenham where this is the club at the moment, the one that's got the glamour, they've taken over from Chelsea and everyone wants to be part of Tottenham. I think Tottenham are going along very nicely and you've got be careful you don't upset the ship.'

Fulham boss Mark Hughes was hardly concerned with the ins and outs of the Beckham saga. He was downhearted after his side's defeat but paid tribute to Gareth's goal, saying it was 'the difference between the two sides' and that it only confirmed what he had felt before kick off – that the boy could now kick on and become one of the greats of the modern game.

As we have noted, Gareth knew it was unlikely he would ever make a major international finals with Wales – although he would never give up hope...that was one other ambition he maintained he was determined to achieve. But at the start of 2011 it became clear he might be able to achieve international recognition in a more unlikely way, as part of a proposed Great Britain team in the 2012 Olympics to be held in London.

There had been rumours during the latter half of 2010 that Gareth and his Welsh team-mate Aaron Ramsey, of Arsenal, could be picked for the GB team. But political in-fighting among the Football Associations of the home nations had thrown that into doubt.

Basically, the Welsh, the Scots and the Northern Irish feared that if they agreed to compete as part of a British team, they faced losing their own individual rights to take part as separate nations at other events. For example, what if FIFA decided that a Great Britain team should compete in the World Cup, or the European Nations Championships? Was that the next logical step if they caved in and agreed to their players competing for Britain at the 2012 Olympics?

In 2008 the Football Association of Wales (FAW) warned that they would not allow any of its players to take part at London 2012. 'If any of our players put their hand up and said they wanted to play in the Olympics, they would not be able to do it,' said Dave Collins, the then-secretary of the FAW. 'They are Welsh players and we would not give them permission.'

I could certainly understand the fears of the Welsh, Scottish and Northern Irish FAs. They quite rightly were reluctant to lose their independence – and were rightly fearful of FIFA. The president of that organisation, Sepp Blatter, was a renowned maverick who could quite easily demand a combined British team so that he could make space for more of the newer, smaller nations who were asking for a place at the World Cup feast.

But by the start of 2011 it was becoming increasingly likely that Gareth would be able to play for the GB team. He had already said that he would like the chance of doing so. The previous November he had said: 'I feel the Olympics would be a great opportunity for a young player like me to play in a major tournament.

'Look, I'm Welsh and we all know Wales don't tend to qualify for too many. I would love to play in the Olympics, especially as it would be a part of a Great Britain team. Of course, I always want Wales to be Wales. That is important and I wouldn't want that to change but if there's a chance for me to play in a GB team that would be a great idea.'

And in 2011 The British Olympic Association (BOA) confirmed they would expect the English FA, who were administering the Olympic team, to select the best possible side – and that included the Welsh, Scottish and those from Northern Ireland. The BOA warned that if they FA did pick an all-England XI, they would be in breach of the Olympic charter, which outlaws discrimination. Jim Shaw, chairman of the Irish Football Association, admitted that the discrimination element meant they and the other FAs now had to look at the GB team in a different way. He said: 'If a player wants to play, we would probably not stand in his way. But I would be doubtful if a player would be happy to play under those circumstances.'

A BOA source told ESPNsoccernet that Gareth was a 'must have' player for the Olympic team, and that discreet enquires had already been made to the Welsh FA about his potential availability.

The source said: 'Gareth Bale has emerged this season as one of the most exciting players in world football, and the plan is not just to field an Olympic football team, but to put together a team that has a chance of going for gold.

'You're not going to achieve that without players of Gareth Bale's quality. But so much depends on the attitude of the Welsh FA as he is a Welsh international. The parameters of the home nations' participation is the subject of wide scale debate.'

Those were concerns for later – there would be an International Board meeting in March to discuss the thorny subject. For now, in the first week of January 2011, Gareth had more pressing matters to deal with. Like the tough-looking fixture away at Everton on Wednesday January 5. Before the match, Gareth revealed a little more about what had turned him into the goliath of a footballer he had become, as it was confirmed that his average of 5.2 dribbles per game was the highest in the season's Champions League so far.

Gareth said the cross-country running at school had built up his energy levels and strength and that he loved running at defences. He said: 'I just think that if you have the chance in a game to go forward into a good area then that's the kind of sacrifice you make for your team. I don't think of it as a way of tiring out full-backs. I just do it until I'm tired.

'I think teams have doubled up on me, but that's a compliment in a way. I'm finding new ways to get past players in different positions - it's interesting and something I enjoy. If someone knocks me over I just get up, and if they keep doing it, eventually they'll get sent off. Someone might decide to "smash" me but it doesn't bother me. I'll just get up and go again.'

Gareth also told *Four Four Two* magazine that he enjoyed playing against the big European teams as they are also not afraid to attack, meaning the games are often more open and entertaining, which suited his game.

The day before the Everton match, former Toffees player Ian Snodin predicted that the encounter could provide a 'left-flank masterclass. He told the *Liverpool Echo*: 'Gareth Bale and Leighton Baines have both enjoyed outstanding seasons so far. And both Everton and Spurs look likely to produce their most threatening work down that wing...I was told about Bale's quality when he was just a 16-year-old. My brother Glyn was working at Southampton with George Burley and I expressed my surprise when they sold Wayne Bridge to Chelsea.

'He told me they already had a kid ready to step straight into the first team – a player with pace, strength, someone who could strike a ball and take a long throw-in – all at the age of 16. When I saw Bale for myself play in the Championship he confirmed everything I had been told, and more.'

BBC Sport also picked up on the potential fireworks Bale

and Baines could provide, saying: 'This match pits arguably the two form left-sided players in the league against each other. Leighton Baines has been outstanding for Everton this season and has buried the ghost of his World Cup snub, while the performances of Tottenham's Gareth Bale have seen his status upgraded to world class.

'Two goals over the Christmas period lifted his tally for the season to 11. Few defenders have been able to shackle the Welsh winger, but the wily skills of Phil Neville neutralised his threat at White Hart Lane in October with a defensive display that turned him into a surprise hit on social networking side Twitter as fans lauded his performance.'

The fans were also busy on the websites and blog sites before the match at Goodison, with many commenting on just how far Gareth had come in the last 12 months. Typical of the sentiments being aired were those from Mark, on The Boys From White Hart Lane blog. He amusingly and cleverly highlighted the Welshman's development by suggesting he had been taken under the wing of a Buddhist monk. He wrote: '...got injured and retreated into his shell to hibernate for about two and a half years. It's not confirmed but rumour has it he spent this time with a Buddhist monk, who taught and trained him the ways of The Force and how to basically run like a freaking bullet. The monk motivated young Bale by placing a poster of Brazilian full back Maicon up on the wall at an unreachable height, slowly lowering the image with every step of progress Bale took. "This", the monk said, "is your destiny. You will one day learn the skills to make this all-conquering right back look like Stephen Carr after a trip to Spurs' Christmas party."'

Another fine football blog site, the Flat Back Four, made the observation that for all Gareth's headline-grabbing speed and skills, the other thing that helped him stand out from previous seasons was his consistency: 'In a team of Luka Modric, Rafael Van der Vaart and William Gallas, Gareth Bale is more than holding his own and is Spurs' Mr. Consistency personified. That's been his main weakness over the years, a lack of consistency. This season, however, he has come of age. There were inklings of his emergence at the tail end of last season but now his performances have made him the top left sided player in Europe.

'The change from defender to winger has helped him most definitely but more importantly, this season, there is more intelligence in his play. His crossing has markedly improved, his awareness and determination to get involved has helped propel him to become one of the most sought-after players in Europe.

'Gareth Bale – Spurs' Mr. Consistency. The transformation from "Jonah" to "Spurs jewel" is now complete.'

The match on Merseyside would certainly test Gareth and Tottenham's consistency after that superb Christmas spell. It had ominous looking omens for Tottenham and boss Redknapp. Spurs had failed to win on their last six visits to Merseyside to play either Everton or Liverpool and Harry had won on just one of 27 visits to the city of Liverpool as a manager – his only ever success being Portsmouth's 3-0 triumph at Everton in August 2008.

And, of course, the last time the clubs had met, at the back end of October at the Lane, Everton had pulled off a 1-1 draw – with the aforementioned dangerman Baines opening the scoring and Gareth finding it tough to break down the spirited resistance of Phil Neville and his helpers.

Gareth arrived on Merseyside in high spirits after a great festive season. He walked into Goodison and was almost immediately asked what he thought about the latest transfer link – one that had him going to Turin and Juventus in the summer. Reports in Italy had claimed that Juve, the old lady of Turin, would make a summer bid for Gareth.

They had apparently initially been set to make a move for Lyon's Michel Bastos but had turned their attentions to Bale after his brilliant form so far in the 2010/11 season. Bianconeri general director Giuseppe Marotta was quoted by sources as saying he remained hopeful he would land the player in the summer – despite the fact that Harry Redknapp had made it clear he had no intention of selling him even if they were offered silly money, and Gareth's repeated protestations that he had no intention of quitting the Lane.

Italian agent Peppino Tirri also stirred up the nonsense by confirming that Juve wanted him – and that there was a good chance of the deal happening in June. Tirri said: 'I can confirm interest from Juventus, but we are talking about June and certainly not January. Milan and Inter have also shown an interest in the Welsh player, especially as Bale would like to play in Italy soon. I'd say there's a good chance of it happening, but more likely in June, as it'd be very difficult for the Italian sides to take him in the transfer window.

'Real Madrid would be the only club capable of signing Bale in January, especially as they are really trying very hard to make it happen. 'Jose Mourinho has set his sights on him and wants to take him straight away, otherwise the conversation will resume in June.'

When asked at Goodison about the comments and the possibility of a move to Italy, Gareth merely laughed and shook his head. Well, he would laugh, wouldn't he? He had already said he had no intention of leaving Tottenham – and why would he go to Juventus, a team who were no longer considered in the top two outfits in Italy, let alone Europe?

They had been playing in the much derided Europa League while Gareth was competing in the Champions League with Spurs. Juve may have been one of the big clubs in Europe in the old days, but now they were not in Tottenham's league in terms of star players or strength in the team itself. No wonder Gareth could afford a wry smile!

'Gareth and the boys were confident they could do a job on Everton,' says a Spurs source. 'Sure, they all knew they had not had much good luck on Merseyside over the last couple of years, but they were full of confidence in their own abilities and were truly starting to believe they could beat anyone. There was a lot of talent in the side and a lot of hope and optimism for the New Year. They were convinced this would be their year – the one in which people finally sat up and took notice of them.'

Long-time supporter Nat McEwan was also convinced this would be the year, saying: 'You just got a feeling, something hard to put into words, that we were watching something special with Harry at the helm – and the likes of Gareth and Rafa and Luka pulling the strings. It was a special team with a special manager at a special time. There was a great optimism among the fans that, yes, after many false dawns, this could finally be our year. And that even if we didn't quite make it, we were certainly on the right tracks to do so next season – as long as we could hang on to Harry, Gareth, Rafa and Luka.'

A few hours before kick off Gareth was asked about Phil

Neville's contribution in negating his usual dynamic performance at the Lane back in October. Gareth said: 'He has a lot of experience but it will be a difficult game for everybody. Hopefully, everyone can win their personal battles and we come out on top. At White Hart Lane it wasn't just him that made it hard for me, he had two or three players helping him. The right winger was right on my toes all the time so I couldn't get the ball and the midfielder or centre-back would come across if I got past him.

'It was the way they set the team up, teams do that against me and Aaron Lennon at the minute. We have to figure ways to get around it now. Every match we go into now will always be tough. Teams are lining up against us in a defensive way and it is hard to break them down. It's a compliment for them to do that and shows how well we are doing. We just have to take advantage of that now. It's nice to have a different challenge and to improve as a player, which is the most important thing. Hopefully, I can keep doing that and keep helping Tottenham.

'We want to continue our run going but it's always tough up at Everton. We know what a good team they are even though they're not in the League position that they'd like. It's still going to be difficult for us, they always make it hard for us. They showed it at White Hart Lane and I think this will be even more difficult up there. They are definitely better than their position in the League suggests. It has been difficult for a lot of teams this season because everyone is beating everyone.

'There are a lot of teams down there who probably shouldn't be. We will be prepared and ready and hopefully get the three points.'

Gareth was right in that it would be tough – but he was

wrong in his anticipation of three more points to help push on Tottenham's top four bandwagon. A resilient Everton would end their 11-match unbeaten run and Gareth would come up against a determined Phil Neville and Co. The only joy from the trip to the frozen North was that Chelsea also lost – 1-0 at Wolverhampton – which meant Spurs kept fourth place, a point ahead of the Blues with both teams having completed 21 games.

Louis Saha put the Toffees ahead within three minutes – his first goal since his brace helped beat Chelsea the previous February – 11 months and 25 Premier League games previous. Saha struck before Spurs had chance to settle, hammering home a 25-yard drive into the corner.

Rafael van der Vaart pulled one back with a header eight minutes later, but Saha proved a thorn in Tottenham's side again on the three-quarter hour mark, indirectly setting up Seamus Coleman for the winner. The Frenchman's sizzling shot was parried by Gomes, but only as far as Coleman who gratefully headed home the rebound.

Relieved Everton boss David Moyes, who had seen his side slip dangerously towards the drop zone, said: 'Everybody knows that is what Louis is capable of. Anyone who has worked or played with him will tell you he's a fantastic talent and can produce that sort of thing. If you are not scoring regularly then it can affect your confidence and to score lifts it immensely. 'Overall he played really well and even if he hadn't scored I would have said he did really well. But the goal is important for him and for us. We are a good team who can play against the good teams and perform well.'

It was Everton's first home win over Spurs in seven years and only their second in the last 11 games and Moyes added:

'I am very pleased with that win, I thought it was a really good game, because whoever beats Tottenham is going to have to play well. I think we are a good team ourselves, but we find it difficult to score. We had improved vigour and determination and made sure we got more balls into the box than recently. We needed to show something tonight – all the players and me. We did that, we were outstanding and we showed we can play against the top sides.'

He was asked about Bale and Van der Vaart and said: 'Both great players, both dangerous players, but tonight was not to be their night – thankfully! Gareth Bale should get the major plaudits because he is an unbelievable talent but Phil Neville did a brilliant job on him. But if you were to talk about a wide player tonight, you can only talk about Seamus Coleman. He should have scored before he did.'

Gareth had a couple of major runs that panicked the Toffees' defence and set up Peter Crouch for what should have been an easy goal before the interval – but the big striker fluffed his lines by straying half a yard offside as Bale flung over the cross for an easy tap-in.

Harry Redknapp was generous in his praise for Everton after the defeat, which meant he had just one win to his name in 28 visits to Merseyside as a manager. He said: 'We started poorly but we came back and got a goal and should have gone in 2-1 up at the break. At half-time I would not have taken a draw but credit to Everton, they upped the pace in the second half.

'They made lots of chances and we had chances on the break. It is not an easy place to come to. We should have scored just before half-time; Crouchy shouldn't be offside there, but credit to Everton. In the second half they were great and had some great chances to score. They pressed us well and worked their socks off.'

Rory Smith in the *Daily Telegraph* suggested that the defeat could hasten the arrival of David Beckham at the Lane. He said: 'If Harry Redknapp had any doubt as to whether David Beckham was worth signing, he will have found all the proof he needed in 90 breathless, frenetic minutes at Goodison Park...What a difference a cool head...a wizened winner of football matches, might have made.

'True, Beckham might have struggled with the pace. His body may not be up to the breakneck speed of the league he left behind. But his calm, his composure would have been valuable as Redknapp's side tried to control their energetic hosts, and his leadership might even have stymied David Moyes's team's rousing crescendo...'

Redknapp also admitted that Beckham could have helped out Gareth and Co, saying: 'I think he can keep the ball and second half we were not keeping hold off the ball. Aaron Lennon didn't get into the game too much and I think Beckham could get it out of his feet and with Crouch playing he could be the perfect foil for him.'

It had certainly not been a night Gareth's would want to dwell on for long – although that was just what he did on the bus home. He was taken off on the hour after a few tough (and a couple of clumsy) tackles from Neville and was quiet on the four-hour journey. 'He never likes to lose and always analyses his own performance and that of the team by himself,' said a Spurs source. 'It seemed a long journey back to London that night.'

Redknapp would later reveal that Gareth had hurt his back and that he was an injury concern for the FA Cup match against Charlton the following weekend after limping off. Redknapp admitted: 'I should have taken him off at half-time. His back went into a spasm and he didn't feel good.'

Ironically, it had been revealed before the match that Gareth was the most fouled Tottenham player so far this season – suffering 37 while only committing six. Even Everton fans were keen to say how much they respected Gareth's dramatic rise to the top. One, writing in the Liverpool Echo, commented: 'Credit to Spurs, no "ten man" defensive tactics from a side full of quality, the result a great free flowing game full of what's best in English football with a result that was more than satisfying, and fully deserved on the night. Most Blues, myself included, didn't rate our chances very highly against the talent of the class act that is today's Spurs – with Bale, van der Vaart and Modric. We had no Cahill or Jags [Jagielka], and recent poor form said a draw would have been a good result for us...'

Yes, Gareth Bale was a fair player as well as a brilliant one. He was also an essentially optimistic lad and soon put the Everton defeat behind him. There was much to play for as the New Year opened up and Gareth wanted to be at the forefront of Tottenham's battle on three fronts – the Premier League, the Champions League and the FA Cup. These were exciting time for the Welsh boy wonder who had now made his home at White Hart Lane, North London.

Chapter 17

PLAYER OF
THE YEAR

In terms of club silverware, the 2010/11 season would peter
out into disappointment for Gareth Bale. The campaign
that had promised so much on the Premier League,
Champions League and FA Cup front would end with no
trophies – and the added agony of also missing out on a return
to Champions League action as they finished fifth in the
English top flight.

Tottenham did manage to make it into the Europa League
courtesy of that fifth-place finish, but that was small change
when compared to the big European glory nights Gareth and
his team-mates had experienced in the continent's No. 1
competition. As a yardstick for the Europa League's merits,
the final in May 2010 would be contested by two Portuguese
sides, Porto and Braga in Dublin – amid hardly a flicker of
interest among fans in the UK.

Certainly, Harry Redknapp was aware that he would have to get Spurs back into the Champions League the following season – or risk losing stars like Gareth and Rafael van der Vaart. These players were happy enough to commit themselves to the Tottenham cause for another 12 months – because they loved the club and the fans and appreciated what the club had done for them – but they were ambitious. Gareth, in particular, wanted to win medals and cups at the very highest level of the game.

His season hit a low when, as mentioned in the last chapter, he was injured in the defeat at Everton on January 5 2011. He played in the 0-0 home draw with Manchester United but then suffered a recurrence of the back problem that had surfaced at Everton, breaking down 11 minutes into Spurs' 1-1 draw at Newcastle on 22 January. It would be nearly seven weeks before Gareth once again pulled on a Spurs shirt, returning as a 69th-minute substitute in the entertaining 3-3 draw with Wolves at Molineux on March 6. Three days later he again emerged just after the hour in the 0-0 draw with AC Milan, a result that sent Tottenham through to the high point of their season, a Champions League quarter-final tie with crack Spanish side Real Madrid.

Even without Gareth, the boys had enough in the tank to beat AC Milan 1-0 in the San Siro a fortnight earlier – thanks to a Peter Crouch goal – to clinch a dream tie against Real Madrid (which, unfortunately, would turn into something of a nightmare).

At the same time, Spurs fans were boosted even more when it was announced that Gareth had signed a new contract with the club. The four-and-a-half year deal would tie him to the club until 2015, replacing his previous contract which ran until 2014.

Gareth said: 'I am absolutely delighted to sign this new contract with the club. I am enjoying my football at Tottenham. I want us to keep going forward as a team and hopefully we can achieve big things. We have got a great squad that is still young and we are going places. It is great to commit to the club, and hopefully we can achieve what we believe we can with this squad.

'The players want what the fans want, and performing in front of these fans is a special experience. I definitely believe we can challenge for a title very soon. That is why I have signed. Every year as a minimum we are aiming to qualify for the Champions League, so we are definitely going in the right direction.

'We have proven in the Champions League this season that we can compete with the best and we are in the last eight now and there is no reason we can't go further this season and in years to come.'

Boss Redknapp was also delighted that his star man had put pen to paper. He said: 'It's great to have Gareth sign a new contract at the club. He is a fantastic player and the type we need to be keeping at Spurs. He's got his whole future ahead and he has everything going for him. Gareth is now one of the top left-sided players in the world. He really is an amazing talent and can only get better. He is a smashing lad as well, which is equally as important.'

On March 19 Gareth finally played a full 90 minutes after his return from injury when West Ham visited the Lane (a 0-0 draw) but broke down again during international week. He had already missed out on Wales' 3-0 Carling Nations Cup defeat by the Republic of Ireland six weeks earlier, but would now not feature in the Euro 2012 qualifier against the English at the Millennium Stadium after suffering a hamstring strain.

Gareth told friends he was 'gutted' to miss out. He had been relishing the fixture and was using it as a target for his rehabilitation after the injury lay-off. Indeed, beforehand, he would admit he was extremely hopeful that he and the Welsh team could get something from the match. He said: 'We're quietly confident in the camp that we've got enough to pull off an upset. People might laugh at us but we fully believe that we've got some good players here and we'll be fully prepared and ready to take it to England.

'A lot of us haven't played against England for the full team. It will be a great occasion and one we all want to play in. I definitely think it will be a great experience for us to play at the highest level and it will stand us in good stead for the future. Now is the time we need to start delivering and there's no better game than to beat England.

'With a full crowd there on the weekend it will give us that extra bit of confidence and belief. You've seen what it used to be like five or six years ago with all the fans there [the last time England played in Wales in 2005 was the last sell-out international football match at the Millennium Stadium].

'I was one of those fans at the time and it was an electric atmosphere. All the fans were with the team. We want to be going out to that and feeling comfortable with everybody on our side. Hopefully we can turn the Millennium Stadium into a fortress and if we do that we've got a great chance of qualifying, maybe not this campaign, but definitely the next one.'

Typically, Gareth was also keen to stress that the Wales team wasn't a one-man band – and that his team-mates were just as important. He added, 'I don't think any player can carry the whole team and it's about the team playing well together and not individuals. As long as we work as a team then I think we can go a long way.'

They were noble, selfless, generous sentiments from a boy who was clearly the star of the show. But it would all end in tears when he was declared unfit the week before the match. The Football Association of Wales released a statement to explain just why he would be absent – and that it was not their fault. 'After playing 90 minutes on Saturday [against West Ham] he felt some muscle tightness. Initially, this was expected to be muscle soreness. On joining up with the Welsh squad he was kept off his feet in training for two days to recover.

'As he still felt tight in the warm-up on Tuesday, Gareth was pulled out of the session. He did not train at all on Wednesday and was sent for a scan. The scan revealed that Gareth Bale picked up his injury last week.'

Wales boss Gary Speed bemoaned the loss of his best player for the biggest game of the campaign on March 26, admitting, 'Any team would miss a player of Gareth's quality.' England's Peter Crouch was sad for his Spurs team-mate that he would miss out, but relieved that a major threat would be absent from the England side's opponents.

Before learning of the injury setback Crouch had rhapsodised about Bale, warning he presented the greatest danger to English hopes. England boss Fabio Capello had been planning on asking Aaron Lennon to drop back from attack to help Glen Johnson cope with Gareth.

And Crouch had stressed just why England feared him so, saying: 'Gareth's been on fire for the last two years. Sometimes he's unplayable. We'll look at videos and I'm sure Gareth will

263

be prominent in a lot of those videos. We might have to double up on him.

'Gareth is only young, developing, and in that position he's got to be up there with the top players in the world. What he did to Inter Milan, over two games, showed people what he is capable of. He's got some way to go to be Lionel Messi's standard. Messi and Cristiano Ronaldo are out there on their own at the moment, with the sheer number of goals they've scored.

'The thing about Gareth is his energy. He's got tremendous pace. He runs the whole length of the pitch with the ball then he runs the whole length back just as quickly. Then he's ready to do it again in a minute's time.

'It's the sheer energy. Sometimes you look at him and think 'how does he do that?' I get tired watching him. He's got fantastic ability and a great left foot as well.

'Gareth is top class and he can really hurt you – it's a shame at times he is not English.'

Crouch had a point. Without Gareth's speed, energy and inspiration, the Welsh crashed 2-0, with Frank Lampard and Darren Bent grabbing the goals.

At least there was the consolation of the Real Madrid encounter looming on the horizon. But that would end in similar – but even worse – disappointment as Tottenham went down 4-0 at the Bernabeu in the first leg of their Champions League quarter-final encounter. Gareth did last the full 90 minutes, but that was essentially thanks to the foolishness of Crouch, who had got himself sent off just a quarter of an hour into the match. The fact that Spurs would now be fighting one of the best club teams in the world for 75 minutes with a man short left boss Redknapp with few options but to keep his best player on the field for the duration. He could have subbed him, of course, but that risked the team suffering an even worse hammering as Bale provided his usual defensive/midfield balance.

Gareth was clearly struggling towards the end of the match, needing treatment for cramp and soreness in his legs as the evening that had promised to be such a great adventure and a highlight in the club's history petered out into disappointment and anguish at the 4-0 battering.

Yet it had all started so brightly and so full of optimism. The Spurs fans had enjoyed a relaxing day in Madrid and were in fine voice and fine fettle as they settled down in the upper tiers of one of the world's greatest football stadiums for a night they hoped would end with even more glory for Redknapp's developing team.

Redknapp had noted how the Spanish media had swarmed all over Gareth when Tottenham had arrived at Madrid airport for the match – and how they had asked if the Welsh sensation could be tempted to leave White Hart Lane for the Bernabeu. When Harry was asked at a pre-match press conference by a British journalist if the obvious fascination in his star player by the Spanish giants worried him, he said, 'If someone is going to come along and offer millions of pounds to move him and he is going to get fantastic wages, it is difficult for them not to get their heads turned.

'It's part of football but Daniel [Levy] deals with it and we don't want to sell him. I saw what happened at West Ham once you start selling off your prized assets. We let Rio Ferdinand and Frank Lampard go and the rest followed. If you are looking to build a club, you can't be selling Gareth as then Luka Modric wants to go and someone else wants to go.

'Then you end up where they were four or five years ago, finishing halfway up the table each year. Yes, Manchester United sold Cristiano Ronaldo but they got £80 million, he's Portuguese and it is more his lifestyle here than Manchester may have been. So, in the end, it was good business.

'But we wouldn't be wanting to sell a player like Gareth at this time, when we're trying to build the club. It would have to be an amazing figure if we ever sold him. But how do you replace a player like that? The day Gareth says he wants to go, or his agent says he wants to move, there is very little you can do about it.

'But I don't see that happening. He signed a deal but maybe he doesn't want to sound unambitious and if people ask him whether he wants to play for one of the top European clubs one day, I am sure that he would.

I don't think he's ready for that, though. He is only a boy and needs a few years playing at home. He has plenty of time to do that later in his career.

'I don't know what he earns but I am sure he is earning big money. He arrived at the airport in Spain and the press were swarming all over him. But he is still learning the game, he has a lot to learn.'

The clash had been set up as a shootout between Bale and Ronaldo and it had all the makings of a great night for Gareth. 'He was really looking forward to taking on Real and showing he was worthy to be on the same field as the likes of Cristiano Ronaldo,' says a Tottenham source. 'This was his chance to do another demolition job a la Inter Milan.'

But it was not to be although Madrid's No. 7, Ronaldo, did highlight how far Gareth had come in an amazing season by specially seeking him out and shaking his hand before kick off. 'Ronaldo had been telling his team-mates how good Bale was – that he had always believed he could be one of the best players in the world when he was playing at Man United,' said Spanish journalist Mark Becerra. 'He told them Bale would be the biggest threat to them making the semis – that they would have to be careful they didn't let him go on one of those dazzling 100mph runs that left defences flailing.'

In the event, Gareth would not get the chance to destroy the Madrid backline all night. After Crouch had been given his marching orders, it took Bale and his team-mates all their concentration to keep Madrid at bay as they struggled with 10 men. They hardly had the opportunity, or initiative, to take them on at their own game.

The omens were not good even prior to kick off when Spurs lost Aaron Lennon during the warm-up. The speedy winger was sidelined with a bug that left him feeling sick and queasy. That meant a last-minute rejig of the formation as Jermaine Jenas was Redknapp's chosen replacement for Lennon. The problem was he was never going to be a like for like replacement. Instead, he moved into central midfield with Luka Modric redeployed on the left and Gareth moved to the right.

It had been a fine season for Redknapp up until this particular night, and my feeling was that he got it wrong tactically after Lennon's late withdrawal. Why sacrifice your two best players – by playing them out of position when you have lost another one? Surely the obvious move would have been to leave Gareth on the left and Luka in the centre of midfield – and moved Jenas out right? That would have been one disruption, rather than three – and you would have had Gareth terrorising Madrid down his usual left channel and Luka causing them headaches from his usual preferred midfield role. It was one long night of calamities and questionable moves – from Lennon's withdrawal, to Harry's deployment of Jenas, Bale and Modric to Crouch's dismissal.

Crouch was sent off for two yellow cards inside the first 15 minutes – lunging wildly for the ball on two separate occasions. Sure, Redknapp wanted his team to be up for a fight but not like that; it defied belief that a player of Crouch's experience in club and international football could have been such an idiot. To rub salt in the wound for Tottenham's travelling 3,000 fans, it was former Arsenal striker Emmanuel Adebayor who effectively killed off any dreams they had of making the last four. The big striker headed two of the four goals, with Angel Di Maria and Ronaldo himself completing the rout.

Gareth was surprisingly upbeat after the match, insisting that the tie was not yet after – that he and his team-mates could turn it round at White Hart Lane the following Wednesday. He said, 'We have to play at our best, stop their best players and score goals at White Hart Lane. It's going to be a difficult task, everyone knows that, but I still think it's possible.

'We are not going to sit back and take another beating from them in the second leg. Hopefully we will win and hopefully that win will be enough. Anything can happen. We will be ready for them.'

Redknapp was more cautious, knowing the odds were heavily stacked against his team. He said, 'It's not over until it's over but we've got a mountain to climb. We lost Aaron Lennon a minute before kick-off, he didn't feel well, just said he had no energy, no strength. We had to change the team just as we were leaving the dressing room. Then we went a goal down and got Crouchy sent off.

'He's certainly not one for getting red cards, but I've not seen it. I haven't spoken to Crouchy to be honest, I'm disappointed obviously, it's all we needed to go down to 10 men so early in the game. It was one of those days where anything that could have gone wrong did go wrong. It was an impossible task with 10. You have to have 11 and be at your best to get a result here.'

The boys were quiet on the return home from Madrid as the full implication of the nightmare result started to hit them. Like Harry said, it would take a miracle if they were to progress to the next stage of the Champions League. Luckily, they did not have too long to dwell on the crushing defeat; four days later Stoke were lined up as visitors to the Lane in the Premier League – and matches against Tony Pulis's dogs of war were always guaranteed to be full-blooded, difficult battles.

Gareth and the boys would need to be focused if they were to keep alive their dream of finishing fourth in the league. It was to their credit that, after the setback in Madrid, they found sufficient reserves to beat Stoke 3-2.

After his personal nightmare in Spain, it was Crouch who emerged the unlikely hero, grabbing a brace with Modric also on the score sheet.

The vital win kept Spurs battling with Manchester City for that fourth spot in the league. They were now just three points behind Roberto Mancini's team – with the teams still scheduled to meet at Eastlands for what could be a decider. Redknapp said of the win over Stoke, 'I knew we'd come back after Tuesday. We've got great players here. I thought it was a pleasure to watch us play in the first half. It was everything I love to watch in football. We moved the ball about, we made angles, we passed it great and I couldn't have enjoyed it more.

'But, from absolutely dominating from first minute to the last in the first half we find ourselves only 3-2 up. Credit to Stoke – they made it difficult for us.'

So everything was now set for the return leg against Madrid at the Lane. Could Gareth and the lads pull off a miracle by extending their debut season in the Champions League to the last four? Unfortunately, it was not to be. The hosts failed to make the most of their chances and were caught out by yet another blunder (in a season of blunders) by keeper Heurelho Gomes, who helped a long-range effort from Ronaldo into his own goal just before the interval. It would be the only goal of the game and condemn Tottenham to a 5-0 aggregate defeat.

Gareth had an impressive game, with several appeals for penalties and a volleyed goal ruled out for offside. Afterwards Madrid boss Jose Mourinho threw his arm around the boy and whispered in his ear. Anxious Spurs fans hoped it was not 'When are you coming to play for me?' or words to that effect. In fact, a reliable source revealed, Mourinho simply said, 'Well done, Gareth, you played really well and caused us problems.' The source added, 'Of course Gareth was disappointed and a bit down – but he is an intelligent boy and realistic enough to know Tottenham were always unlikely to win the thing. Like the boss, he enjoyed the journey to the last eight and it certainly whetted his appetite to compete in it every year.'

Redknapp himself made a plea to chairman Levy to invest in more quality players if Gareth's dream of playing Champions League football every season was to have any chance of materialising. Harry said, 'If this club wants regular Champions League football then you have to add quality players to the squad each season. It has become so hard to qualify now as all the teams at the top are spending big on top players.

'If Tottenham can make the top four again it would be a great achievement, arguably better than last season because City have spent millions trying to make sure of fourth place. City have probably spent in the region of £150 million trying to make sure they finish above us and they could probably spend the same amount again. 'What we have to do is to make sure next year Tottenham keep on building and creating a team capable of getting into the Champions League. It is no good doing it once and not having a go at doing it again for another 15 years or something like that. To do it every year, you have to keep improving your squad. We have seen the players you have to bring in. Everyone has seen the talented players we have got and how they are capable of playing at this level. But you need to tweak your squad a little bit if you are to qualify every year. There is no reason Tottenham cannot do that. The players will give it their all to reach the top four but it is going to be tough.'

He was right about that. So tough, in fact, that Manchester City, the team Spurs had been battling with for that fourth place spot all season, eventually finished third – with Arsenal ending up fourth. Redknapp and Bale would have to be content with a fifth place finish and, as we outlined at the start of this chapter, a place in the Europa League.

Gareth would play in all four games that followed the home defeat to Madrid – the 3-3 draw with Arsenal at the Lane, the 2-2 draw with West Brom, also at home, the 2-1 loss at Chelsea and the 1-1 draw at Blackpool. It was in the latter that his season would end three games prematurely. 65 minutes into the match, he was the victim of a dreadful tackle by the Seasiders' star man, Charlie Adam. The Scot caught Gareth late and hard on his left ankle, and the winger was carried off on a stretcher and later left the ground on crutches.

Amazingly ref Lee Probert did not even award a free kick against Adam for the diabolical challenge. Afterwards Harry Redknapp said, 'Gareth's done his ankle, it looks quite bad. It's quite swollen but we're not sure whether he's done his ligaments A few people told me it was nasty but I didn't have a good look at it.'

Four days later it was revealed that Bale had suffered ruptured ankle ligaments and would not play again that season. 'Gareth will remain in a protective boot for up to 12 days before beginning rehabilitation,' said a statement from Tottenham. 'The player is expected to be fit for the start of pre-season.'

It was a sad end on the field to a campaign that had offered so much – both for Gareth and Spurs, who now would lose out on that much coveted fourth place in the Premier League and a consequent Champions League spot. But off it, Gareth at least had the consolation of winning worldwide plaudits and the PFA Player of the Year award for his remarkable efforts during the season.

Naturally enough, he also made the PFA Team of the Year, which read: Van Der Sar (Manchester United), Sagna (Arsenal), Cole (Chelsea), Vidic (Manchester United), Kompany (Manchester City), Nani (Manchester United), Nasri (Arsenal), Wilshere (Arsenal), Bale (Tottenham), Tevez (Manchester City), Berbatov (Manchester United).

Gareth beat off tough competition to win the Player of the

Year award – including the captains of Manchester United and City, Nemanja Vidić and Carlos Tevez respectively, Scott Parker and his Tottenham team-mate Rafael van der Vaart.

He also became the fourth Welshman to win it after Ian Rush, Mark Hughes and Ryan Giggs and was 'over the moon' with the decision. He said: 'It is an honour really when you look at the names that have won it before and it just makes you go "wow" really. It's such an honour to be even mentioned in the same breath as them.

'I am more than delighted really. It is a massive award and it is a great honour to receive, especially from other fellow professionals.

'When I first joined Spurs, it was hard for me when I was not playing although I felt confident that I would show what I could do if I could get into the side. It was the same when I had a bad injury and couldn't get back in.

'Then suddenly it took off. I went from strength to strength, because now I was playing regularly and not just training. My confidence grew with each and every one of those games and there's no doubt that you learn more from playing than training, and you get better with every experience.'

He added, 'There haven't been too many Welshmen to have won the trophy but it is great and it is great for me personally. And it is not just for me, it is for all my team-mates that have helped me through the season and it is kind of for everyone really.'

That was typical of the boy: humble, honest and respectful even in his proudest moment. Along with his remarkable speed, skill and strength it is what marks Gareth Bale out to be potentially the greatest player of his generation.

Chapter 18

THE REAL DEAL

'If we sell him, we've had it haven't we? It would only be a Barcelona, a Man City or a Real Madrid who would be able to pay for him. He's an amazing player. He's got everything, there's not a weakness in his make-up. He can head the ball, he's as strong as an ox, he can run, dribble and shoot. Most important of all, he's a smashing lad.'
Harry Redknapp, then Tottenham manager, December, 2011.

Some pundits had erroneously believed that Gareth Bale had reached his zenith when he won the Player of the Year award at the end of the 2010-11 season. That, OK, he might go on to have a few good-to-great seasons with Spurs and maybe be in the running for future awards, but that his 2011 win and his destruction of Maicon Sisenando and Inter Milan in November 2010 was probably going to be as good as it got.

How very wrong they would be proved to be. As it

transpired, those accolades and honours from 2010-11 would eventually be seen as merely the *start* of the Bale legend, rather than its conclusion, as he stepped up another gear or two and eventually became the most wanted man in world football in the summer of 2013.

In June of that summer the first whispers could be heard on football's grapevine that the biggest outfit in world club football were contemplating a move for Gareth. By July, Real Madrid's interest was common knowledge and a month later negotiations were taking place between the powerbrokers of the Spanish club and their north London counterparts over a possible transfer.

But it would be the transfer fee that would dominate conversations in both Spain and England as it was revealed that Real would pay up to £90 million for the Welsh wonder boy. If that was correct, it would mean he would be walking away from White Hart Lane for a new world record fee, even dwarfing the £80 million Real had paid Manchester United for Cristiano Ronaldo four summers previously.

In the event, the final fee would be 100 million euros (£86 million). Real tried to massage Ronaldo's ego by claiming they had only paid £78 million as the Portuguese was unhappy to lose the mantle of the world's most expensive player. But I was reliably informed by sources at White Hart Lane that the fee was indeed that incredible 100 million euros.

Gareth's transfer was finally confirmed on Sunday September 1, and he was unveiled as a Madrid's new No 11 at the Bernabéu on the last day of the transfer window the following day. The Wales star had agreed a £300,000 per week, six-year deal – and expressed his delight that the long, drawn-out saga had finally been resolved.

'I have had six very happy years at Tottenham but it's the right time to say goodbye,' he said. 'We've had some special times together and I've loved every minute of it. I am not sure there is ever a good time to leave a club where I felt settled and was playing the best football of my career to date. I know many players talk of their desire to join the club of their boyhood dreams, but I can honestly say, this is my dream come true. Tottenham will always be in my heart and I'm sure this season will be a successful one for them. I am now looking forward to the next exciting chapter in my life, playing football for Real Madrid.

'I am well aware I would not be at the level I am today were it not for firstly Southampton and then Spurs standing by me during some of the tougher times and affording me the environment and support they have. I would like to thank everyone at the club; the chairman, board, staff, coaches and players, and, most of all, the fantastic fans who I hope will understand this amazing career opportunity.'

Tottenham chairman Daniel Levy may have received the biggest cheque in football transfer history, but he was still unhappy at losing Gareth. He had not been impressed when Real had erected a stage for Gareth's unveiling during the previous week and that they had publicly courted the player during the summer.

His ire was reflected in his rather biting comments after the deal was finally completed. Levy said, 'Gareth was a player we had absolutely no intention of selling as we look to build for the future. He is a player whose career we have fostered and developed and he was only a year into his new four-year contract.

'Such has been the attention from Real Madrid, and so great

is Gareth's desire to join them, we have taken the view that the player will not be sufficiently committed to our campaign in the current season. We have, therefore, with great reluctance, agreed to this sale and do so in the knowledge that we have an exceptionally strong squad to which we have added no fewer than seven top internationals.

'More importantly, we have an immense team spirit and a dressing room that is hungry for success.'

Gareth rose above the furore expressing his thanks to Levy for pushing the deal through. And, after his unveiling in Madrid, he returned home to Wales for two World Cup qualifying matches. He would play no part in the games, but did reveal a little more about the stresses and demands behind his big-money move.

Gareth said, 'It's obviously been a whirlwind few days, but it was great being unveiled. It's quite nice to come back and relax – and get back to normality, really. It's been very stressful, to say the least. I knew they were interested from the start and I was always confident the move would go through but obviously the chairman, Daniel Levy, had to do his business and do Tottenham well, so I kind of understood that.

'But at the same time, thinking of myself, it was a hard time. It was stressful and I just had to be patient and try and focus and I believed Real would get the deal through, and finally they did.'

Talking to BT Sport ahead of the World Cup qualifiers against Macedonia and Serbia, Gareth added, 'When I was younger I had some close friends who always loved European football and Real Madrid at that time were the dominant force. I remember family holidays when we used to go to

Spain and we'd bring back replica shirts of Real Madrid and pretend to be the players when we played in the park.

'I've followed them ever since and the football they played, the team they had, was amazing and it's just great to be there.'

It was a wonderful achievement for the boy from Cardiff – and he had certainly come a long, long way since joining Spurs as a raw left-back six years earlier. And he wasn't making it up when he said he had always wanted to play for Real – as the picture of him wearing a Real Madrid shirt as a boy had confirmed at his unveiling in the Spanish capital.

It was hardly surprising that Real had made their move. From the end of the 2010-11 season – after Gareth had won the coveted PFA Player of the Year award and famously roasted Inter Milan's Maicon – and right up to the summer of 2013, the Welsh boy wonder had developed into one of the world's best players.

So much so that by mid 2013 he was universally accepted as the best footballer in Britain, and the third best in the world after Ronaldo and Barcelona's Lionel Messi. Hence the massive price tag that would have made him the most expensive player on the planet.

Gareth had got to that stage by sheer hard work and sheer quality. He had always had the potential to make it to the very top, but during those two years he had made a point of upping his efforts and application both in training and on the pitch. It showed: he had become virtually unstoppable, whizzing past defenders as if they did not exist and scoring from free kicks and difficult positions as if he were Ronaldo himself.

Like Ronaldo, he was big, strong and almost impossible to halt when in full flow. In fact, some Tottenham fans told me he could even have been mistaken for Ronaldo as he hammered down the touchline, causing mayhem in his wake.

His efforts would be rewarded in April 2013 when he once again won the PFA Player of the Year award – and he also won the PFA Young Player of the Year trophy.

By doing so Gareth, then 23, became only the third man to win the double accolade, following then-Aston Villa striker Andy Gray in 1976-77 and Cristiano Ronaldo six years previously. He also joined Mark Hughes, Alan Shearer, Thierry Henry and Ronaldo as the only men to have won the main award twice, after his first triumph in 2010-11.

Gareth came out on top of a shortlist that included Manchester United's Robin van Persie and Michael Carrick, Chelsea's Juan Mata and Eden Hazard, and Liverpool's Luis Suarez. Gareth said: 'It's a massive honour. To be voted by your peers is one of the biggest things in the game. It's great to win it and I am delighted. When you look at the list there are some massive names on it but I couldn't have done it without the team.

'They have been fantastic this year and so has the manager, so I would like to give them all a big thank you as well. The other nominees have been unbelievable, they have been outstanding for their clubs and it's a massive moment to win, especially as it's both awards. It's something that I'm extremely proud of.'

A week later, Gareth would complete the set by scooping the Football Writers' Association Footballer of the Year, becoming the first Spurs player to win the award since David Ginola in 1999 and the first Welshman since goalkeeper Neville Southall in 1985.

Gareth won over half of the votes to lift the trophy and said:

'It is a huge honour to receive the Footballer of the Year award from the Football Writers' Association. It means a lot to win this award when you consider the number of players that have been outstanding for their clubs in the Premier League this season.

'I have been very fortunate to be playing in such a fantastic team and I owe a lot to my team-mates and, obviously, the manager who has shown such faith in me. This award has been won in the past by some of the greatest names in football and I consider it a privilege that the FWA has selected me to be named alongside them.' Gareth became the 15th man to win the PFA and FWA awards in the same season, with former Arsenal striker Thierry Henry and the aforementioned Cristiano Ronaldo completing the double twice. Ronaldo's triumph in 2007 was the only other occasion when the same player had won the FWA and both the PFA player and Young Player of the Year awards.

FWA chairman Andy Dunn summed up Gareth's achievement and acknowledged that he was closing in on Ronaldo and Messi as the world's greatest footballer. Dunn said, 'In a contest for votes that took so many late twists and turns, Gareth's penchant for the spectacular captured the imagination. He is a player who is rising inexorably towards the rarefied levels of world stars such as Lionel Messi and Cristiano Ronaldo.

'Twice the PFA Player of the Year and now, two months before his 24th birthday, the FWA Footballer of the Year. Let's all hope he lights up the Premier League for many seasons to come.'

The latter comment did, of course, shine a light on the elephant in the room as English football came to terms with the fact that it had a true genius on its hands. Would he be lighting up the Premier League for seasons to come – or would he be headhunted by the likes of Madrid or Barcelona?

Amid the euphoria of winning those awards and propelling Tottenham towards the top of the table, Gareth would also soon suffer torment as he himself came to terms with the fact that he was wanted by the world's leading football clubs. He had given his all to Tottenham and had been the key factor in their drive to the upper realms of the Premier League. But was he outgrowing them?

Sure, they were among the English elite, but there was a romance and magnetism about the likes of Real Madrid that possibly only Manchester United in the realms of English football could match. Who wouldn't be enthusiastic if Madrid came calling? Even Cristiano Ronaldo had left United for the bright lights of the Bernabéu, so you can understand Gareth's reaction when Madrid made it clear they wanted his signature.

For Gareth the seasons 2011-12 and 2012-13 had been the ones in which he had made the huge strides that would leave the power brokers of Real Madrid purring. Sure, leaving Maicon for dead in 2010 and winning his first PFA Player of the Year award a year later had pushed his name to back page prominence throughout Europe but his exploits in the following two seasons – as he developed stronger physically and mentally – was what brought the Continent's footballing superpowers to the gates of White Hart Lane. In 2011-12 he again excelled, inspiring Spurs to fourth place in the league. Probably the best month of that season for Gareth was January 2012 when he enjoyed a triple celebration.

On January 5, he was voted into the UEFA Team of the Year 2011. It was no mean achievement – the team was chosen by nearly 400,000 football fans on UEFA.com, with Gareth the only representative from the Premier League. Five players from European champions Barcelona – Dani Alves, Gerard Piqué, Xavi, Andres Iniesta and Lionel Messi – made the line-up along with Real Madrid trio Iker Casillas, Marcelo and Cristiano Ronaldo. Bayern Munich forward Arjen Robben and AC Milan centre-back Thiago Silva completed the team.

Gareth declared himself 'proud' and 'delighted' at the honour.

At the end of January 2012, he claimed his third brace of the season as he scored twice against Wigan.

Then he iced the cake on a terrific month as he was named the Premier League Player of the Month for the second time in his career – his three goals and two assists during the month helping him secure the award.

But his dreams of playing once again in the Champions League would be cruelly dashed as Chelsea won that competition, meaning they and not Tottenham would be England's fourth representative.

It was a devastating blow for Gareth and it would ultimately contribute to then Spurs manager, Harry Redknapp, losing his job. The papers were full of stories about how Gareth would now quit the club to join one that had qualified for the Champions League. The Guardian's Sachin Nakrani best summed up the situation, 'There is a financial shortfall to come for Spurs – they made £25.34 million from reaching the quarter-finals of the Champions League in 2010 and will receive only a fraction of that even if they go on to win next season's Europa League – and a possible loss of key players too, with Gareth Bale having already suggested that he may leave should Spurs fail to qualify for the top competition. Luka Modric, who tried to leave White Hart Lane last summer is sure to agitate again for a move away.'

In the event, Modric would leave – ironically, to join Real Madrid. But Gareth showed his loyalty to Tottenham by pledging to stay for another year. In other words, he would stand by the club to see if they could make the Champions League the following season. If they failed again, well, then he would reconsider his position. It was a fair deal all round.

On June 27 Gareth showed he was keen to stay if Champions League football could be achieved by signing a new four-year contract with Tottenham, which would commit him to the club until 2016.

He said, 'The club is progressing and I want to be a part of that, so it was great to get the deal done. I've been here for five years now and I've enjoyed every minute. I love the club and the fans.

'We've a good, young squad and we need to work together to get back on the biggest stage again. The fans have been great to me and I'd love to repay them and do the very best for them. I want to play my part in trying to get us back into the Champions League – where we belong.'

It was all about the Champions League in Gareth's mind – and the need for Tottenham to get back in the competition. After the disappointment of being usurped by Chelsea for a place in the competition in May 2012 – and the sacking of Redknapp – Spurs supreme Daniel Levy came up with his own blueprint to hopefully ensure that Champions League ambition could be achieved.

He decided to bring in a young, ambitious new manager to take the club that final step up the table and into the holy grail of Europe's top club tournament. Someone Levy hoped would bring enough success to convince Gareth Bale to stay at White Hart Lane for the long haul. On July 3, Levy announced that Andre Villas-Boas would be the man to lead them to the promised land.

It was a calculated gamble by Levy. The Portuguese manager had not brought the level of success desired at nearby Chelsea. He lasted just eight months in the job at Stamford Bridge.

But Levy is a shrewd operator and his belief was that Villas-Boas could do a job at Tottenham if he was backed fully – and that he was hungry enough to do the job after his sacking at Chelsea. Levy argued that Villas-Boas would want to prove Chelsea were wrong not to stand by him – and that this desire would be of benefit to Tottenham... and would prove to Gareth that the club could match his own ambitions.

Gareth made an immediate statement of intent at the start of the 2012-13 campaign when he revealed he had changed his squad number from number 3 to number 11. In his earlier days at Spurs, he had often played at left-back – hence the number 3 – but now he felt his game had developed and he was no longer a mere fullback.

He had worn the number 3 since joining the club in 2007 but now felt he was more of an all-round attacking player and should take number 11. For 18 months previously he had been deployed as a winger and during Tottenham's pre-season tour of North America had starred as a striker, wearing the number 9 shirt. Gareth confirmed he felt he was 'not a left-back any more' and that he had asked the club for a 'higher number'.

It was an indication of his burgeoning self-belief and as the season got going, so did Gareth. Playing in a more advanced role, he was regularly among the goals. He notched his first

Premier League hat-trick in the 4–0 win at Aston Villa on Boxing Day, 2012.

After the match, Villas-Boas was full of praise for his efforts. 'He's up there with the best,' said the Portuguese manager following Spurs' sixth victory in eight games. 'And I think he is improving every game. His left foot is wonderful and the power and direction he applies is wonderful too. It was an excellent performance from him and obviously he gets the goals and reward. But it was a very good team performance from start to finish.

'We fully deserved it. It didn't happen for us in the first half but we kept our concentration and came on very strong in the second half. If one team was going to win it, it was us and overall it was a very good performance.'

Asked about the possibility of Bale leaving in January, Villas-Boas shrugged and dismissed the prospect, saying: 'There's no release clause in his contract. He has a market value that is unobtainable to most clubs.'

Afterwards Gareth had his own celebration to mark the hat-trick as he posted a Twitter picture of the match ball on top of his Christmas tree, and tweeted: 'Amazing feeling to get my first league hat trick today but more importantly a great team performance to get us up to 4th #matchball'.

It was appropriate that Villas-Boas should be asked about his superstar and how he was attracting the attention of the world's biggest clubs – because it was the manager who had given Gareth the encouragement to play a more advanced role and to get among the goals. To his credit, Villas-Boas, upon arrival at White Hart Lane, had told Gareth he would build the team around him.

He wanted the Welshman to have the freedom to roam from

central midfield, out to the wing and into the centre of the attack. He believed, correctly as it transpired, that Gareth would be virtually unplayable if he had the freedom to dictate proceedings. It was a brilliant move by the young manager and one that propelled Tottenham into third position in the Premier League by February 2013.

If Gareth owed a debt of gratitude to Villas-Boas for having the belief in his ability to play the role that Cristiano Ronaldo played for Real Madrid, he certainly paid it back with his thrilling play and goals that 2012-13 season. At the start of March 2013, Gareth scored a goal that would have ensured he had legendary status at the Lane even if he wasn't already one of the club's greatest ever players. Yes, against Spurs' most bitter rivals, Arsenal!

Gareth – with his 10th goal in his past eight games – and Aaron Lennon grabbed the goals that killed off the Gunners and kept Spurs in third place with 10 games of the season to go. It seemed Gareth was carrying the club into the Champions League on his own – as if it were his personal mission to do so. A few days later he was on the scoresheet against old rivals Inter Milan, nabbing the first goal in the 3-0 Europa League triumph.

His superb form led to his winning the Premier League Player of the Month for February and the BBC's Goal of the Month in January and February for his strikes against Norwich and West Ham respectively.

And he still wasn't done. On May 4, Gareth scored the winning goal against his former club Southampton. The 1–0 win meant he had notched his 20th Premier League goal of the season for the club in his 200th appearance for them. He had also become the first Tottenham player to score 20 league goals in a season since Jurgen Klinsmann in 1994/95. Gareth said, 'I saw the space open up and got a good strike away. It's a massive three points and keeps our Champions League hopes alive. Southampton played very well. The first half we didn't play well, the second half we were more confident.'

Even disappointed Saints boss Mauricio Pochettino took time out to pay a particular tribute to Gareth. He said, 'When a team has a player of those characteristics, they can light up those moments. There is nothing you can do against that.'

A fortnight later Gareth was at it again, lashing the ball home from 20 yards out in the last minute as Tottenham beat Sunderland 1-0.

But his celebrations were muted, for the goal was not enough to clinch Spurs a spot in the Champions League the next season. For all his wonderful efforts and goals, he would be condemned to another Europa League campaign if he stayed at White Hart Lane.

It was time to move on and no one at Tottenham could truly begrudge the boy his big-money exit to Real Madrid. He had put in a magnificent season's work for them but Spurs had still fallen short of keeping their end of the bargain they had agreed 12 months earlier. The failure to make the Champions League meant Gareth was now entitled to leave and join a club that could provide him with that platform to exhibit his world-class skills.

Even in April 2013, Villas-Boas had publicly conceded that Gareth would only stay if they made the Champions League. The Spurs boss explained on Saturday April 27 that the club's owners had told him that Gareth would not leave if that ambition was achieved. Villas-Boas said: 'That's the information I have. The club is committed to keeping the best assets. That's the only way we can ensure we are in the top four every year. Gareth is part of that project bearing in mind he has been amazing this season.'

But they weren't in the top four and the writing was on the wall – and everyone at the Lane knew what was about to happen. Real Madrid called and Gareth Bale was on his way out. As always with Daniel Levy, determination and negotiating skills underpinned the deal and you could bet your house on Spurs getting the best possible premium for the boy. But he was on his way to Spain and the Champions League.

And the chance to prove that, yes, he was worthy of being mentioned in the same breath as Lionel Messi and Cristiano Ronaldo. For the 100 million euros man, his time had come...

SOURCES

Western Mail
Gwyn Morris
Rod Ruddick
Carl Morgan
Georges Prost
The *Sun*
The *Guardian*
The *Daily Telegraph*
The *Daily Mirror*
The *Mail on Sunday*
The *Independent*
The *Daily Mail*
Four Four Two magazine
www.saintsfc.co.uk
www.canaries.co.uk
BBC Sport

Sam Lyon
Paul Abbandonato
Birmingham Mail
BBC Wales Sport
John Toshack
Sport magazine
Paul Hayward
The *Observer*
Kenny Dalglish
Tottenham Hotspur official website
Steve Featherstone
Henry Winter
The *People*
Pat Sheehan
Paul Jiggins
Shaun Custis
Soccer365.com
Andrew Fifield
Sam Wallace
Soccer magazine
Chris Kamara
Jamie Redknapp
North Wales Daily Post
The *Independent*
Yahoo Eurosport
on footballfancast.com
Goal.com
ESPNsoccernet
Inside Soccer